T0305800

The speed of technology advancement has never been faster! This book is an invaluable resource for anyone looking to successfully navigate the challenges and opportunities presented to us in this rapidly changing digital landscape!

Mr Roy Lim Long Hei, Founder and CEO of Robocore,
Tung Hing Automation and Founder member of temi

The collection of writings provides fascinating and kaleidoscopic insights for businesses and working professionals on how to embrace and thrive in the digital economy, and to face the challenges of the Fourth Industrial Revolution.

Professor Cham Tao Soon, President (Emeritus),
Nanyang Technological University

I recommend this book for managers who are trying to grasp the multifaceted implication of digital disruption to businesses. It delves into different ways that digital technologies have both upended traditional approaches to business, as well as opened new opportunities for innovative approaches to take root. The authors hail from a spectrum of disciplines in the School of Business at the Singapore University of Social Sciences, showcasing the industry-relevant and applied orientation of the School toward business education and intellectual development.

A/P Calvin Chan, Assistant Provost & Director
(Graduate Studies), Singapore University of Social Sciences

LEADING IN A DIGITALLY DISRUPTIVE WORLD

LEADING IN A DIGITALLY DISRUPTIVE WORLD

Edited by

LEE Yew Haur
Amy WONG Ooi Mei

Singapore University of Social Sciences, Singapore

World Scientific

NEW JERSEY · LONDON · SINGAPORE · BEIJING · SHANGHAI · HONG KONG · TAIPEI · CHENNAI · TOKYO

Published by

World Scientific Publishing Co. Pte. Ltd.

5 Toh Tuck Link, Singapore 596224

USA office: 27 Warren Street, Suite 401-402, Hackensack, NJ 07601

UK office: 57 Shelton Street, Covent Garden, London WC2H 9HE

Library of Congress Cataloging-in-Publication Data

Names: Lee, Yew Haur, editor. | Wong, Amy Ooi Mei, editor.

Title: Leading in a digitally disruptive world / edited by Yew Haur Lee,
    Amy Ooi Mei Wong, Singapore University of Social Sciences, Singapore.

Description: New Jersey : World Scientific, [2024] | Includes bibliographical references and index.

Identifiers: LCCN 2023029014 | ISBN 9789811278563 (hardcover) |
    ISBN 9789811278570 (ebook) | ISBN 9789811278587 (ebook other)

Subjects: LCSH: Technological innovations--Management. | Leadership.

Classification: LCC HD45 .L336 2024 | DDC 658.5/14--dc23/eng/20230706

LC record available at https://lccn.loc.gov/2023029014

British Library Cataloguing-in-Publication Data

A catalogue record for this book is available from the British Library.

For any available supplementary material, please visit
https://www.worldscientific.com/worldscibooks/10.1142/13477#t=suppl

Desk Editors: Sanjay Varadharajan/Yulin Jiang

Typeset by Stallion Press
Email: enquiries@stallionpress.com

Printed in Singapore

About the Editors

Lee Yew Haur is an Associate Professor and Deputy Director in the Business Intelligence & Analytics unit at the SUSS. He holds a PhD in Statistics from the Virginia Polytechnic Institute and State University, USA. His research interest is in the application of text mining and data mining in education.

Amy Wong Ooi Mei is an Associate Professor in the School of Business at the SUSS. She holds a PhD in Management from Monash University, Australia. Her research interests include online brand communities, celebrities, and influencers.

About the Contributors

Dianna Yan Li Chang is a Senior Lecturer in the School of Business at the SUSS. She holds a PhD in Marketing from Melbourne Business School, University of Melbourne, Australia, and an MBA from the Business School of HK University of Science and Technology. Her research interests include consumer well-being, sustainability, and interdisciplinary research.

Eng Joo Tan is a Senior Lecturer in the School of Business at the SUSS. He holds a PhD in Finance from the University of Minnesota, USA. He teaches contemporary business strategy at the undergraduate level and innovation and strategy at the graduate level. His research examines the implications of financial intermediation for asset pricing and corporate finance, and has been published in the *European Accounting Review*, the *Journal of Business Finance and Accounting*, and the *Journal of Financial Research*, from which he has also received an Outstanding Article Award. His works have been presented at the London Business School, the American Accounting Association Annual Meeting, and the Financial Intermediation Research Society Conference.

Huong Ha is an Associate Professor and is currently Head of Business Programme, School of Business, SUSS. She holds a PhD from Monash University, Australia. Her research interests include corporate social responsibility (CSR)/ESG, change management, consumer protection, sustainability, e-commerce, e-government, governance, etc.

James Tan is an Associate Professor and Head of Business Analytics Programmes in the SUSS. He holds a PhD in Information Technology from Monash University, Australia. James has a passionate interest in working with local and overseas organizations to develop novel analytics solutions for real-world problems. For example, he has worked with the US Airforce Office of Scientific Research to develop a novel technology in anomaly detection for data streams. Locally, he has completed many analytics projects, with a focus on helping several small and medium enterprises improve organizational performance.

Jimmy Wong is an Associate Professor in the School of Business at the SUSS. He holds a PhD in Marketing (Consumer Psychology) from the University of Illinois at Urbana-Champaign, USA. His research interests focus on the social effects of power and cultural differences on consumption behaviors in contexts including service marketing, product and brand management, as well as AI Marketing. His publications appeared in several peer-reviewed journals including the *Journal of Business Review*, *Journal of Service Research*, the *European Journal of Marketing*, etc. Prior to his academic career, he worked for corporations across a wide range of industries including FMCG, electronics, and pharmaceutical. Now, he continues to participate in consulting projects with local enterprises in the domains concerning social media marketing and branding, and adopts an industry-led approach in his classes.

Karin Sixl-Daniell is a Professor of Management and Entrepreneur and has been a pioneer in online and blended learning, facilitating such courses since 2003. In addition to her being Associate Faculty at the SUSS, she has been working in Austria, Canada, Dubai, Germany, Hungary, India, Malaysia, and Singapore. She was also Co-Programme Director for the blended Programme on Family Business and Entrepreneurship at the Indian Institute of Management (IIM) in Bangalore. Before focusing on e-learning, Dr. Sixl-Daniell was Assistant Professor and Deputy Head at the Institute of International Management, University of Graz, Austria. She was also a member of the Advisory Panel to the INSEAD Financial Education for Women initiative FinEdX and co-authored the book *Wealth Wisdom For Everyone* which was accompanied by a 26 episode TV series on Channel NewsAsia in 2006. She also established her own research and advisory businesses and holds a Doctorate in Social and Economic Sciences (Business Administration) and two Masters degrees — one in economics and one in healthcare management.

Marcus T. H. Lee is Vice-Dean, School of Business at the SUSS. He holds a PhD in Marketing from the Joseph L. Rotman School of Management at the University of Toronto, and a B.A.Sc. in Computer Engineering from the Faculty of Applied Science and Engineering at the University of Toronto, Canada. Prior to SUSS, Dr. Lee was Director, Customer Engagement and Strategy, at the Land Transport Authority of Singapore (LTA) where he led a team in conceptualizing, designing, and implementing customer strategies to enhance LTA's ability to be citizen-centric and pro-enterprise, as well as to create collaborative partnerships for greater affinity toward public transport as a way of life. Prior to his role at the LTA, Dr. Lee was the founding academic director of the Institute of Service Excellence at the Singapore Management University and was the primary person responsible for the design, execution, and evolution of the Customer Satisfaction Index of Singapore (CSISG) from 2007 to 2016. In 2011, Dr. Lee led the team that created and launched the inaugural Singapore Service Excellence Medallion — designed as the pinnacle service award given out by the Singapore government. Dr. Lee specializes in the areas of customer satisfaction measurement, service experience design, data visualization, and data-intensive analytics, and has led more than 40 consulting projects to help senior leaders identify and solve core issues with the service experience in their organizations.

Mun Wei Chan is an Associate Lecturer in the School of Business at the Singapore University of Singapore (SUSS). He holds an MA in Education from Stanford University and an MBA from National University of Singapore. He runs a consulting business — SustainableSG — that helps organizations develop and implement effective sustainability strategies. His professional interests include decarbonization pathways, circular business models, sustainable development, and corporate citizenship.

Niak Wu Koh is the CEO + CTO of Cosmiqo and specializes in supply chain analytics, strategy execution and operations management innovation. He received the IEOM Distinguished Industry Achievement Award in 2021 for his outstanding achievements in supporting growth and transformation of the profession of industrial engineering and operations management. In 2019, Niak Wu received the Intellectual Transcendence Award from the China Productivity Center for his contributions to ASEAN. He codes, believes in the power of operational analytics and how it shapes business decisions. Niak Wu holds a Doctor of Philosophy in

Mechatronics from the National University of Singapore and a Bachelor of Engineering in Mechatronics (1st class) from King's College London.

Peter Chuah is a Senior Lecturer and the Head of Visual Communication and Experience Design Programmes in the School of Business at the SUSS. He holds a PhD in Design from The Hong Kong Polytechnic University, Hong Kong SAR. His research interests include critical thinking and reflective thinking in communication design education and information design.

Poh Ling Neo is a Senior Lecturer at the SUSS. She holds a PhD in Engineering from Cambridge University, UK. Her research interests are in the fields of quantitative finance and asset management.

Priyanka Gupta is a Senior Lecturer in Business Analytics Programmes in the School of Business at the SUSS. She holds a PhD in Quantitative Marketing from Nanyang Technological University, Singapore. Priyanka had worked in the FMCG industry across Sales and Marketing, which has given her a good exposure to field realities and managerial issues. Her training as an empirical researcher combined with her managerial experience puts her in good stead to connect the methodological rigor of her analysis to real-world solutions. Her research answers the intriguing question regarding how and to what extent spatial interaction affects marketers' and retail managers' decisions. In addition to research, Priyanka has a passionate interest in teaching.

Seyed Mehdi Zahraei is a Senior Lecturer in the School of Business at the Singapore University of Social Sciences. He holds a PhD in Logistics and Supply Chain Management from Nanyang Technological University, Singapore. His research focuses on supply chain management, sustainability in logistics and transportation systems, circular economy, and urban logistics.

Contents

Introduction

Digital disruptions are occurring every day in an increasingly volatile, uncertain, complex, and ambiguous business environment. Organizations need to respond to these disruptive changes and proactively develop their own disruptions for organizational transformation and growth. Focusing on emerging trends in business management and technology innovation, this book presents the market-driven forces of digital disruptions propelled by the Fourth Industrial Revolution, which has dramatically improved the efficiency of business decision-making and organizational processes.

Utilizing practice-oriented approaches, the book discusses the accelerators of digital disruptions, the soft skills, knowledge, and competencies for digital success, the business revenue generators for digital impact, and the typology and practices of sustainability and ethics for business growth. In addition, the book covers the digital leadership challenges associated with operating in a digitally disruptive environment and provides innovative solutions on how organizations and knowledge workers can prepare themselves to reap the benefits of the digital revolution by designing, managing, and leading organizations in a future-forward manner.

The book is organized into five sections. *Part I: The Accelerators of Disruption* presents the wave of technology disruption across the entire value network and the restructuring of organizations to ride the exponential change. In addition, the section covers the relevant digital transformation tools that can be used for structuring organization transformation.

Part II: Embracing Digital Skills, Knowledge, and Competencies examines the polymathic mindset, a key success factor within the context of the future of work as well as the emerging technology trends and the role of technology in transforming the customer experience. Moreover, the section presents practical tools for the delivery of better, happier, and more enjoyable customer experiences.

Part III: Enhancing Business Revenues through Digital Ventures discusses the use of business analytics to help organizations make better decisions and improve business outcomes in the age of disruption. The section also describes the rise and motivations behind blockchain-based solutions and how the wider business community can benefit from these blockchain solutions.

Part IV: Fostering Sustainability in the Disruptive Environment offers insights into how organizations adopt digital-related technologies to fulfill their corporate social responsibility in an innovative manner to demonstrate their commitment to ethical business conduct via new practices. Further, the section details the benefits of sustainability, the implementation challenges and future trends, and how technological innovations can enable a transition from linear models to circular business models.

The final section, *Part V: Leading in the Digital Era,* outlines the foundations and applications of everyday leadership and presents recommendations on how to design, manage, and lead companies in a future-forward manner. Consequently, the section discusses how organizational structure and culture need to be adjusted in order to provide a conducive environment for innovation.

It is our hope that this book will provide readers with a good overview of the emerging trends and changes that are taking place in the fast-paced digital economy. Equipped with the knowledge and understanding from this book, readers should be able to formulate their own technology disruption, structure organizational transformation, incorporate the polymathic mindset, deliver enjoyable and innovative customer experience, understand the use of analytics and blockchain solutions, and lead companies in a future-forward and sustainable manner.

PART I

THE ACCELERATORS OF DISRUPTION

Chapter 1

Riding the Wave of Exponential Change

Niak Wu Koh

Introduction

Starting back in 18th century in Great Britain, the Industrial Revolution has transformed agriculture and handicrafts into economies based on largescale industry, mechanized manufacturing, and factory systems. This acceleration in the processes of technical innovation has brought about a wide variety of new tools and machines which involved practical improvements in various fields that impact labor, production, and resource use.

Today, the world is at an inflexion point and it is propelling toward new normals at a formidable rate. As a result, the future of anything has been a topic of intense discussion and it is also one that is intensely hypothesized. People may view the world through the lens of the most significant frame, but no matter which perspective one adopts, one needs to agree that technology will be disrupting entire value networks and this will chart a new direction for the future.

In today's amazing times, organizations with no assets are positioned to dominate global logistics, retail, accommodation, and media industries. For example, Flexport owns no trains, planes, or ships of its own, but it is one of the fastest-growing players in digital freight forwarding[1]; Amazon

Marketplace, which allows third-party sellers gain access to Amazon's customer base. Moreover, Amazon expands the offerings on its site without having to invest in additional inventory.[2] Airbnb, which acts as broker by connecting hosts and travelers, and facilitates the process of renting without owning any rooms itself[3]; and YouTube, a video sharing service that allows registered users to upload and share video clips online.[4] Whichever the industry, one is now expected to reimagine business models for exponential change. As can be seen, software is still eating the world[a] and organizations will have to restructure around different economics.[b]

Supply chains and logistics are unnecessarily complex due to their spatial reach. This complexity is exacerbated by the dynamism of each industry that they enable, and in recent years, the tightening clockspeed of the double helix — a situation in which basic cyclic frequencies (such as a product or process) driving evolution of an industry, increase over time. Such complexity not only creates high barriers to entry but also a competitive force that can influence the balance of economic growth.

As an entrepot that is also a gateway to ASEAN, Singapore is well-positioned to coordinate business operations throughout the region and assume the role of a control tower that orchestrates the network of supply chains in Asia. Such a function will allow organizations to both create value for the ultimate end user and capture value through symbiotic relationships. In order to maximize these values, it is imperative that one understands the different facets of technology, ascertain how each facet can play a fundamental role in reshaping an entire industry, and subsequently, embrace that change. "It's not about ideas. It's about making ideas happen." To realize these changes, it is important to build strong business competencies and follow through with the execution.

This chapter presents the various stages in the industrial revolution, the different waves of growth, and how organizations are transforming themselves with innovative business opportunities. To illustrate the wave of exponential change in the era of digital disruption propelled by the industrial revolution, several case studies in different countries, namely Singapore, Indonesia, Thailand, and Vietnam, are discussed in detail.

---

[a]A claim made famous by Marc Andreesen predicting software companies disrupting traditional industries.

[b]The mode of value creation and how it facilitates new exchange of value.

Growth

The birth of the industrial revolution marks a major change in an economy driven by the general introduction of power-driven machinery, which impacted the prevailing methods of machine usage. An underlying trait that persists across each industrial revolution is one of meeting unmet demand, driven primarily by consumerism,[c,5] the intensification of which resulted from the emergence of the middle class in Europe and North America due to their higher income levels. These changes were exhibited by the following:

- the move from a domestic approach of production[d] to one that is factory-driven in the First Industrial Revolution,
- advancements of factory-driven approaches for widespread use to large-scale businesses over vast areas in the Second Industrial Revolution (aka the Technological Revolution) and
- a shift from mechanical and analogue electronic technology to digital electronics in the Third Digital Revolution (aka the Digital Revolution) that, incidentally, persists to the present day.

The patterns of industrial growth are similar — an increase in per capita income accompanied by a rise in the share of industrial output,[6–8] most people are much better off than their ancestors were and the proportion of the world's population living in extreme poverty has decreased significantly in the last two centuries.[9]

In each revolution, there was a fundamental change in which technology was developed. This stemmed from the professionalization of invention and design work which subsequently resulted in the ability to sustain the process of innovation.[10] The premium on knowledge is high and such growth would almost certainly not have been possible without readily accessible practical skills and scientific knowledge.[11]

There was a decisive break from the pre-industrial world of slow technological advance to the modern world of sustained technological progress. This *slowness* is exhibited in the modest productivity growth

---

[c]In current times, this is reflected in the growth of e-Commerce.

[d]A production system, also known as a putting-out system, widespread in 17th-century western Europe in which merchant-employers "put out" materials to rural producers who usually worked in their homes but sometimes labored in workshops or in turn put out work to others.

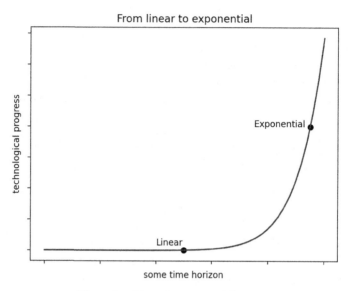

Figure 1: Linear to exponential: $y = e^x$.

rates of the First Industrial Revolution. Having said that, it is owed mostly to productivity gains in one sector (i.e., textile manufacturing) and the productivity of the economy was fixed, with demography determining the marginal product of labor.[12] The Second Industrial Revolution was fueled by the steel industry for construction, automobiles, and railroads[13]; and the Third Industrial Revolution, an era of rapid technological progress associated with the development of information technologies giving rise to the information age,[14] the digitization of manufacturing,[15] and the shift to renewable energy.[16]

The Third Industrial Revolution is the last of the great Industrial Revolutions and laid the foundational infrastructure for an emerging collaborative age.[17] Conventionally, centralized business operations will increasingly be subsumed by the distributed business practices; and the traditional, hierarchical organization of economic and political power will give way to lateral power organized nodally across society.[18] This shift to lateral power gives rise to a new economic narrative. Figure 1 abstracts this general idea of localized growth spurts (linear) to growth spurts that have succumbed to the irresistible force of globalization (exponential).

Moore's Law[e] is the most famous distillation of the exponential development of digital technology (see Figure 2), serving as a guide to the

---

[e]An observation that the number of transistors in a dense integrated circuit doubles about every two years.

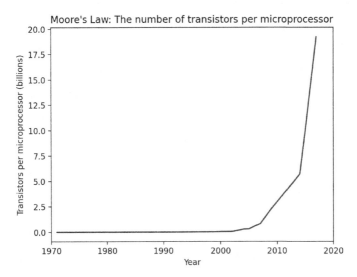

Figure 2: Growth of transistors per microchip from 1971 to 2017. Observe that the number of transistors on an integrated circuit doubles approximately every two years.

Source: Adapted from Roser and Ritchie,[21] Rupp.[22]

dynamics of the silicon revolution, and following that, the proliferation of silicon chips into nearly every aspect of contemporary life.[19] Even with the tyranny of numbers,[f] scientific endeavors persisted and this eponymous law serves as an emblem for the whole of technological change.

This exponential growth is unique to computing, information technologies and their related markets and it seems to occur at all levels of the ecosystem. Denning and Lewis[20] speak about such an ecosystem at three levels: (i) the chip, (ii) the system, and (iii) the community. The study posits that each of these levels are mutually reinforcing and the full potential can be realized with rapid adoption by the user community. This potential can be modeled with an S-curve the most interesting of which is when technology jumps occur at the inflexion point supported by new business models. These series of S-waves experience continuous exponential growth as businesses hop from one wave to the next. Such continuing achievement (see Figure 3) signified by Moore's Law is critically important to the digital economy and, more generally, progress.[23]

---

[f]A problem faced in the 1960s by computer engineers as engineers were unable to increase the performance of their designs due to the huge number of components involved.

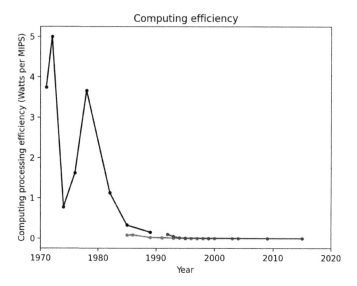

Figure 3: Exponential progress in computing efficiency. Computing efficiency is measured as the number of Watts (a measure of electrical power) needed to carry out a million instructions per second (Watts per MIPS).

Source: Adapted from Roser and Ritchie,[21] Kurzweil.[26]

Lateral power has given rise to the sharing economy and the sharing economy needs machine intelligence. In the case of Airbnb, the amount of compute capacity dedicated to analytics and machine learning grows relative to the transaction processing portion of the business.[24] Apart from finding a place that satisfies both the renter and the host, machine intelligence is used to set prices.[25] For Google and Meta (formerly Facebook), an auction model is used where companies bid on each keyword. This also means that pricing is fluid and based on how much competition is present and how much the competitors are willing to pay.[27] Such multi-sided marketplaces are made possible precisely because of the chip, system, and community which in turn have shown further sustained technological progress in computing (see Figure 4). Interestingly enough, Google owns more than 2 percent of all the world's servers[28] and innovations on data center performance are widespread.[29]

A computing system that benefited from this growth is the application of artificial neural networks (ANNs) to a vast array of problems, from

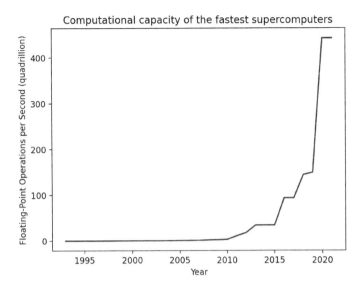

Figure 4: Growth of computational capacity from 1993 to 2021. Number of floating-point operations carried out per second by the fastest supercomputer in any given year.
Source: Adapted from Roser and Ritchie.[21]

spotting manufacturing defects to translating between languages, from voice recognition to detecting credit card fraud, and from discovering new medicines to recommending the next video to watch. This was made possible with AlexNet,[30] a leading architecture for any object detection task, and thereon, neural networks that have changed every aspect of machine intelligence with GPT-3 (Generative Pre-trained Transformer 3)[31,32] and GPT-4 (Generative Pre-trained Transformer 4).[33] These language models leverage deep learning to generate human-like text (i.e., output) such as code, stories, and poems to name a few. For these capabilities and reasons, it has become such a hot topic in the area of natural language processing. A fundamental comparison between these neural networks is the number of trainable parameters which, once again, is exponential in nature (see Figure 5).

Underpinning this foundation, it is imperative that attention now turns to the exploration of how industries are capitalizing on this wave and transforming themselves with innovative business opportunities.

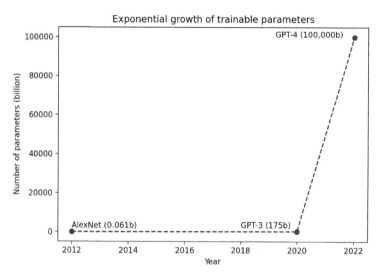

Figure 5:   Observe the 571x growth of GPT trainable parameters in a short 2-year period.

Impact

Living in this exponential age can be exciting, yet daunting. With its inherent compounding nature, changes occur at rates that increase with time once an inflection point is reached. An inflection point may be driven by technology that has been in development for a long time, eventually reaching a critical performance metric or a perceived value threshold. Such a development (or transition) may represent an evolution spanning several decades. This transition has made a significant shift in industrial capitalism and is one that has brought forth relatively larger unpredictability. As a result, topics concerning a change by assimilation,[34] human capital needs for tomorrow,[35] and views by thought leaders on navigating the exponential age[36] that help bring directionality to the surface through a dynamic understanding of the connections between economic, social, and technological forces have begun to surface. Further, there have also been concerns that organizations might not be able to adapt and governments could fail to employ and regulate new technologies to capture their benefits. This may cause a shift in power, create new security concerns, or propel inequality among different fragments of societies.[37] Faster digitalization reveals the growing gap between current economic terminology understanding and new digital business models. Concisely, the impact of nonlinearity is unpredictable.

The rapid change to technology, industries, and societal patterns and common processes in the 21st century due to increasing interconnectivity and smart automation is now better known as the Fourth Industrial Revolution (4IR) or Industry 4.0.[38] A part of this phase of industrial change is the joining of technologies such as artificial intelligence and gene editing, to advanced robotics that blur the lines between the physical, digital, and biological worlds.[39] The vision was and still is compelling because it puts people in the center, promising significant progress for the economy and society at large. This conceptual framework has now become an international brand, where the idea is to merge real and virtual spaces in what is now known as cyber–physical production systems.[40]

The initial focus of this framework in the manufacturing sector in Germany was well understood as it was widely accepted that economies with a strong industrial backbone recovered faster and better from global financial and economic crises. Today, the confluence of underlying technologies and its proliferation has enabled the birth of myriad innovative business models within traditional industrial practices and across multiple industry clusters. New and exciting megatrends have spurred governments to rethink, reshape, and restructure their modus operandi and transform entire industries.

Singapore

A notable example is the Industry Transformation Programme[41] led by Singapore's Ministry of Trade and Industry the goal of which is to put forth a strategy that promotes growth and competitiveness. This has materialized as an Industry Transformation Map (ITM) that integrates productivity improvement, skills development, innovation, and internationalization across 7 industry clusters:

(1) Advanced Manufacturing and Trade (AMT)
(2) Connectivity
(3) Human Health and Potential (HHP)
(4) Urban Systems
(5) Resource and Environmental Sustainability
(6) Modern Services
(7) Lifestyle Cluster

As industries evolve, so do ITMs, now refreshed as ITM2025,[42,43] to address structural shifts in the economy by riding on the digital revolution, closer integration with research and innovation, greater focus on jobs and skills, and heightened pursuit of greater sustainability and inclusive growth.

SimplyGo,[44,45] a contactless bank card, is one such initiative that showcases the significance of smart ticketing technology for cities worldwide by transport providers in their mission to create a seamless passenger experience. Commuters can enjoy the convenience of tapping in and out with contactless bank cards or mobile wallets when in transit, removing the need to carry a separate travel card or make any upfront top-ups. It taps into digital payment technology to provide commuters with a more convenient way to pay for public transit.

Another particularly inspiring transformation under the Connectivity cluster is the Next Generation Port (NGP) at Tuas, Singapore,[46–48] which is expected to be the world's largest fully automated terminal in a single location. The NGP is planned to be an intelligent, sustainable, and green port where automated guided vehicles (AGVs) that are electric and driverless will be picking up the containers and transporting them between the wharf and the yard. These AGVs have a carbon footprint that is 25 percent smaller than regular AGVs, making the port greener and more sustainable. Data and technology will be used at the NGP to help predict arrival times for ships, to allow faster turnaround times, and to help them with just-in-time port calls. Intelligent control systems will also be present to predict traffic hotspots for ships, allowing the ship master to plan the best route to take, and preventing possible collisions in busy waterways. The port's goal is to make itself more efficient for ships to carry out all their needs: from banking to refueling to unloading container cargo and storing it there until the next ships become available.

A refreshed Financial Services Industry Transformation Map 2025,[49] which builds upon the previous roadmap launched in 2017, was initiated to deepen capabilities and grow in areas such as sustainable and transition financing, private credit, philanthropy, and the digital asset ecosystem. It lays out the growth strategies to further develop Singapore as a leading international financial center in Asia, which aims to connect global markets, support Asia's development, and serve Singapore's economy.

Indonesia

The resulting shifts and disruptions mean that the current era is a time of great promise and great peril. This also presents itself as an opportunity to overhaul entire value chains with a digital-first approach to unlock value from the most significant frame. Southeast Asia's largest economy has designed "Making Indonesia 4.0" as an integrated roadmap to implement a number of strategies to progress into the Industry 4.0 era with a focus on technology mastery.[50] Susilo[51] examines the feasibility of this strategy by considering Indonesia's readiness given the archipelago's diversity and puts forth suggestions to realize Indonesia 4.0 with digital education.

The five industries, selected based on economic implementation and feasibility, primed to capitalize on 4IR are as follows:

(1) Food and beverage
(2) Textile and apparel
(3) Automotive
(4) Chemicals
(5) Electronics

As a result of this national policy roadmap, concepts that aim to improve productivity across industries through a technological lens have surfaced. For example:

- Hidayatno et al.,[52] Otles and Sakalli[53] conceptualize a systemic relationship structure that highlights the interactions between policies and key variables of technology adoption in the food and beverage industry.
- Rezqianita and Ardi[54] identify drivers and barriers of Industry 4.0 adoption in the manufacturing industry.
- Kurniawan et al.[55] ascertain that digital technology (i) promotes the resource recovery of non-biodegradable waste for a circular economy and (ii) enables the local community to do online transactions of recycled goods through mobile-based applications, i.e., adding economic value to recycled waste.

This digital-first approach has also given rise to multi-sided platforms (MSPs) such as Tokopedia, Go-Jek, and Bukalapak[56,57] and are prime examples that have grown exponentially in a compressed time frame. In start-up parlance, these are the much coveted unicorns[g] with the exception of Go-Jek, which is a decacorn.[h]

---

[g]A privately held start-up company valued at over US$1 billion.
[h]A privately held start-up company valued at over US$10 billion.

Tokopedia provides a customer-to-customer (C2C) platform that is free to use for merchants and buyers; it provides technological solutions that empower millions (more than 150 million users as at the first quarter of 2022[58]) of merchants and support consumers to participate in the future of commerce.

Go-Jek is an on-demand, multi-service technology platform that provides access to a wide range of services including transport, payments, food delivery, and logistics for over 170 million users across Southeast Asia[59]; its popularity is due to the convenience it offers and a nationwide network.

Bukalapak started as an online marketplace to facilitate online commerce for small and medium enterprises (SME) and later expanded to digitize small family-owned businesses serving over 100 million users as at 2021.[60]

The digital economy has brought about multi-sided platforms as superior configurations for value co-creation.[61,62] Platforms play an important role throughout the economy as they minimize transaction costs between market supply and demand for complementary products and services and the coordination of suppliers and buyers to deliver customer value. MSPs appear to be the most powerful business models in the digital economy due to their adaptability and ability to handle complexity, rapid scale-up, and value capture (see Figure 6). It is an ecosystem in which network

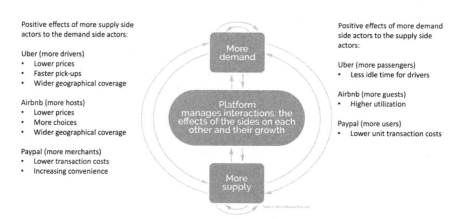

Figure 6:　Multisided platform network effects.

Source: Adapted from Innovation Tactics.[63]

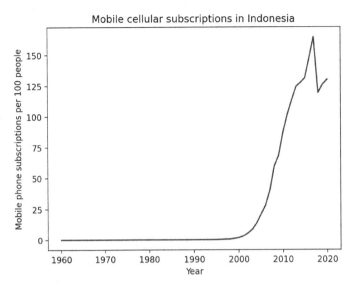

Figure 7: Growth of mobile cellular subscriptions in Indonesia from 1960 to 2020. *Source*: Adapted from World Bank.[66]

effects increase as the number of ecosystem participants (see Figure 7) and the quality of their participation increase. The co-evolution of such an ecosystem is typically reliant on the technological leadership of firms that provide such a platform.

Thailand

The development of each industrial revolution builds upon its predecessor. Thailand, the second largest economy in Southeast Asia, has abstracted its innovation cycles with *S*-curves (see Figure 8), which reflects the goal of attaining *Thailand 4.0*. This economic model aims to unlock the country from several economic challenges resulted from past economic development models which place emphasis on the agriculture industry (Thailand 1.0), light industry (Thailand 2.0), and advanced industry (Thailand 3.0).[64] With this model, Thailand 4.0 aims to achieve the following:

- Economic prosperity that is driven by innovation, technology, and creativity.

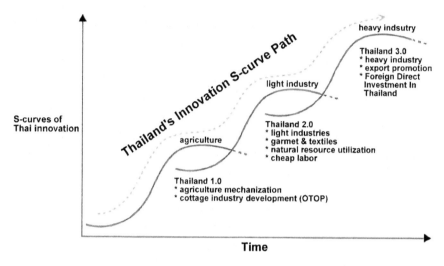

Figure 8: Innovation S-curves from Thailand 1.0 through Thailand 3.0.[73]

Source: Jones and Paltoon (2017)

- Social well-being to create a society that moves forward without leaving anyone behind (inclusive society) through realization of the full potential of all members of society.
- Human values to transform Thais into "Competent human beings in the 21st Century" and "Thais 4.0" in the first world.
- Environmental protection to become a liveable society that possesses an economic system capable of adjusting to climate change and a low carbon society.

This transformative shift to a technology-driven economy promotes the Eastern Economic Corridor (EEC) initiative,[65] which targets the following industries:

(1) next-generation automotive
(2) intelligent electronics
(3) agriculture and biotechnology
(4) food for the future
(5) medical tourism
(6) automation and robotics
(7) aviation and logistics

(8) medical and comprehensive healthcare
(9) biofuels and biochemicals
(10) digital
(11) defense
(12) education and human resource development.

Results arising from this are shown rather quickly with the formation of automotive clusters[67] and, subsequently, the preparedness of the automotive industry entrepreneurs for Industry 4.0.[68] With these clusters, an extension to value chain discussions[69] have ensued. Consequently, small and medium enterprises (SMEs) can ride this wave through a people, process, and technology framework.[70] Thailand is determined to develop the next generation industry with a digital-first approach.[71,72] The spillover effects extending from these initiatives have resulted in unicorns such as Flash Group (logistics and e-commerce), Ascend Money (fintech), and Bitkub (crypto):

Flash Group is an integrated logistics company that is best known for its delivery service, Flash Express. Offering a variety of services including free door-to-door pickup and delivery, this start-up handles a daily peak parcel volume of 2 million items.[74]

Ascend Money uses digital technologies to provide financial services to people in the region — particularly those who lack access to banking. Following a shift toward cashless payment, they service 14 million active users as at the first quarter of 2022.[75]

Bitkub is a cryptocurrency exchange with a share of 90 percent of crypto transactions based on 2021 data from regulated exchanges.[76]

Interestingly, these companies are achieving such rapid growth across various nodes in the value chain and rightly so, since under this backdrop Thailand intends to play its part by working with Northeast Asian countries to develop a single chain of production within mainland Southeast Asia,[77] consisting of Cambodia, Laos, Myanmar Vietnam, and Thailand (CLMVT). Strengthening CLMVT connectivity will greatly enhance ASEAN integration and merge mainland ASEAN into a single market and production base.

Figure 9: Three essential flows of the supply chain.

An abstraction of the Thailand 4.0 approach can be viewed as that of a supply chain comprising the three essential flows as follows (see Figure 9):

- **Material Flow** involves the movement of goods from a supplier to a customer. This supply chain management flow also concerns customer returns and service needs.
- **Information Flow** centers on transmitting orders and updating the status of delivery.
- **Financial Flow** involves credit terms, payment schedules, and consignment and title ownership arrangements.

Such a view provides a holistic approach to the intended transformation. For example:

- Kittipanya-ngam and Tan[78] discuss how digitalization allows food supply chains to be highly connected, efficient, and responsive to customer needs and regulation requirements. More importantly, the study discusses the challenges of augmenting a traditional food supply chain.
- Choosung et al.[79] explore the current situation of mulberry fruit supply chain management in Nan province and propose a new supply chain model for fresh mulberry. The study recommends an online ecommerce platform as an additional channel for fresh mulberry fruit distribution.
- Jaipong et al.[80] review how data analytics can enable businesses to accurately predict demand spikes and decreases which allows organizations to adjust material volumes and routes. This study extends the research to the adoption of Artificial Intelligence (AI) in highly complex agricultural supply chains factoring its applications to production, distribution, and consumption of food.

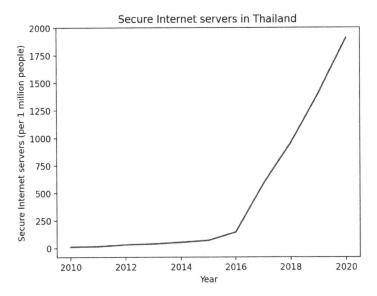

Figure 10: Secure internet servers in Thailand from 2010 to 2020.
Source: Adapted from World Bank.[81]

Today, Thailand is actively working on its transition into an increasingly digitalized world and continues to make great strides toward complete digitalization (see Figure 10). Industry 4.0, AI, e-payments and cutting-edge technologies form part of the daily realities for most who live in the country. With a strong industrial policy that favors digitalization, Thailand is on the cusp of becoming the next Asian digital behemoth through its adoption of the 4.0 digital revolution.

Vietnam

As Industry 4.0 requires a new agile mindset and cultural shift, economies across the globe are witnessing a new industrial model, built on the integration of digital technologies and physical systems. This includes innovating thinking, unifying perceptions, and perfecting institutions to facilitate the process of national digital transformation.[82]

To realize this, Vietnam, the third largest economy in Southeast Asia, has put forth a National Strategy for the Fourth Industrial Revolution and is building a digital government (see Figure 11) which consists of six important solutions[83],[84] as follows:

(1) heightening the quality of institutionalization and capacity for policy formulation
(2) developing infrastructure for interconnection and database usage
(3) human resource development
(4) developing e-government and digital government in the long term
(5) enhancing national innovation capability and
(6) investing in Industry 4.0 technologies.

A value chain approach was adopted and the action plan has identified that without supporting industries, dependence on material imports will weaken Vietnam's competitiveness and make it difficult to sustain economic growth. Key sectors that have been prioritized for development, based on the highest competitive advantage, in order to accelerate participation in global supply chains[85] are as follows:

• electronics and mechanical engineering
• garment and textile
• leather and footwear

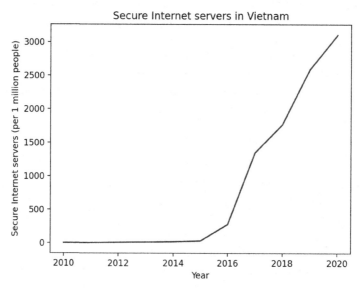

Figure 11:   Secure internet servers in Vietnam from 2010 to 2020.

Source: Adapted from World Bank.[81]

- high-tech
- automotive

Following this, research on systematic and extensive factors affecting the adoption of Industry 4.0 by SMEs in Vietnam have surfaced. For example:

- Nguyen and Luu[86] explore the impact of factors that influence the actual adoption of Industry 4.0 by SMEs in Ho Chi Minh City. The study suggests that managerial efforts aimed at increasing the factors' perceptions of adoption of Industry 4.0 and individual's relevance of the technology will contribute to implementation success.
- Ha *et al.*[87] focus on assessing the status and proposing solutions to develop the electronics industry in the Thai Nguyen province. The results show that although the electronics industry in the Thai Nguyen province does not have a large number of enterprises, it has the largest number of employees in the group of industries in the province. As such, appropriate strategic directions and solutions are needed to improve the efficiency of electronic industry enterprises to ensure sustainable development in the future.
- Tang *et al.*,[88] Cuong and Tien[89] study the effects of food loss when supply chains are disrupted and analyze technology solutions used by Vietnamese enterprises to prevent food loss, as well as existing and potential technologies around the world that can help to lessen food loss. The study provides insights into each "critical loss point", the required solutions, and potential technologies needed to address these concerns, and showcases how the availability of low-cost technologies can produce high efficiency gains.

Vietnam's digital transformation is well underway and accelerated by the pandemic as businesses consider the possibilities of a virtual world having experienced sudden and overwhelming restrictions on physical mobility.[90] Major industries driving the growth of Vietnam's digital economy include e-commerce, Fintech, ICT, and Edtech. This is reflective of unicorns such as the following:

VNG is a technology company specializing in digital content and online entertainment, social networking, and e-commerce. Their four main businesses, which include online games, platforms, digital payments, and cloud services, have over 80 million users.[91]

VNPAY is a financial services company which provides electronic payment solutions in Vietnam. The company offers mobile banking, phone recharge, and bill payment solutions and services for local banks, telecommunications companies, and e-commerce businesses to enhance and promote consumer adoption of e-payments[92] for over 22 million users.

Sky Mavis is a video game developer that brings the benefits of blockchain through fun and practical applications.[93] It specializes in the fields of information technology, blockchain, and video game and has more than 2 million daily active users.

A sizable mobile-first (see Figure 12), unbanked population in a country with gradually maturing regulations is a positive factor supporting the growth of FinTech firms in Vietnam. The pandemic-triggered rapid digitalization of financial services may open up even more opportunities in this space for implementing tech start-up models, especially with 64 percent of the population using the Internet, along with the young generation that are technology-savvy, the explosion of e-commerce, and the support of the government.[94,95]

Even with the labor-cost advantage, there is a common understanding that Vietnam has to upscale technology levels in these industries to

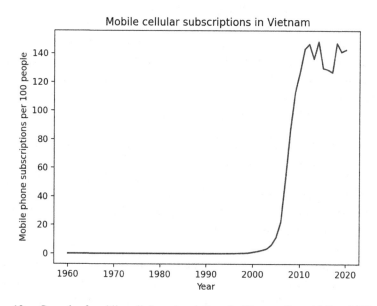

Figure 12: Growth of mobile cellular subscriptions in Vietnam from 1960 to 2020.
Source: Adapted from World Bank.[66]

increase productivity to remain competitive. Capitalizing on the benefits and potentials of Industry 4.0, Vietnam is leapfrogging to close the gap with other ASEAN countries by leveraging on advanced technologies to boost its economy.[96] With a great determination to embark on Industry 4.0, Vietnam will experience a great economic growth along with developments in science and technology, and create a fundamental change in the growth model to ascend the global value chain.

Human capital

In 2020, the media became concerned about the effects of automation in the workplace, raising the prospect of mass redundancy. This, however, is a notion that is not unfamiliar as it has happened in the 19th century[97] and was popularized in the 1930s, as "technological unemployment".[98] Such a notion fundamentally boils down to a skills gap (or structural unemployment) caused by a mismatch between the skills that workers in the economy can offer, and the skills demanded of workers by employers. Today, this manifests as an exponential gap between working arrangements, enabled by rapidly improving technologies, and the outdated norms.

Transitions have never been easy, but once the transition is completed, there will most likely be positive impact on employment. This latency is caused by the necessary adaptations to new technologies and working methods. A certainty is that innovation generates growth and technology will revolutionize the way people work.

One such success is the Global Lighthouse Network initiative,[99] which was launched to close the gap between frontrunners and laggards while accelerating the widespread adoption of advanced manufacturing technologies. These lighthouses[i] keep people at the center of their Fourth Industrial Revolution transformation with a focus on inclusive growth, thus ensuring organizations have the opportunity to realize their full potential to build an innovative and creative future at the heart of a reimagined industry. For example:

- Petronas Malaysia has boosted engagement by coupling targeted upskilling and innovative learning approaches like gamification with a culture that fosters experimentation among empowered workers.[100]

---

[i]Organizations with the courage to invest in new ideas, new approaches, and altogether new methods that are collectively transforming the very nature of operations.

- HP Inc. Singapore shifted from labor-intensive, reactive, manual work to highly digitized, automated work. This freed up considerable tasks and responsibilities offering new opportunities for upskilling.[101]
- Western Digital, Batu Kawan (Malaysia) rolled out a comprehensive IIOT[j] Academy program to educate and nurture its talents to cultivate a new way of thinking with the adoption of 4IR technologies.[102]

The body of knowledge on human capital development in a 4.0 era has been growing. An underlying commonality is the need for new competencies to ensure the success of digital transformation, and life-long learning should be integral to an organization's strategic goals.[103,104] Bordel et al.[105] leverage on sensing technologies to increase the global production process efficiency and worker well-being in the European bakery industry. This is an extended application from sensor nodes to obtain actionable insights for evidence-based decision-making.

Collaboration has a special role in supporting knowledge-sharing mechanisms for the adoption of Industry 4.0 technologies.[106] Mentorship through the support of other less advanced firms can facilitate the emergence of a collaborative culture in the regional ecosystem, which can influence the adoption of new digital technologies. Similarly, research and development collaborations with scientific and business partners can contribute to digital transformation.[107] Eventually, business success is also dependent on how disruptive technologies are used to value-add to the enterprise. Turning to the challenges of workforce,[108,109] highlight how a lack of IT/digital skills can impact analytical thinking and adversity when dealing with complexity.

Exponential growth, increasing job complexity, and technology integration, have led to significant changes in competency requirements across industries. A positive note is that in this day and age, the dissemination of knowledge, learning, and education is more accessible, to more people, in more places, and in more ways than ever before.[110] The success of this transition, as with the previous ones, depends not only on technology but also on the ability of people to ride this wave of change. Ultimately, the character of a nation is determined by the character of its people. In this industrial revolution, the premium on knowledge is high and that is exactly why education is pivotal.

---

[j] Industrial Internet-of-Things.

Path Forward

As the world transitions into a future system where the contours and parameters are not yet clear, it is encouraging that more discussions are taking place to better appreciate each other's perspectives. In the midst of this transition, individuals need to maintain the impetus to perform, the latitude to be creative, and the motivation to contribute to the common cause. This chapter provided an overview of the various stages in the industrial revolution along the different waves of growth. Relevant examples from Singapore, Indonesia, Thailand, and Vietnam are presented. Finally, the chapter covers the Fourth Industrial Revolution transformation, made possible through the ever-important resource, human capital. With this exponential wave of change, it is important that discussions are made about using the right technology as an enabler and how a more progressive society will lead to a more inclusive economy. What role will you play in shaping this new revolution?

References

1. Alex Konrad. (2022). Flexport is silicon valley's solution to the supply chain mess — why do insiders hope it sinks? *Forbes*.
2. Your Marketing People. (2021). What is the difference between Amazon and Amazon Marketplace? https://yourmarketingpeople.com/blog/what-is-the-difference-between-amazon-and-amazon-marketplace/.
3. Investopedia. (2022). How Airbnb works. https://www.investopedia.com/articles/personal-finance/032814/pros-and-cons-using-airbnb.asp.
4. TechBoomers. (2022). What YouTube is and how to watch videos. https://techboomers.com/t/what-is-youtube.
5. Fine, B., & Leopold, E. (1990). Consumerism and the industrial revolution. *Social History*, *15*(2), 151–179.
6. Chenery, H. B. (1960). Patterns of industrial growth. *The American Economic Review*, *50*(4), 624–654.
7. Kuznets, S. (1955). Economic growth and income inequality. *The American Economic Review*, *45*(1), 1–28.
8. Hartwell, R. M. (1971). *The Industrial Revolution and Economic Growth*. Taylor & Francis Group, London.
9. Koyama, M., & Rubin, J. (2022). *How the World Became Rich: The Historical Origins of Economic Growth*. Polity Press, Cambridge.
10. Hanlon, W. W. (2022). The rise of the engineer: Inventing the professional inventor during the industrial revolution. *Working Paper 29751*, National Bureau of Economic Research. DOI: 10.3386/w29751.

11. Kelly, M., & Grada, C. O. (2020). Connecting the scientific and industrial revolutions: The role of practical mathematics. *Working Papers 202017*, School of Economics, University College Dublin.
12. Clark, G. (2014). The industrial revolution, in P. Aghion, & S. Durlauf (eds.) *Handbook of Economic Growth*, Vol. 2, Chap. 5. Elsevier, North Holland, pp. 217–262. DOI: 10.1016/B978-0-444-53538-2.00005-8.
13. Mokyr, J. (1992). *The Lever of Riches: Technological Creativity and Economic Progress*, no. 9780195074772 in OUP Catalogue. Oxford University Press.
14. Greenwood, J. (1997). *The Third Industrial Revolution: Technology, Productivity, and Income Inequality*. American Enterprise Institute for Public Policy Research. ISBN 0844770930.
15. The Economist. (2012). The third industrial revolution (Manufacturing).
16. Rifkin, J. (2012). The third industrial revolution: How the internet, green electricity, and 3-d printing are ushering in a sustainable era of distributed capitalism. *The World Financial Review*. pp. 21–34.
17. Cooper, C., & Kaplinsky, R. (1989). Consumerism and the industrial revolution. *Technology and Development in the Third Industrial Revolution*, *1*(1), 1–3.
18. Rifkin, J. (2011). *The Third Industrial Revolution: How Lateral Power Is Transforming Energy, the Economy, and the World*, 1st edn. Palgrave Macmillan, New York City.
19. Brock, D. (2006). *Understanding Moore's Law: Four Decades of Innovation*. Chemical Heritage Press, Philadelphia.
20. Denning, P. J., & Lewis, T. G. (2016). Exponential laws of computing growth. *Communications of the ACM*, *60*(1), 54–65. DOI: 10.1145/2976758.
21. Roser, M., & Ritchie, H. (2013). Technological change. *Our World in Data*.
22. Rupp, K. (2018). 42 years of microprocessor trend data. https://www.karlrupp.net/2018/02/42-years-of-microprocessor-trend-data/.
23. Thompson, N. C., Ge, S., & Manso, G. F. (2022). The importance of (exponentially more) computing power. DOI: 10.48550/ARXIV.2206.14007.
24. Rice, J., & Matlin, A. (2021). Our journey towards cloud efficiency. *The Airbnb Tech Blog*.
25. Hill, D. (2015). The secret of Airbnb's pricing algorithm. *IEEE Spectrum*.
26. Kurzweil, R. (2005). *The Singularity Is Near: When Humans Transcend Biology*. Viking, New York.
27. He, X., Pan, J., Jin, O., Xu, T., Liu, B., Xu, T., Shi, Y., Atallah, A., Herbrich, R., Bowers, S., & Candela, J. Q. (2014). Practical lessons from predicting clicks on ads at Facebook. *Proceedings of the Eighth International Workshop on Data Mining for Online Advertising, ADKDD'14*. Association for Computing Machinery, New York, NY, USA, pp. 1–9.

28. Data Center Knowledge. (2017). How many servers does google have? https://www.datacenterknowledge.com/archives/2017/03/16/google-data-center-faq.

29. Google Data Centers. (2022). Innovations.

30. Krizhevsky, A., Sutskever, I., & Hinton, G. E. (2012). Imagenet classification with deep convolutional neural networks. *Proceedings of the 25th International Conference on Neural Information Processing Systems — Volume 1, NIPS'12.* Curran Associates Inc., Red Hook, NY, USA, pp. 1097–1105.

31. Brown, T. B., Mann, B., Ryder, N., Subbiah, M., Kaplan, J., Dhariwal, P., Neelakantan, A., Shyam, P., Sastry, G., Askell, A., Agarwal, S., HerbertVoss, A., Krueger, G., Henighan, T., Child, R., Ramesh, A., Ziegler, D. M., Wu, J., Winter, C., Hesse, C., Chen, M., Sigler, E., Litwin, M., Gray, S., Chess, B., Clark, J., Berner, C., McCandlish, S., Radford, A., Sutskever, I., & Amodei, D. (2020). Language models are few-shot learners. DOI: 10.48550/ARXIV.2005.14165.

32. Floridi, L., & Chiriatti, M. (2020). Gpt-3: Its nature, scope, limits, and consequences. *Minds and Machines, 30,* 1–14. DOI: 10.1007/s11023-020-09548-1.

33. GPT-4. (2022). Ai is the future, and the future is now. https://www.gpt-4.co.

34. Cassard, A., & Hamel, J. (2018). Exponential growth of technology and the impact on economic jobs and teachings: Change by assimilation. *Journal of Applied Business and Economics, 20*(2). DOI: 10.33423/jabe.v20i2.328.

35. Zain, S., & Yahya, F. B. (2019). Working in industry 4.0: IPS seminar on human capital needs in industry 4.0 report. *Workshop,* Lee Kuan Yew School of Public Policy.

36. Azhar, A. (2021). *The Exponential Age.* Diversion Books, New York City.

37. Schwab, K. (2017). *The Fourth Industrial Revolution.* Crown Publishing Group, New York City.

38. Kagermann, H., & Wahlster, W. (2022). Ten years of industrie 4.0. *Sci, 4*(3). DOI: 10.3390/sci4030026. https://www.mdpi.com/2413-4155/4/3/26.

39. Philbeck, T., & Davis, N. (2018). The fourth industrial revolution: Shaping a new era. *Journal of International Affairs, 72*(1), 17–22. https://www.jstor.org/stable/26588339.

40. Monostori, L. (2014). Cyber-physical production systems: Roots, expectations and R&D challenges. *Procedia CIRP, 17,* 9–13. DOI: https://doi.org/10.1016/j.procir.2014.03.115. Variety Management in Manufacturing.

41. Ministry of Trade and Industry. (2017). What are ITMS? https://www.mti.gov.sg/ITMs/Overview.

43. Ministry of Trade and Industry. (2021). Future economy council welcomes new members, embarks on ITM 2025 to refresh ITMs and develop new

strategies for a post-COVID-19 world. https://www.mti.gov.sg/Newsroom/Press-Releases/2021/04/Future-Economy-Council-welcomes-new-members.

44. Yeo, T. G. (2019). SimplyGo signals change for ticketing in Singapore. *Intelligent Transport*.

45. Smart Nation (Singapore). (2019). Breezing through public transport. https://www.smartnation.gov.sg/initiatives/transport/contactless-fare-payment.

46. Koh, A., & Park, K. (2022). Singapore's $14 billion mega-port takes aim at shipping chaos. *Bloomberg*.

47. Andres, G. (2022). PSA Singapore, A*STAR to develop large-scale fleet management solution for AGVs at Tuas Port. *Channel News Asia*.

48. Mindur, M. (2020). Significance of the port of Singapore against the country's economic growth. *Zeszyty Naukowe. Transport/Politechnika Slaska, 106*, 107–121.

49. Monetary Authority of Singapore. (2022). MAS launches financial services industry transformation map 2025. https://www.mas.gov.sg/news/media-releases/2022/mas-launches-financial-services-industry-transformation-map-2025.

50. Indonesia Investment Coordinating Board. (2017). Making Indonesia 4.0: Indonesia's strategy to enter the 4th generation of industry revolution. Ministry of Investment.

51. Susilo, D. (2020). Industry 4.0: Is Indonesia ready? *Management Analysis Journal, 9*(3), 262–270. DOI: 10.15294/maj.v9i3.39695.

52. Hidayatno, A., Rahman, I., & Rahmadhani, A. (2019). Understanding the systemic relationship of industry 4.0 adoption in the Indonesian food and beverage industry. *Proceedings of the 2019 5th International Conference on Industrial and Business Engineering, ICIBE 2019*. Association for Computing Machinery, New York, NY, USA, pp. 344–348.

53. Otles, S., & Sakalli, A. (2019). 15 — Industry 4.0: The smart factory of the future in beverage industry, in A. M. Grumezescu, & A. M. Holban (eds.) *Production and Management of Beverages*. Woodhead Publishing, pp. 439–469.

54. Rezqianita, B. L., & Ardi, R. (2020). Drivers and barriers of industry 4.0 adoption in Indonesian manufacturing industry. *Proceedings of the 3rd Asia Pacific Conference on Research in Industrial and Systems Engineering 2020*.

55. Kurniawan, T. A., Dzarfan Othman, M. H., Hwang, G. H., & Gikas, P. (2022). Unlocking digital technologies for waste recycling in industry 4.0 era: A transformation towards a digitalization-based circular economy in Indonesia. *Journal of Cleaner Production, 357*, 131911. https://doi.org/10.1016/j.jclepro.2022.131911.

56. Santoso, A., & Sari, W. (2018). Maximizing strategic alliances in the multi-sided platform firms. *International Journal of Business, 23*(1), 26–52.
57. Soegoto, E. S., & Akbar, R. (2018). Effect of the internet in improving business transactions with online market methods. *IOP Conference Series: Materials Science and Engineering, 407*, 012051. DOI: 10.1088/1757-899x/407/1/012051.
58. Statista. (2022). Leading e-commerce sites in Indonesia as of 1st quarter 2022, by monthly traffic (E-Commerce).
59. Wikipedia. (2022). Gojek.
60. Florence, U. (2021). Bukalapak raises new funds from Microsoft, eyes local listing, report says. *KrASIA*.
61. Poniatowski, M., Lüttenberg, H., Beverungen, D., & Kundisch, D. (2022). Three layers of abstraction: A conceptual framework for theorizing digital multi-sided platforms. *Information Systems and e-Business Management, 20*(2), 257–283. DOI: 10.1007/s10257-021-00513-8.
62. Sanchez-Cartas, J. M., & León, G. (2021). Multisided platforms and markets: A survey of the theoretical literature. *Journal of Economic Surveys, 35*(2), 452–487. DOI: https://doi.org/10.1111/joes.12409.
63. Innovation Tactics. (2022). The complete guide to the revolutionary platform business model. https://innovationtactics.com/platform-business-model-complete-guide/.
64. Royal Thai Embassy, Washington D.C. (2017). Thailand 4.0. https://thaiembdc.org/thailand-4-0-2/.
65. Asian Robotics Review. (2018b). Thailand's $45 billion leap to industry 4.0. https://asianroboticsreview.com/home92-html.
66. World Bank. (2022a). Mobile cellular subscriptions (per 100 people). World Development Indicators.
67. Kuroiwa, I., & Techakanont, K. (2017). Formation of automotive manufacturing clusters in Thailand. *Economic Research Institute for ASEAN and East Asia*, 1–12.
68. Phungphol, W., Tumad, S., Sangnin, K., & Pooripakdee, S. (2018). Creating passion for preparedness of automotive industry entrepreneurs for industry 4.0 era in the southern part of Thailand. *International Journal of Business and Economic Affairs, 3*(1), 1–12.
69. Nupra — in, A., & Junsang, T. (2020). Logistics and Thailand 4.0 industrial development. *WMS Journal of Management, 9*(1), 118–129.
70. Sopadang, A., Ramingwong, S., Anantana, T., & Tamvimol, K. (2021). *Implementation Strategies for SME 4.0: Insights on Thailand*. Springer International Publishing, Cham, pp. 393–422.
71. Asian Robotics Review. (2018a). Is Thailand next to go digital? Sure looks that way. https://asianroboticsreview.com/home254-html.

72. Charoen, D. (2018). Digital Thailand. *NIDA Case Research Journal, 10*(2), 4–35.
73. Jones, C., & Pimdee, P. (2017). Innovative ideas: Thailand 4.0 and the fourth industrial revolution. *Asian International Journal of Social Sciences, 17*, 4–35. DOI: 10.29139/aijss.20170101.
74. Suchit Leesa-Nguansuk. (2021). Flash Group becomes first Thai unicorn. *Bangkok Post.*
75. Suchit Leesa-Nguansuk. (2022). Financial unicorn takes flight in Asean. *Bangkok Post.*
76. TripleA. (2021). Cryptocurrency information about Thailand. https://triple-a.io/crypto-ownership-thailand/.
77. Srisamoot, A. (2022). *China, Thailand and Globalization.* Springer Singapore, Singapore, pp. 181–191. ISBN 978-981-16-8086-1. DOI: 10.1007/978-981-16-8086-1 23.
78. Kittipanya-ngam, P., & Tan, K. H. (2020). A framework for food supply chain digitalization: lessons from Thailand. *Production Planning & Control, 31*(2–3), 158–172. DOI: 10.1080/09537287.2019. https://doi.org/10.1080/09537287.2019.1631462.
79. Choosung, P., Wasusri, T., Utto, W., Boonyaritthongchai, P., & Wongs-Aree, C. (2022). The supply chain and its development concept of fresh mulberry fruit in Thailand: Observations in Nan Province, the largest production area. *Open Agriculture, 7*(1), 401–419. DOI: 10.1515/opag-2022-0102.
80. Jaipong, P., Sriboonruang, P., Siripipattanakul, S., Sitthipon, T., Kaewpuang, P., & Auttawechasakoon, P. (2022). A review of intentions to use artificial intelligence in big data analytics for Thailand agriculture. *Review of Advanced Multidisciplinary Science, Engineering & Innovation, 1*(2), 1–8.
81. World Bank. (2022b). Secure internet servers (per 1 million people). World Development Indicators.
82. Guzikova, L. A., & Lo Thi, H. V. (2020). Industry 4.0 in Vietnam: Strategic planning experience. *Asia and Africa Today, 8*, 64–68. DOI: 10.31857/S032150750010453-0.
83. Vietnam Investment Review. (2020). A Vietnamese perspective on the evolution of Industry 4.0. https://vir.com.vn/a-vietnamese-perspective-on-the-evolution-of-industry-40-77078.html.
84. Vietnam Law & Legal Forum. (2021). National Strategy for Industry 4.0 introduced. https://vietnamlawmagazine.vn/ national-strategy-for-industry-40-introduced-27590.html.
85. Vietnam Briefing. (2020). Vietnam sets ambitious goals in new national industrial policy but can it stay competitive. https://www.vietnam-briefing.com/news/vietnam-sets-ambitious-goals-in-new-national-industrial-policy.html.

86. Nguyen, X. T., & Luu, Q. K. (2020). Factors affecting adoption of industry 4.0 by small- and medium-sized enterprises: A case in Ho Chi Minh City, Vietnam. *The Journal of Asian Finance, Economics and Business*, 7(6), 255–264.

87. Ha, N. T. T., Long, N. T., & Trang, T. T. T. (2022). Development of the electronics industry of Thai Nguyen province, Vietnam: Achievements and limitations. *European Journal of Development Studies*, 2(2), 66–71. DOI: 10.24018/ejdevelop.2022.2.2.87.

88. Tang, M. H., Ho, T. T. H., Do, D. T., Nguyen, Q. P., Nguyen, Q. L., & Vo, T. C. (2022). Tackling food loss in Vietnam logistics sector via technology. *Binh Duong University Journal of Science and Technology*, 5(2). DOI: 10.56097/binhduonguniversityjournalofscienceandtechnology.v5i2.42.

89. Cuong, T., & Tien, N. (2022). Application of ICT in logistics and supply chain in post-Covid-19 economy in Vietnam. *International Journal of Multidisciplinary Research and Growth Evaluation*, 3, 493–501.

90. World Bank. (2021). Digital Vietnam: The path to tomorrow, report. *Open Knowledge Repository*.

91. Bloomberg. (2021). Vietnamese unicorn VNG to seek funds ahead of U.S. listing. https://www.bloomberg.com/news/articles/2021-12-06/vietnamese-unicorn-vng-said-to-seek-funds-ahead-of-u-s-listing.

92. Dinh, V., Nguyen, H., & Nguyen, T. (2018). Cash or cashless? Promoting consumers' adoption of mobile payments in an emerging economy. *Strategic Direction*, 34(1), 1–4. DOI: 10.1108/SD-08-2017-0126.

93. Culannay, R. C. (2022). Analysis on the factors that influence the investment on online crypto games. *International Journal of Arts, Sciences and Education*, 3(1), 143–154.

94. UOB. (2021). FinTech in Vietnam 3Q2021: Payments flourish, though cash still king. https://www.uobgroup.com/techecosystem/news-insights-fintech-in-vietnam-3q-2021.html.

95. Hao, V. T. (2020). Developing a fintech ecosystem in Vietnam: Opportunities and challenges for startups. *SHS Web of Conferences*, 89, 04001. DOI: 10.1051/shsconf/20208904001.

96. Vu, T., Anh, H., & Office, F.-E.-S. V. (2017). *The Fourth Industrial Revolution: A Vietnamese Discourse*. Friedrich Ebert Stiftung.

97. O'Rourke, K. H., Rahman, A. S., & Taylor, A. M. (2013). Luddites, the industrial revolution, and the demographic transition. *Journal of Economic Growth*, 18(4), 373–409. http://www.jstor.org/stable/42635331.

98. Keynes, J. M. (2010). *Economic Possibilities for Our Grandchildren*. Palgrave Macmillan UK, London, pp. 321–332. 1007/978-1-349-59072-8_25.

99. World Economic Forum. (2021). Global lighthouse network: Reimagining operations for growth. https://www3.weforum.org/docs/WEF_GLN_2021_Reimagining_Operations_for_Growth.pdf.

100. World Economic Forum. (2022). The global lighthouse network playbook for responsible industry transformation. https://www3.weforum.org/docs/WEF_The_Global_Lighthouse_Network_Playbook_for_Responsible_Industry_Transformation_2022.pdf.
101. The Straits Times. (2021a). HP Singapore among 15 global firms joining WEF's leading-edge manufacturers network (World). The Straits Times. (2021b). Industry transformation maps to be refreshed, strengthened over next 5 years: DPM Heng (Politics).
102. Malaysian Investment Development Authority. (2021). Western digital WEF lighthouse network. https://www.mida.gov.my/media-release/western-digital-wef-lighthouse-network/.
103. Li, L. (2022). Reskilling and upskilling the future-ready workforce for industry 4.0 and beyond. https://doi.org/10.1007/s10796-022-10308-y.
104. Ertz, M., & Skali, A. (2022). *Impact of Industry 4.0 on Human Resources Systems: The Emergence of Work 4.0.* IGI Global, Pennsylvania, United States, pp. 278–303.
105. Bordel, B., Alcarria, R., de la Torre, G., Carretero, I., & Robles, T. (2022). Increasing the efficiency and workers wellbeing in the European bakery industry: An industry 4.0 case study, in Á. Rocha, C. Ferrás, A. Méndez Porras, & E. Jimenez Delgado (eds.) *Information Technology and Systems.* Springer International Publishing, Cham, pp. 646–658.
106. Lepore, D., Dubbini, S., Micozzi, A., & Spigarelli, F. (2022). Knowledge sharing opportunities for industry 4.0 firms. *Journal of the Knowledge Economy, 13*, 501–520.
107. Rocha, C., Quandt, C., Deschamps, F., Philbin, S., & Cruzara, G. (2021). Collaborations for digital transformation: Case studies of industry 4.0 in Brazil. *IEEE Transactions on Engineering Management*, 1–15. DOI: 10.1109/TEM.2021.3061396.
108. Ozkan-Ozen, Y. D., & Kazancoglu, Y. (2022). Analysing workforce development challenges in the industry 4.0. *International Journal of Manpower, 43*, 310–333.
109. Cater, T., Cater, B., Cerne, M., Koman, M., & Redek, T. (2021). Industry 4.0 technologies usage: Motives and enablers. *Journal of Manufacturing Technology Management, 32*, 323–345. DOI: 10.1108/JMTM-01-2021-0026.
110. SkillsFuture. (2019). Additional initiatives to prepare workforce for industry 4.0. https://www.skillsfuture.gov.sg/NewsAndUpdates/DetailPage/32cccc6a-f6e9-4452-9b36-11645d8a4cec.

Chapter 2

Digital Disruption and Transformation

Marcus T. H. Lee

The notion of digital disruption is often thought of as a form of environmental turmoil caused by digital innovation which results in the erosion of existing boundaries and a significant reduction in efficacy of organizational approaches that had previously served as fundamentals for capturing and delivering customer value. As a consequence, digital disruption often holds a negative connotation for leaders who view it as an attack on their existing business model. In fact, the change brought about by digital disruption is only negative when leaders choose to ignore the impending transformation within their industry or try to contest them head-on in a futile attempt at halting the revolution within their industry. Rather than create chaos and turmoil, digital disruption has been found by astute leaders who embrace it to be immensely beneficial for their businesses, leading to their continued success.

An illuminating example is the initial responses of the incumbents in the taxi industry and their respective governing bodies around the world with the arrival of the immensely popular ride-hailing platforms such as Uber, DiDi, Grab, and Gojek. Taxi industry incumbents moved from initially trying to prevent these ride-hailing platforms from operating in their markets, to learning how to thrive in this new industry landscape by working with, as well as competing with, these new platform business model entrants. It is not uncommon to see taxi drivers in Singapore today offering their taxi services on multiple platforms. Similar observations across the world indicate that the different markets have (independently) settled at an equilibrium point that allows the different stakeholders to benefit from the platform business model in their industry.

Beyond the taxi industry, it is unsurprising to find digital disruptions occurring in the VUCA (i.e., volatile, uncertain, complex, and ambiguous) business environment. For incumbents in these industries to retain their competitive edge requires forward-thinking leaders who are willing to bring about their own disruptions for the transformation and growth of their organization. To be effective, transformation needs to involve both taking advantage of technological advancements as well as mobilizing all stakeholders to appreciate the need for change and be motivated to move away from the status quo.

This chapter offers guidance on how organizational transformation can be structured within the context of digital disruptions. Specifically, this chapter introduces a framework and tools relevant to structuring organizational transformation and responding to a changing environment, with recommendations on how transformation and innovation activities should be approached.

What is Digital Disruption?

Digital disruption of an industry occurs when a new entrant, operating on a radically different business model, enters a market and dramatically changes the landscape in their favor. In digital disruption, the novel business model introduced to the market is enabled through the use of digital technologies and facilitated by the pervasiveness of the internet in the everyday lives of consumers. The value proposition of this new business model to consumers dominates the incumbents' offerings to the point that the market leaders are compelled to adapt their business models to offer consumers a similar value proposition.

The importance of digital disruption in business

A business needs to be able to grow and deliver customer value in order to stay competitive and relevant. In the current climate, digital disruption performs the integral role of creating the competitive advantage which businesses need to survive in the evolving landscape of their respective industries.

Today's business and consumer environments are characterized by internet-enabled technologies such as mobile apps, social media platforms, cloud computing services, and Internet-of-Things (IoT) devices. Advances in machine learning (ML) have dramatically increased the usefulness of artificial intelligence (AI)-enabled applications and devices. Many industries are looking toward extended reality technologies such as virtual reality, augmented reality, and mixed reality as the next big wave of industry disruption. The application of these advanced technologies is believed to have a major impact on consumer attitudes and buying behavior, which can generate new customer expectations and therefore encourage organizations to renew and optimize their processes in an attempt to meet these changing expectations. In addition to existing practices of customer experience management, digital technologies can transform and impact other critical organizational functions such as leadership, corporate culture, and organizational competitive strategy that require a completely different way of thinking and acting. As such, digital disruption is often seen as a revolutionary change for people, culture, organizations, and technology.

Disruption from digital technology

Digital technology is all around us, creating opportunities for major transformations. There is artificial intelligence (e.g., a fully autonomous car that drives you to the destination you provide), augmented intelligence (e.g., a navigation app that maps out the fastest route to your destination based on current traffic conditions), as well as IoT devices, where billions of devices are connected to the internet (e.g., Apple AirTags, smart fridges, or a service robot at the frontline).

In the automotive industry, drivers now enjoy the luxury of easily connecting to the outside world from within their cars, with innovations which have since expanded the frontiers of autonomous-navigation and in-vehicle entertainment. The navigation capability built into smartphone map apps have made dedicated in-vehicle navigation devices obsolete. In photography, digital single lens reflex (SLR) cameras have made film-based SLR cameras obsolete, and smartphone cameras have improved enough in quality to act as a viable replacement for dedicated digital cameras for many consumers. This last point underscores one important characteristic of digital disruption — digital innovations occurring in one industry (e.g., improved camera quality in the mobile phone industry) have the potential to disrupt another seemingly unrelated industry (e.g., the digital camera industry). As such, prudence dictates that organizations invest resources in keeping abreast of innovation activities beyond the specific industries their businesses operate in.

In the public service sector, there are e-government platforms which allow citizens and businesses to access government services through websites or apps without having to physically visit the specific agency's office premises to transact or interact with them. Beyond the convenience these online services bring to citizens and businesses, allowing stakeholders to interact with agencies asynchronously and remotely also allows these agencies to reallocate their (human) resources to other areas of work. The next logical step in citizen services would be to move from having each agency offer services limited to their own scope of authority, to amalgamated one-stop service websites or apps that allow citizens to initiate a single complex request that triggers multiple agencies to work on it. An example of this would be the LifeSG app by the Singapore Government (see Figure 1). Among other things, this app allows citizens to (1) submit feedback about municipal issues without having to wonder which agency or group of agencies the feedback should be directed to; (2) register the birth of a child, which would trigger the relevant agencies to disburse applicable subsidies as well as trigger an application for a membership with the National Library Board; and (3) arrange for virtual appointments with different agencies and ministries.

The use of sensors, big data, and analytics in the logistics industry has allowed organizations to improve the efficiency of their supply-chain operations. Tracking and tracing has improved in speed and accuracy with the advent of these sensors and devices, which has a knock-on effect on both logistics organizations as well as end-users of their services. IoT devices allow for real-time tracking of goods, which enable warehouses to plan the receiving and handling of goods in advance, which in turn facilitates more efficient use of warehouse space with less of a need to set aside space for unexpected changes in delivery schedules. In cold-chain transport, IoT devices go beyond location tracking and include temperature, humidity, and shock sensors. This allows all parties to ensure that the goods are not damaged in transit.

In service industries of all kinds, organizations are evolving their business models. In healthcare, there is a rise in popularity of telemedicine through mobile apps such as WhiteCoat and Dr Anywhere. These apps

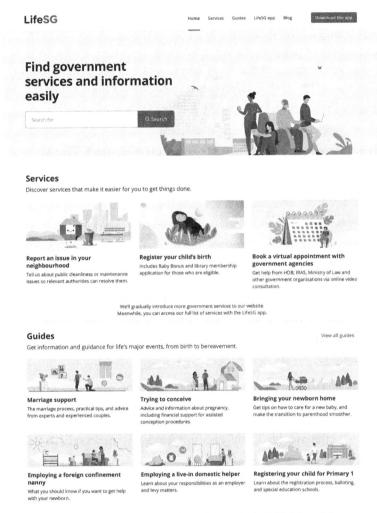

Figure 1: A description of the services offered through the LifeSG mobile app.
Source: www.life.gov.sg.

allow patients to video consult with a general practitioner remotely though a mobile app from the convenience of their homes, with the prescribed medicine couriered to them within the day.

During the COVID-19 pandemic period, the education industry across the world embraced digital technology and experienced a rapid expansion of e-learning and online offerings. While many educational institutions have returned to in-person lessons for most of their offerings, the lasting impact the lockdown has had on the education industry is that the perception of distance-based education (e.g., remote/e-learning) programs has improved in the eyes of employers and the general public.

The examples above demonstrate the wide-ranging impact digital disruptions have had across disparate industries.

Digital Transformation Frameworks and Tools

This section highlights a framework and the tools relevant to structuring digital transformation.

Diffusion of innovation theory

The Diffusion of Innovation (DOI) Theory by Rogers[1] is useful in explaining how adoption of an innovation progresses through a specific population, with different segments of the population possessing differing adoption propensities.

Specifically, the population can be partitioned into five adopter categories, namely,

Innovators	Tied to these individuals' sense of self is the need to be acknowledged as one of the first to test or try an innovation. Innovators are generally risk takers and highly curious about the world. Little encouragement is necessary for them to adopt an innovation.
Early Adopters	These are individuals, comfortable and open to adopting new ideas, who are often opinion leaders others look to for guidance. As early adopters typically embrace change, the information businesses need to provide this segment should not focus on convincing them on the need for change. Instead, this segment is looking for implementation details for the innovation.
Early Majority	This segment adopts innovations just ahead of the average individual. The early majority generally needs assurance that the innovation works before considering adopting it. Communicating success stories and evidence of the innovation's effectiveness to this segment will increase the likelihood of adoption.

Late Majority	This segment considers adopting an innovation only after the majority of users have adopted it, as they are skeptical of change. Information on the number of people who have already tried and successfully adopted the innovation will increase the likelihood of adoption.
Laggards	This final segment values tradition and is typically conservative in their decision-making. Laggards are the most challenging group to bring on board as they are skeptical of and resistant to change. A multi-prong approach that includes conveying success statistics, fear appeals, and peer pressure from other adopter groups should be considered when trying to convince this group to adopt.

A key takeaway from Roger's Diffusion of Innovation theory is that the appeal and unique value proposition of innovative products/services should be tailored to each adopter category. Diffusion principles can be operationalized to accelerate the rate of adoption and broaden the reach of innovations to the different categories.

Challenges of Digital Transformation

While other forms of disruption have preceded today's digital technologies (e.g., the commercialization of the Internet in 1995), the rising emergence of digital disruption has blurred the boundaries of affected industries, lowered existing barriers for entry, altered value chains, and propelled a host of business model shifts. Cameron[2] identified four key challenges to digital transformation, as follows:

Understanding the Customer	Key to customer-focused digital transformation is the need to understand customers. Instead of emphasizing the technology involved, organizations should align the digital transformation process with customers' needs and aspirations. To ensure strong internal focus on the digital transformation project, organizations should develop a strong narrative about the need for the transformation project based around the customer. For a successful digital transformation project, organizations should adopt an empathetic mindset when tapping into their customer research, customer journey mapping, and data analysis.

The "Always-on" Business	Organizations need to constantly be on their guard to proactively seek new and unconventional ways of doing things or acquiring new skill sets or modus operandi. They need to tie their business strategies and tactics to their customers' ever-increasing expectations. Ideally, leaders should kick-start conversations with their key customers before forming their transformation project teams.
Business Model Velocity	Implementation of technology can be confounding for organizations without a clear and focused strategic vision for their digital transformation efforts. As businesses are addressing their customers' unfulfilled needs by leveraging on technology to disrupt the existing environment and redesign the whole market, it is important to not conflate the business model with the technological considerations. While they are often inextricably linked, a successful business model should center around business strategy and competitive advantage.
The Data Dialog	Successful businesses often have the practice of considering the data on hand and developing a conversation that is focused on delivering a service that a specific segment of customers value significantly and are willing to pay for. While it may be possible to analyze all the available data for the purpose of creating more defined segmentation and targeting, doing so will most likely be costly and difficult to begin. Instead, a better approach is to identify and use the data points that will provide the most value to the customer base. Considering how digital transformation focuses on the use of digital tools and techniques to transform a business, leaders need to be open to new ways of thinking and working. It is important to note that the biggest digital transformation challenges are typically related to leadership and communication, rather than the technology involved.

Failed digital transformation initiatives

"While understanding the challenges of digital transformations, it is also good to reference three failed digital transformation initiatives to draw some valuable lessons on things to avoid." One example of a company that has not been successful in its digital transformation attempt is Ford's Smart Mobility unit, a new segment created by Ford to promote the production of digital cars that are equipped with functional mobility. From the start of the transformation process, the entity was seen as a separate business, which resulted in its lack of integration with Ford's other business units due to lack of support from the Ford headquarter. Clearly, the alignment of both the business model and corporate strategy are crucial for the optimization of digital disruption. In relation to Ford's case, the company did not align the mission, vision, and business model for the Ford Smart Mobility segment with its other strategic business units. For instance, the lack of integration of this new segment with other established segments resulted in the failure of positioning the competitive advantages of the Ford Smart Mobility unit in the market. Although the Ford Smart Mobility unit is an innovative approach that is geared toward digital transformation, the inability to highlight its business value through a coherent business model and strategy negatively impacted its performance. Therefore, it is crucial that organizations interlink their business model and technology development to promote customer value and competitive advantage within the market and industry.

Another notable example is General Electric (GE) and its subsidiary business, GE Digital. GE had the overarching goal of owning the industrial Internet. To reach the goal, the company established a separate entity called GE Digital in 2015 with the aim of centralizing all its IT operations. By constructing a massive IoT platform and overhauling its industrial goods business models, GE had a vision of becoming one of the top 10 software companies by 2020. However, GE Digital failed to meet that vision. Its resources were spread too thin, its projective objectives were unrealistic, and its implementation timelines were rushed. GE Digital failed to bring in the profits that GE had hoped for Baumann.[4] Its stock prices fell and its industrial internet platform was unable to compete with rival companies due to delays and technological issues, resulting in a platform failure. Consequently, GE decided to sell GE Digital and went for a more focused strategy while abandoning its plans to become a major player in the software space Toesland.[5] One possible reason for the failure could be a reluctance to integrate GE's legacy assets with the new digital assets of GE Digital. The fact that they formed a separate entity rather than conduct a total digital transformation within their own company implies that GE was reluctant to dispose of its existing legacy assets. Although GE attempted a digital transformation, it failed due to underestimating the need to change its structure, a reluctance to dispose of legacy assets, no alignment with its overarching goal and the expertise that GE Digital could offer, and a lack of a clear project vision to tackle challenges that arise from digital transformation initiatives.

Another company that made a failed attempt at digital transformation is ComfortDelGro. With the rise of e-commerce and more things becoming digital, the private hire consumer market and spending power was also making a shift toward a younger consumer base. This group of digital natives enjoyed the convenience and ease of booking rides directly on their phones and ComfortDelGro was slow in adapting to this change in consumer preferences, as the company stuck to its traditional means of hailing rides by waiting in long lines at taxi stands under the hot sun, or booking through a hotline, which often included long waiting times and expensive booking fees. ComfortDelGro only launched its Zig app for ride-hailing in 2021, several years after platforms like Grab and Uber had disrupted the industry. As the Zig app cost millions to develop, it was not a successful venture. It was shut down less than a year after it was launched and was merged with the existing ComfortDelGro app. Due to its lack of expertise to lead digital transformation initiatives, ComfortDelGro did not have an overarching strategy for digitalization. In addition, the Zig app had multiple uses, which include booking a taxi, searching for restaurants and staycations, and making bookings. The complex user interface made it difficult to navigate, which discouraged app adoption.

Responding to a Changing Environment

Kotter's eight-step change model

A useful model for implementing change is the Eight-Step Change Model by Kotter.[3] This framework is best suited for senior leaders in organizations to scaffold corporate transformation activities. By adopting this framework, organizations will be assured of not missing out any crucial steps in their transformation journey. In this framework, the following eight steps are listed for leaders to adopt to increase the likelihood of a successful organizational transformation journey.

1. *Create a sense of urgency* — Change the narrative within the organization and help relevant parties recognize and acknowledge the urgent need for organizational change.
2. *Build a guiding coalition* — Select and assemble a suitable group of senior leaders and grant them with the necessary power to lead the change collaboratively.
3. *Form a strategic vision and initiatives* — Design a compelling and persuasive vision that change efforts can strive for.
4. *Enlist a volunteer army* — Create organizational buy-in and encourage an enthusiasm for change throughout the organization.
5. *Enable action by removing barriers* — Make visible changes by eliminating existing barriers to change and encourage risk-taking and positive action.
6. *Generate short-term wins* — Engineer quick wins and then celebrate, recognize, and reward employees involved.
7. *Sustain acceleration* — Implement further changes to systems, structures, and policies to create alignment with the strategic vision. Promote, develop, and hire individuals capable of implementing the vision.
8. *Institute change* — Secure and strengthen the new corporate culture by explicitly connecting the dots for employees. This will help employees realize how their new behavior and attitude have helped improve organization performance, which in turn anchors the desired culture within the organization. Additionally, in terms of succession planning, leaders should redesign the organization's criteria for promotion and succession to ensure that future organization leaders genuinely believe in the same vision.

The eight-step framework for organizational transformation

While the steps in Kotter's change model are most suitable for senior leaders at or close to the apex of the organization, the Eight Steps Framework offers a step-by-step guide on orchestrating effective organizational transformation efforts for leaders at all levels within an organization. The eight steps are outlined in more detail in the rest of this section (see Figure 2).

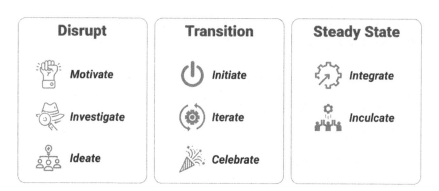

Figure 2: The eight steps framework for organizational transformation.

Motivate   The first step in effecting successful organizational transformation efforts begins with convincing all relevant stakeholders that the organization has outgrown and outpaced its existing organizational structures and their accompanying processes. Change management frameworks prescribe the need to provide the appropriate motivation to stakeholders, as this creates the right environment for an agile and willing workforce, one which is open to considering new approaches in the implementation and execution of core work.

For example, when a bank in Singapore wanted to improve the turnaround time for their credit card replacement process and initiated ideation workshops with the teams of staff involved in the process, they motivated the staff involved, not by emphasizing the need to deliver better customer service or to strive to meet the ever-increasing expectations of their customers, but by getting everyone to realize that each additional day a customer goes about their life without the bank's credit card is an additional day they are getting used to using another bank's credit card for their daily purchases. If the bank takes too long to replace the credit card, the customer may end up not returning to using the bank's credit card. The takeaway from this example is that effective appeals should be based on things that matter to your audience.

In this case, the frontline as well as backend bank staff care more about the bottom line (i.e., the potential negative financial impact on the bank losing a customer would have, and the consequence that would eventually have on their remuneration and jobs) than they do about pleasing customers.

Providing the motivation for change creates within the organization a sense of collective purpose and responsibility, which in turn encourages inter-department cooperation and pre-empts organizational inertia and learned helplessness. Motivation supplies the impetus for change and progression, from which organizations can then proceed onto the next step of challenge identification.

Investigate The next step in managing organization transformation involves a thorough investigation into the ongoing processes of the organization. Knowing what to work on is as important as knowing how to get it done. Understanding the status quo is an essential element of the transformation process.

The investigation begins with characterizing and categorizing stakeholder segments into different levels of priority, followed by an evaluation of the activities each segment engages the organization on. After which, ground sensing exercises are encouraged in order to gain a deeper appreciation of the experiences of stakeholders in relation to the current processes in place.

Many organizations, especially those in the public sector, generally consider their customers in an undifferentiated manner. Service processes in such organizations are designed with the average customer in mind because they believe they serve the general public. In this step of the framework, it is important to help the internal stakeholders recognize that their customer base is made up of many different segments of customers, and that each of these segments come with their own, possibly unique, requirements, constraints, expectations, and desires. Facilitating discussions to identify and collectively agree on the relative importance of each customer segment is an important prerequisite for the downstream innovation activities.

For example, as part of crafting a new land transport master plan that would spell out the Singapore Government's strategic vision and plans that would unfold over a 20-year period, there were many discussions about the characteristics of the different segments of land transport users, including their needs, constraints, expectations, and motivations. Great emphasis is placed on having assurance that the identified segments were comprehensive and their characteristics were accurate as the design of the subsequent ground sensing, engagement activities, and ideation workshops are based on this.

Prioritizing the segments and processes within each group enables a decision to be made in an objective, structured, and defensible manner. A thorough investigation will provide an understanding of the impact each segment has on the organization, as well as the impact each process, product, or service has on the respective segments. These investigative efforts will help organizations identify the appropriate process, product, or service which requires reformative action.

Ideate

Upon identifying the areas within the organization which require transformation, leaders now have the responsibility to collectively agree on a digital transformation strategy statement that will guide the selection of potential innovations for further development. With the overarching direction set, internal stakeholders who are directly or indirectly connected to focal processes, products, or services should be engaged in guided ideation sessions.

Service blueprinting workshops provide a platform for employees from different departments to arrive at a common understanding of mechanisms behind a specific customer process. The acts and responsibilities of each stakeholder and the sequence of steps which a customer follows impacts the manner in which information and work are channeled to the respective parts of the organization, all of which are a consequence of a specific process triggered by the customer. As such, incidental streamlining of customer processes often occurs as a result of these blueprinting sessions.

As part of a process reengineering exercise at a large Singapore based organization, multiple service blueprinting workshops were conducted in which all 18 internal departments involved in various stages of a complex service transaction were present. Not unexpectedly, at the end of the workshop, multiple departments realized that they were duplicating the work of other departments present at the workshop.

The findings from these sessions also act as a starting point for other innovation tools, such as design thinking, to attempt to achieve greater transformational changes within the organization. With these findings, senior leaders within the organization should now be able to choose the most promising designs to pilot, as they embark on initiating transformation within their organization.

Initiate   With promising designs endorsed by organization leaders, the initiation stage involves designing one or more prototypes with core features that can be released quickly. The availability of monetary and non-monetary resources as well as the length of the applicable time horizon will determine the number of designs to prototype and the extensiveness of each prototype produced.

The start of the iterative process should focus on the design and launch of an initial product with minimal viability. This pilot design will provide preliminary insights on its functionality, which should then spark further innovation through the observation of how staff and customers navigate and experience the new process, product, or service.

The objective behind the implementation of prototypes is to discover and learn from the current prototypes, and then incorporate the insights gained from the first prototype into the next iteration of the design. This objective ties in closely with the key purpose of any organizational transformation journey. Thus, the success of the initial pilot is inconsequential, instead, staff should be encouraged to be adventurous in creating novel designs, with their key performance indicators tied to lessons learned and how those lessons have been applied to the next iteration.

This approach benefits the organization in two ways, (1) it unshackles staff from the compulsion to rely on safe, tried, and tested designs to ensure a well-received pilot, thus resulting in greater exploration of the possible solution space when designing the pilot; and (2) it shifts the mindset of staff to one of continuous improvement, which is essential in the next stage of the transform process.

Iterate   The intent of this stage is to launch a prototype design, learn from observations of the experiences of staff and customers during their interaction with the prototype, and then incorporate changes into the next iteration. This process is repeated until the successive inter-iteration changes taper off. During this stage, adopting a continuous improvement mindset is necessary in order for stakeholders within the organization to appreciate that products and services should be considered to be dynamic systems created for their specific purposes and contexts. As the context changes, the relevance of the respective parts may also change.

As an example of this, consider the design of each stretch of road in a familiar neighborhood. Each stretch of road was designed to accommodate a predetermined volume of vehicular and human traffic journey in between a set of origin and destination points. Over time, emergent behavior arises from patterns of journeys made by residents as part of their formation of daily habits. This emergent behavior reveals the under- and over-utilization of certain routes, which gives planners the information they need to update the road and network design to better reflect the realized patterns of travel habits.

The organizational processes, products, and services that customers and staff experience are similar. Each was initially designed to address a specific need with a specific context in mind. Yet to remain relevant, periodic reviews are necessary based on changes to the context and needs of the stakeholders.

Celebrate Celebrating the successes after the iterate stage is essential in ensuring a smooth transformation, as it acknowledges the challenges involved in any organizational transformation. Amidst the ongoing changes throughout the transformation process, this phase underscores the importance of taking sufficient opportunities to reassure employees of their continued value to the organization and affirm their willingness to embrace the uncertainty that comes with transformation.

In addition, celebrating success reinforces the objective that success in a transformation focuses on the learning process and the implementation of changes to each successive iteration based on what was discovered at the earlier stage. Celebrating these successes lowers the perceived risk associated with transformation activities and communicates to all levels within the organization that these activities are the building blocks to secure the future of the organization.

Integrate When the iterative process is completed, the transformed process, product, or service has to be considered in terms of scalability. Specifically, attention should be focused on the manual elements within the process and steps taken to eliminate them. As part of this exercise to remove manual elements, the continued relevance of existing policies should be considered in relation to the changing contexts that the organization is operating in as organizational processes are generally designed to enforce policies. Any policies deemed irrelevant would allow the removal of associated processes from the workflow, which would consequently reduce the time and effort associated with the transformed process, product, or service.

Inculcate The final stage in the transformation process is inculcating culture change. An organization-wide shift in culture is required in order to successfully implement radical changes to existing processes. Successful transformation requires the willing cooperation of the entire organization.

Organizations can achieve this by adjusting employee KPIs to shift the focus toward the facilitation of transformative efforts, such as to reward collaborative effort, attempts at new approaches, and efforts in the facilitation of transformation across departments. Adjusting KPIs will shape the behavior of each person within the organization, which will in turn influence the overall success of the organizational transformation.

Conclusion

This chapter discusses how organizational transformation can be structured within the context of digital disruptions. Several frameworks and tools for structuring organizational transformation are highlighted, including the Diffusion of Innovation Theory, Kotter's Eight-Step Change Model, and the Eight Steps Framework for organizational transformation.

References

1. Rogers, E. M. (2003). *Diffusion of Innovations*, 5th edn. Simon and Schuster, New York (NY).
2. Cameron, M. (Jun 14, 2016). Digital transformation key challenges. Available from https://www.marketingmag.com.au/hubs-c/four-key-challenges-digital-transformation-tackle/.
3. Kotter, J. (Aug 16, 2003). The 8-step process for leading change. Available from https://www.kotterinc.com/8-steps-process-for-leading-change/.
4. Baumann, B. (Sep 1, 2021). 4 lessons learned from the GE digital transformation failure. Panorama Consulting Group. Available from https://www.panorama-consulting.com/ge-digital-transformation-failure/.
5. Toesland, F. (Mar 24, 2020). Digital transformation failure: What to learn when it goes wrong. Raconteur. Available from https://www.raconteur.net/digital/digital-transformation-failure/.

PART II

EMBRACING DIGITAL SKILLS, KNOWLEDGE, AND COMPETENCIES

https://doi.org/10.1142/9789811278570_0003

Chapter 3

Developing a Polymathic Mindset for the Future of Work — A Personal Reflection

Jimmy Wong

At the time of writing this chapter, I was leading a course called The Future of Work at the university I was working for. It was a postgraduate course in which my students were mostly working adults pursuing a degree in the Master of Management. In my preparation, I chanced upon the concept of polymathy and I was deeply captivated by it. So, I incorporated it as the final topic for my class where students reviewed how a polymathic mindset could enhance one's career in the future of our work. To my surprise, among all the concepts covered in this course, the feedback was most positive for this topic. Consequently, given the demands of the high-intensity work culture here in Singapore, I felt compelled to put down my thoughts in this chapter on how the concept of polymathy could prepare the local workforce for the future of work.

Nevertheless, before we dive any deeper, I shall declare that it is not my ambition to help readers *become* polymaths (as we shall see in the later sections, considering the achievements and profiles of impactful individuals that are commonly recognized as polymaths, it is certainly not easy to be one). Instead, my main purpose is to highlight the benefits of polymathy and hope that readers can invest time to develop a polymathic approach toward their work. Once you see the benefits, I strongly believe that you will experience a sense of empowerment in your work and a renewed sense of freedom toward your life. This is what I hope for in this chapter.

In the subsequent sections, we shall first evaluate the meaning of being a polymath, followed by a discussion on why a generalist approach of polymathy contradicts the social norms of raising specialists. We then expand the conversation further by examining why we should entertain the idea of developing a polymathic mindset within the context of our work and evaluate the benefits. Lastly, we review the context of the future of our work and discuss how we can train our minds to be polymathic by assessing various aspects of developing the habit of lifelong learning.

What is a Polymath?

So what exactly is a polymath? According to the Macmillan dictionary, the word polymath is a noun used to refer to individuals who possess great knowledge and are well-informed across a wide domain of topics.[1] In fact, the term is a derivative of two Greek words — *poly* means "much" and *manthanein* refers to the "process of knowledge acquisition". According to many scholars, the word polymath was used traditionally to describe individuals who excelled in many different domains ranging from philosophy, history, poetry and arts, politics, economics, and very often, it also included mathematics, physics, and astronomy. At this moment, some may raise the question, "so what is the difference between a scholar and a polymath?" Let's try to peel this a little further.

According to writer Peter Burke,[2] who reviewed the profiles of over 500 polymaths, ranging from traditional polymaths to modern ones, although the concept of polymathy started during the age of the "Renaissance Man" (1400–1600), the term polymath was not used until much later. Instead, "a universal man (uomo universale)" was used to describe the numerous *many-sided* scholars that emerged during this period of high Renaissance. Among them, the one that typified a polymath was none other than Leonardo da Vinci (1452–1519). Unbeknown to many, Leonardo was more than a painter (of great works such as the Mona Lisa and The Last Supper). He was also a sculptor, architect, inventor, and engineer who made various discoveries in stage design, music, hydrodynamics, military hardware, civil engineering projects, and even geology, botany, zoology, and human anatomy. Nevertheless, most of these works were kept in his notes and were never published (possibly incomplete as well). However, one cannot deny that his motivation to gather and connect different domains of knowledge was a trait that qualified him to be a polymath. He was so passionate in acquiring new knowledge that he was often distracted by them as well. Hence, compared to the numerous projects that he had started, Leonardo completed relatively few of them. Scholars termed this weakness (common among polymaths) the *Leonardo Syndrome*.[3]

Another prominent scholar during the late Renaissance, albeit less popularly cited as a polymath, was Galileo Galilei (1564–1642). Similarly, Galileo had immense interest in a wide range of knowledge domains, not just astronomy, physics, and mathematics which he was most well known for. In fact, he studied medicine and philosophy, and was also a critical scholar on paintings, sculpture, and poetry. Pushing past the 1600, the next commonly recognized polymath was Isaac Newton (1642–1727) who was initially known as a philosopher before he gained his reputation as a polymath scientist. In fact, he first started publishing in theology rather than science. Like Galileo, Isaac Newton was a mathematician who practically created the scientific field of physics through his book called the *Mathematical Principles of Natural Philosophy* that laid down the foundations of gravity and established the three laws of motion. (For a more complete review of renowned polymaths, please refer to the excellent book written by Peter Burke.[2]) As such, based on the traditional approach of defining polymathy, I assert that most polymaths are indeed very scholarly by nature. However, to dwell any further on discerning the two will be too academic for our current purpose, so let's just settle on the general definition that a polymath is a *many-sided* man who is extremely knowledgeable.

At this juncture, I would usually pause and ask my students to share their thoughts. Many would tell me that these examples were not exactly relevant to them. First, these polymaths were all from a bygone era and, second, these polymaths were all geniuses to begin with. While I would usually proceed to showcase examples of 21st century polymaths (who are still alive at the time of writing this chapter) such as Bill Gates and Elon Musk, and praise their entrepreneurial achievements, students would once again remark that it was easy for these billionaires to be polymaths since they had the resources to do so. Regrettably, most of the students would also admit that they do not envision themselves to be as successful as Bill Gates or Elon Musk, these students just want to have a better pay check.

I can certainly empathize with my students given that most of them are common men in the streets; they are not seeking ways to contribute to the society on a grand scale and I do not expect them to do so. As such, I usually remind the class that the purpose of our discussion on polymathy is focused more on developing a polymathic mindset to help us improve our work and enhance our career. It is not my intention to train students to be polymaths because the expectation of becoming one is very high indeed. Instead, all I am trying to highlight is just some attributes of polymathy and demonstrate some benefits that can be obtained by simply applying some of these polymathic traits. Specifically, I raise the question: can we be proficient in several domains of knowledge (without spending too much time to become an expert or a specialist) and learn to weave these domains together to make us more effective in our work? We turn our attention to this question by examining the pros and cons of specialization.

Polymathy — From Generalization to Specialization?

The discussion so far suggests several observations concerning polymathy. First, interdisciplinary knowledge is a prerequisite; you will need to be knowledgeable in not just one, but several other domains. Second, it seems that successful scholars, scientists, entrepreneurs, and even politicians share the common denominator of being highly motivated and curious in gathering information without necessarily knowing if the information is immediately useful for their next endeavor. Does this then imply that polymaths are typically a jack of all trades (and master of none)? How should we reconcile the brilliant contributions by Leonardo, Galileo, and Newton if these were not considered masters of their fields? To examine this, we shall begin from the evolution of knowledge creation and curation.

Tracking back to the early medieval era, knowledge taught in schools and cathedrals were broadly categorized as arts.[2] This was further broken down into two streams, one concerning words (grammar, logic, and rhetoric) and another concerning numbers (music, arithmetic, geometry, and astronomy). However, the proliferation of knowledge creation went into high gears during the fifteenth and sixteenth centuries (i.e., the Renaissance Era) as European scholars focused on restoring ancient texts and artifacts that were left behind by the Greeks and Romans. It was also a time where printing was invented, which further accelerated the spreading and sharing of views and knowledge. During this period, scholars added the fields of poetry, history, and ethics to the study stream concerning words and the field of humanities was conceived. This was also the era where polymathy flourished. Scholars were in high gears gathering information, knowledge creation went into overdrive toward the late Renaissance until a state of information overload occurred during the seventeenth century. It was during this era where scholars began questioning each other's depth of knowledge which started the debate between specialization and generalization. The generalist scholars were criticized for being too superficial in terms of their claim to knowledge, and that they suffered from the previously mentioned Leonardo Syndrome. The specialist scholars, on the other hand, were being mocked for missing the beauty of true knowledge by over examining unnecessary details, thereby missing the forest while focusing on the trees.

Regardless of whichever approach toward knowledge acquisition was better, there was another reality occurring. Raw information was meaningless until it was processed and categorized, and the volume of information grew at an uncontrolled pace during the eighteenth century, to the point where knowledge itself became fragmented. In fact, it was cited that "Polymathy is often nothing but a confused mass of useless knowledge which is offered to put on a show".[4] The word "charlatan" was also used very often to describe polymaths; it was not a good time for them. Scholars recognized that there was an urgent need to categorize knowledge so that it could be seen as relevant and useful; hence began a new evolution, marking the rise of discipline specialization in scholarly institutions. Universities started branching into deeper specializations and disciplines based on existing ones. In fact, specialization became so foundational during this era that it found its way into the economy and production processes. This was evidenced in Adam Smith's famous Jurisprudence lecture in 1763[5] where he asserted the eventuality and usefulness of categorized and specialized knowledge in the process of production.

Subsequently, the idea of specialization was formalized as the "division of labor" in Adam Smith's *Wealth of Nations* publication. Following the conceptualization of the division of labor came the rise of the modern corporation in the late nineteenth and early twentieth centuries. There about the same time, *The Principle of Scientific Management*,[6] which promoted specialization as a means of production efficiency, was published. Ideas from this publication were epitomized in the mass production process made popular at the Ford car factories.

The ideas of specialization also spilled into the education system designed to support the economic forces required to sustain the wealth of a society. As much as we deny it, schools' curriculum was indeed designed to mass produce graduates that could operate as useful agents of production, serving the manufacturing machines of the society. School subjects were compartmentalized and often taught in isolation without any emphasis on uniting these specializations to make them useful and relevant. For example, wouldn't Algebra be more useful when applied to the context of Geometry? Likewise, to fully appreciate Geography, one may need to understand the history of a particular location. In the words of Alfred Whitehead (a British philosopher of education), the flaw in modern day education was that we failed to recognize that specialization only produced a laundry list for regurgitation; we overlooked the importance of teaching children to weave and synthesize knowledge so that life's problems could be better appreciated. Unfortunately, as we moved into the 21st century, the culture of hyper-specialization as observed with the development of so many fields of disciplines in higher education had already become a societal norm.

But what is so wrong with a focus on specialization? From the lens of a polymath, the problem with specialization was that learning only one or two topics allowed you to understand half-truths about the world. In fact, the bigger issue was that fragmented understanding of how the world functioned could pose a greater danger than pure ignorance. From the perspective of the students or adult learners, it could not be any more torturing attending lectures and reading journal articles while wondering about the practicality of this knowledge in their current career. The disjointed education style of hyper-specialization was based on a factory model meant to mass produce like-minded students. So, what's the impact on our work? We turn to this aspect next.

Impact of Specialization for the Modern Employee

Every human is born with multifarious potential. Why, then, do parents, schools and employers insist that we restrict our many talents and interests; that we 'specialise' in just one?

— *Waqās Ahmed*

According to writer and polymath Waqās Ahmed,[7] we are now faced with the most unfortunate reality of modern times in which a large proportion of the world's corporate employees is stuck in their career that is personally and financially unfulfilling. Through social norms, these individuals were told to specialize in a particular field during the earlier phase of their lives, typically because of various financial and social circumstances at the time. What happened next was a vicious cycle that was hard to break. As university students, they would enroll into a specific discipline and graduate with a core specialized skill. This core skill would then be the foundation of recruitment by employers, which usually led to an accumulation of more specialized years of practice (which we proudly called "work experience"). Then, the next employer seeking individuals with that core skill would offer a better remuneration package based on the individual's accumulation of "specialised work experience". This vicious cycle motivated employees to continuously invest their time and lives to the practice of that one specific specialization for the next bigger pay check.

This form of employment practice in our society can be seen as a form of slavery[7] because, for as long as people continue to be sucked into this bondage of practicing only just one core skill, they will find it difficult to switch careers, particularly at the later stages of their lives (and we all know the sad stories when mid-career retrenchment hits). However, what is even more unfortunate is that the general populace is often brainwashed by our education system into believing that lifelong specialization is the only way to make a living. This usually creates a sense of disillusionment and work–life imbalance, leading to a global employee engagement crisis.[8] Specifically, between 2000 and 2015, only 32 percent of US employees and 13 percent of worldwide employees were engaged in their work (i.e., employees who self-reported that they were enthusiastic and committed to their work and workplace).[a] Put differently, these figures suggested that about three-quarters of the US workforce was feeling miserable at work and a great majority of the global workforce felt the same way, especially, the millennial cohort. Accordingly, the disengagement at work was caused by the monotony of their specialized job. A study by the School of Life revealed that almost 60 percent of employees, when given a chance, would learn or study something else, and choose a vastly different career path.[7]

---

[a] *Interestingly, an updated survey by Gallup (2021) in 2021 revealed improved engagement levels in the US (36 percent) and worldwide (20 percent). It was argued that these positive results were due to the flexible work-from-home norms triggered by the COVID-19 pandemic.*

To combat this pandemic of workplace disengagement, there is an increased need to seek work–life balance. This can be seen in the rise of flexible work arrangement by companies as well as the increased application of technology to facilitate a "work from anywhere culture" (a practice that is also reinforced by corporations due to the COVID-19 pandemic). The explicit motivation behind this trend is to empower employees to have greater control of their time and, perhaps, engage in non-work-related activities such as white-collar boxing or volunteering at non-profit organizations. Nevertheless, according to Ahmed,[7] such a flexi-work culture has the potential to encourage a work–life balanced lifestyle, but it also highlighted our deep ingrained feelings toward work — "that work is toil... an activity in which one spends the majority of one's time and which results in the financial remuneration required to survive..." If specialization in our work is contributing to a disillusioned workforce, perhaps it is time to consider polymathy (i.e., let's generalize!) and challenge our current perception toward the nature of work.

Benefits of Developing a Polymathic Mindset

In the beginning of this chapter, I mentioned that polymathy is one of the topics covered in the Future of Work course that I am teaching at my current university. Very often, at the mid-point of this topic, a few students will inevitably say that they do not wish to be a polymath because it is just too difficult (and time-consuming); they do not see how it can benefit them at work or enhance their life. I shall dedicate this section to elaborate a little more.

1. *Polymathy helps solve problems more innovatively and effectively*
If you are a company employee, you should be familiar of the cultural norm of firms to set up ad-hoc project teams to implement various strategic initiatives. Very often, the level and frequency of participation in such teams are criteria used for employees' performance appraisal. Even within the university that I work for, I need to participate in different committees ranging from strategic curriculum planning to social media marketing design. Being nominated by your supervisor as a representative is usually considered a good thing because it implies that you are perceived as an important member of your organization and your supervisor thinks that you can add value to it. (If you feel that these committees are a waste of

time, I urge you to change that perception because such teams offer you not just the chance to learn about the functions of the other departments of your organization, but your participation also increases your visibility among your bosses).

These project teams are typically formed to address abstract problems (such as designing a Sustainability Business Framework for a company) that involve stakeholders (who are usually the specialists) from different departments and fields. However, it is not uncommon for these specialists to disagree with each other because they do not understand the constraints that each is experiencing within the context of the abstract problem. This is the main issue when you work in a multidisciplinary team. In the cultural norm of workforce specialization, most management thinks that pooling the minds of specialists is an effective way to solve problems. But is this the most productive approach? Most modern-day business problems (such as how to design an Artificial Intelligence (AI) Marketing Model) are wicked problems that need to be addressed via an interdisciplinary approach. As described by polymath Herbert Simon,[9] a polymath is the *interdisciplinary generalist* that can help galvanize the different specialists in a multidisciplinary task force to work as a team. Being polymathic, this individual will be quicker in acquiring and synthesizing knowledge across different specialized fields compared to the other specialists within the committee. Hence, if you train your mind to be polymathic and it has been actively accumulating a wide range of knowledge that is beyond your current work scope, you will be able to seize upon the inputs made by the specialists during committee discussions. Using cross field inputs (such as applying design thinking skills in the context of developing AI driven Apps to facilitate App-based selling), you may be able to think out of the box far better than specialists who are used to working in silos. In the long run, your visibility in an organization will increase and you will be valued as a great problem solver. This makes you a highly versatile and adaptive employee, which should reduce the chances of you being on the retrenchment list.

2. *Polymathy creates value by synthesizing different domains of knowledge*
In most discussions concerning polymaths, the literature tends to focus on the diversity in the range of knowledge fields in which these polymaths excel in. However, we need to understand that most of these polymaths achieve success in multiple fields not simply because they are geniuses

and are excellent learners. Most often, it is because they have applied related experience gain from their previous successes (or even failures) in different fields, thus creating a positive cycle of continuous success in many other fields. This "accumulated advantage", sometimes termed as the Matthew Effect, can be observed in many successful polymaths including politicians, entrepreneurs, celebrities, and sportsmen. For example, it is quite common for a successful sportsperson, bodybuilder, or wrestler to switch careers and become a Hollywood actor or actress. Most of these celebrities will further leverage on their accumulated fame and knowledge to venture into other forms of businesses. Although not all of them will succeed, it shows how polymathy creates value by synthesizing and applying one's past knowledge from different fields into a pursuit *in a related domain*. (Note the last few words in italics, which I shall return to shortly).

At this point, some of my students will once again lament that whatever I have just said is not realistic, "I am not a celebrity, neither am I successful in any fields, how is this even relevant to me?" This is a common question I get not just in class, but during public forums as well. This is also the moment I remind my students that I am not advocating that all of us must train to be a polymath. All I am suggesting is for us to entertain the idea of developing a polymathic mindset. I get it! Being a polymath is scary because it takes years of commitment (and requires a lot of resources). Not everyone has the time and discipline to follow through. However, what I am hoping is for this chapter to introduce this concept and sensitize the reader to understand how a polymathic mindset can enhance your life by simply appreciating the value in picking up skills from different domains. But you will need to be smart about how you gather and apply these accumulated skills and experiences; for optimal effect, they should be *in related domains*.

For example, bodybuilders' expertise is in fields that are related to their training. They will be well-versed in multiple sub-fields such as muscle building-related diets, the management of a sports gym, or perhaps in the latest software that tracks muscle development. If a bodybuilder ventures in any of these fields as an entrepreneur, the chances of success will be relatively higher compared to him or her switching career paths to be a dentist. It is from this lens that I urge my students to develop a polymathic mindset; I am not asking them to take up a vastly diverse portfolio of courses or multiple career specializations. Instead, I am asking them to practice weaving their knowledge in related fields to start a simple gig, project, or business.

Let's imagine that a university marketing student is passionate about yoga. This student completes a yoga instructor certification course and is about to start teaching yoga in a gym on a part-time basis. Up to this point, this student is mainly motivated to do this as a hobby. But the COVID-19 pandemic forces the gym to close indefinitely. So, this student decides to apply what is taught during her social media marketing class to start an online yoga channel on YouTube. She takes up an elective in school that teaches mobile phone videography and photography to make her video uploads more appealing. She also takes up elective courses related to branding and Search Engine Optimization (SEO) to make her channel more attractive to Gen-Z and Gen-Y mothers (because she is targeting to teach yoga to these two segments of consumers). Over a 6-months period, the number of subscribers on this student's YouTube yoga channel gradually increases and some yoga accessory brands start to place advertisements on her channel; she receives her first ad-payment remuneration from YouTube. Note that the student starts this channel as a hobby and she does not have the intention to monetize her videos initially. Is she a polymath? NO! I will not consider her one (yet), but she has certainly demonstrated the application of a polymathic mindset.

From a simple passion to teach yoga, she takes conscious steps to collect and synthesize parallel knowledge that she feels will help her achieve her goal. But she does not need to go out of her way to pick up these skills; she is already a marketing student so the opportunity cost of learning the skills is very low. This is what I am advocating among working adults. Apply an "intra-field" polymathic mindset within the context of your work and pick up parallel skills and knowledge. In this manner, it is hopeful that you will remain motivated to pursue these skills because you can see the linkages and hence the benefits of these skills to your career development. The more you learn about these parallel fields and learn to find linkages in them, the higher the chances for you to solve problems innovatively and effectively, thereby creating value for your company.

3. *Polymathy helps to future-proof your career and aids changing of career paths*

The third benefit of having a polymathic mindset is related to the interactive and accumulated effects brought on by the two previous benefits.

For a fresh graduate who has just landed the first job, there is not much prior work experience to build on (other than the courses that were taught during the individual's formal education). But this is where someone with a polymathic mindset will be more superior in the corporate race because he or she will be motivated to understand and learn about the different job functions in an organization. This polymathic person will probably want to understand how other people's job functions can enhance his or her own performance. As such, this individual will strive to learn much more than is necessary and is able to overcome steep learning curves with ease. He or she will be more participative in ad-hoc projects than someone who just wants to do enough to earn his/her monthly salary. After a few years, the capability of a polymathic rookie will far exceed those who just want to stay in their comfort zone. As such, when it is time to pick the next generation of corporate leaders, it is quite easy for management to select the few with great (polymathic) potential.

The characteristic of a polymath's inquisitiveness to acquire knowledge maps well with the discussion on the importance of lifelong learning in the 21st century. Given that globalization has resulted in the development of new business processes, the need to upgrade and upskill becomes paramount for mid-level managers. Before the 90's, managers around the age of 40s would have accumulated sufficient skills to last till their retirement. But this is no longer the case given the rapid global development in technology and AI, making the debate on the importance of lifelong learning a rhetorical one. In current times, mid-career managers with the old school thinking that specializing in skills pertaining to only one career and staying loyal to just one company will be most vulnerable as there is a higher chance of being retrenched. On the other hand, mid-career polymathic managers would have accumulated a wide range of knowledge to stay relevant to the workforce and, chances are, these managers will appreciate the importance of being flexible and adaptive to take up new jobs in different industries. In fact, these managers are more likely to change jobs once they feel that their learning curve in an organization has plateaued, hence it is more likely that they will "fire" their bosses and not the other way round. In this manner, the virtuous cycle of knowledge accumulation, which the corporate world perceived as "having a wide range of industry exposure", provides polymathic managers the chance of gaining entry to senior management jobs across different industries at a much younger age that those who specialize in just one single industry.

As such, it is easy to see that with a polymathic mindset, one could easily transit across different industries.

4. *Polymathy helps to enhance your life*
So far, I have kept my discussion of the benefits of polymathy within the context of career development. In this section, I shall expand it a little by adapting the idea provided by an American author who is most popular as the Dilbert comic creator, Scott Adams. In a blog post on career advice,[10] he says that it is quite easy for most people coming from average income households in developed countries to achieve average lives; you just need to stay out of trouble from the law, attend school diligently and complete your university degree, get a stable job, manage your finances, spend wisely, and plan early for your retirement. However, if you want your life to be extraordinary so that you can be more satisfied and happier, such as being a world-class entrepreneur, sportsman, actor or actress, or celebrity chef, etc., then you must be ready to take one of two paths.

The first path is to strive for mastery and perfection in one domain, but this takes many hours of practice. In his famous book *Outliers: The Story of Success*, Malcolm Gladwell (2008) argued that to attain mastery in a particular skill, such as in sports, playing a musical instrument, or in the culinary field, etc., it takes almost 10,000 hours or 10 years of pure practice before one becomes an expert. Nevertheless, there have been numerous articles written to debunk this idea, claiming that mastery achievement is not just about investing 10,000 hours of practice; it also requires the conscious effort to synthesize experiences gained through practice. However, we cannot deny that you need strong commitment to be able to practice a skill for so many years. In addition, didn't we claim that specialization is risky in our modern society? And how many working adults can really achieve such a feat while keeping their day jobs?

As a result, Scott Adams recommended the second path — *you do not need to be an expert in one area, but you should aim to be very good in a few areas.* Notably, when Scott Adams wrote about this in his blog back in 2007, he did not talk about polymathy. However, he seemed to be alluding to similar ideas associated with polymathy when he said that you would be valued by others if you had an extra skill which others did not have. For example, an engineer with an MBA will sound more impressive in a business meeting, throwing in another skill of being a toastmaster will certainly increase this engineer's persuasiveness, which is helpful not just in the boardroom, but in many other social situations. Hence, the combination of skills (even at the average level) can bring value into one's life far beyond one's imagination. This mirrors my assertion at the beginning of this book chapter; I am not recommending that we must train to be polymaths; I am saying that one should try practicing a polymathic mindset and *be proficient* in a few skills (there is no need for mastery). You will be amazed by the benefits not just in your career development, but also your personal life.

At this point, some of my students will follow up with yet another helpless comment, "this still feels tough because I really do not have time to pursue any skills, I hardly have time for myself." In the next section, I shall discuss a few approaches to develop one's polymathy and the attributes required to have this mindset.

How Do You Develop a Polymathic Mindset?

In this section, we shall first examine how our new economy has shifted our life blocks (see Figure 1) and in doing so, it is hoped that you will develop an appreciation of the new work mindset that is required. Next,

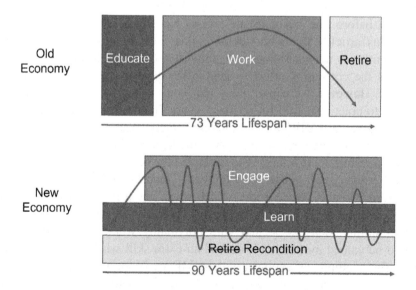

Figure 1:   Life blocks will need to change for the future of work.

Source: Adapted from the work by Heather E. McGowan, see www.futureislearning.com.

we review the natural qualities of a polymath and evaluate how these qualities are necessary to thrive in the new knowledge-based economy. Finally, we shall review a few techniques to help individuals practice the ways of a polymath.

1. *How has the new economy resulted in a new work mindset?*
We shall adapt the work by career strategist, future of work expert, and author, Heather McGowan.[11] As she asserts, in the old economy, most manufacturing processes emphasize specialization because of the belief that repetition increases efficiency, thereby reducing production cost. This mirrors our previous discussion related to companies' tendency to depart-mentalize different functions for the sake of efficiency which, in turn, encourages the factory style of education in our universities. Consequently, employees from the old economy usually envisioned their relatively mun-dane life as a single career arc over the blocks of education, work, and retirement as shown in Figure 1. However, the success and fulfillment of this single career arc is predicated on the assumption that the education one receives is sufficient to last a lifetime. Such an assumption is no longer realistic now. The new economy is one that is based on the application of knowledge; companies now rely heavily on technology and artificial intelligence to refine work processes. Consequently, Heather McGowan explains that to thrive in the new knowledge-based economy, one needs to periodically disengage oneself from the corporate race and recondition the mind to pick up new skills. Instead of just one peak in the single career arc, we should envision multiple peaks and troughs as we live through our lives with greater sense of purpose. As such, against this backdrop, to engage in lifelong learning, you will need to awaken your inner traits of passion and curiosity.

2. *Main qualities required for the future of our work (and lives)*

(a) Passion Quotient (P.Q.) and Curiosity Quotient (C.Q.)

The winners (in the future of our work)...will be those with more P.Q. and C.Q. to leverage all the new digital tools to not just find a job, but to invent one or reinvent one, and to not just learn but to relearn for a lifetime.

— Thomas Friedman

Three times Pulitzer Prize winner and American author, who is also a weekly columnist for *The New York Times*, Thomas Friedman made a popular comment that "P.Q. plus C.Q. is greater than I.Q."[12] Like Heather McGowan, Tom also asserts that the education we receive during our formative years as well as our undergraduate training are no longer sufficient to last a lifetime. In our current state, our society is so hyperconnected digitally that "the skills required for every decent job are rising as is the necessity of lifelong learning".[13] Consequently, only those who have the passion and curiosity to learn continuously will have a purposeful and meaningful career. If like many working adults, you go through the week with all your senses dulled and behave like a vegetable, lamenting that your life is boring and without purpose, perhaps it is time to change; you need to be in more control of your work, and develop a sense of agency so that your passion and curiosity can be awakened.

(b) Sense of agency

Polymaths learn because they are passionate and curious about the events that surround them. They are not bothered about how others feel about the usefulness of the things they learn. This is because polymaths feel totally at ease pursing their own personal goals and they are in total control of their lives. Nevertheless, I am not positing that you should do likewise; the aim of this chapter is to help readers develop a polymathic mindset so that, in a more pragmatic sense, you can see the relevance and benefits of a polymathic mindset within the context of your work. Hence, I am not suggesting that you should quit your job tomorrow to pursue your childhood dream of being a botanist or painter. However, I am highlighting that it is important to develop a strong sense of agency so that you are in control of your life and that you are cognizant to the purpose of your endeavors and invest your time wisely to pick up new and useful skills.[b]

To continue with our previous example about the university student with an interest to be a yoga instructor, her main endeavor at that

---

[b] *During my presentations at public forums, I usually stop at this moment to highlight that I understand I am deviating from the traditional meaning of polymathy. A traditional polymath learns from multiple fields out of passion and curiosity, and not because of an ulterior motive of making money or to be famous. What I am advocating here is the pragmatic view of developing one's interests while retaining one's career ambition, so that we can face the challenges of the future of our work.*

moment is to complete her university education. However, she is also keen to pursue her personal goal as a certified yoga instructor. If she has no sense of agency, she would have given up her personal goal because it makes no sense to be wasting time on a pursuit that will not help improve her school grades. Her parents may object to this seemingly useless hobby. Some may call it stubbornness, but I would attribute it to her strong sense of agency (as well as her passion for yoga) that led to a successful outcome from her efforts. In addition to this, there are also a few other qualities worth mentioning. These include her ability to find a parallel interest on top of her current obligation as a university student, to find time to learn other additional skills (e.g., how to set up and monetize a YouTube channel), and to develop linkages on all these skills to help make her goal a successful one. In the next section, we shall review specific techniques to develop a polymathic mindset.

3. *Specific techniques to develop a polymathic mindset*
In the previous section, we have briefly discussed the importance of developing our P.Q. and C.Q., as well as a sense of agency. I would call these the foundational traits which people should have if they want to develop a polymathic mindset in a very short time. If you think you have these traits, then the next few techniques will help even further.

(a) Set aside time to read and learn — the 5-hour rule.
According to entrepreneur and writer Michael Simmons,[14] to be successful, one needs to set aside at least 5 hours a week to read or learn about something useful. This is called "deliberate learning" and it is a worthwhile investment in the new knowledge economy. As discussed, the trend in the future economy is that we are going to see an explosive reliance on technology and AI. If the philosophy behind the application of technology and AI is to free us from our daily mundane chores in our work, how then should we make use of the free time given to us? We need to learn something new so that we can add value back into the society. It is against this backdrop that Michael Simmons argues that intellectual knowledge is certainly a worthy investment to thrive for in the future of our work (and lives). A quick review of successful and impactful individuals such as former US President Barack Obama, billionaire investor Warren Buffet, and billionaire entrepreneur Bill Gates reveal that they spend a considerable amount of time reading and learning from books and different sources.

(b) Stop finding excuses, find time instead!
At this moment, many of my adult students will comment that I do not understand how busy they are at work, and that they do not have the luxury of time to be reading anything. Some will even add that they do not have the ambition to be "impactful individuals in the society". I am usually empathetic and say that at least they are devoting time to learning by being enrolled in my class. So, it is a very good start. However, I will also ask if they have watched any Netflix series recently and the answer is usually yes. If that's the case, I would argue that they do have time to spare to read up on something useful.

> We spend our lives collecting, spending, lusting after, and worrying about money — in fact, when we say we "don't have time" to learn something new, it's usually because we are feverishly devoting our time to earning money, but something is happening right now that's changing the relationship between money and knowledge.

> — Michael Simmons

Another common view is that reading is a waste of time because of the uncertainty that the materials being read are going to help enlarge people's pay checks. This is a very common attitude toward reading and learning (the primary reason why people pursue post-graduate qualifications is because they believe that will enhance their careers). Recall that a skill which a polymath possesses is the ability to develop linkages across multiple disciplines to help solve problems innovatively. But in order for that to happen, you will need to gather sufficient knowledge and skills from a diverse range of domains in order to come up with useful linkages; it is naïve to think you can achieve this by simply reading a book or two. Hence, it is important to remember the new economy model proposed by Heather McGowan. We must be prepared that at certain moments of our lives, we may need to focus on learning, reconditioning, and updating our existing skills. At this moment, an impatient and overwhelmed student will often comment, "but this is so risky, how do you know what you learn will ever be useful? And where do you even start?" I will make a suggestion next.

(c) Learn to identify linkages and pick up skills that will expand the role of your current career
Let us recall the example about the university student who learns yoga and combines different business skills she picks up from her university

education to enhance her YouTube channel. She is guided by her interest in yoga and her endeavor is motivated based on her hobby. Many adult students feel that this example is not realistic because their job is not their hobby. I agree to this. Hence, in the context of one's work, I suggest that you learn to identify skills and knowledge that will not only expand your role in your current career, but also help you to pivot to other industries.

For example, if you are working in the sales department of your company, you start reading about technological trends that will impact sales and marketing to find out how your current job will be affected in the future. (Do you now see how important it is to spend time reading? If you have done so, you should be aware of such trends and be ready to identify these opportunities to introduce these initiatives to your company.) As it is, many forward-looking companies are already investing in Customer Relationship Management (CRM) systems that capture data on all touchpoints with customers so that AI marketing models can help with effective targeting of customers in their marketing campaigns. As such, if you want to increase your market value in the sales domain, you should invest time in understanding how these CRM systems work, and how they can be optimized and implemented efficiently. Next, seek out the courses, possibly online ones, related to this and get your company to pay for these courses. This is how you signal to your superior that you have a polymathic mindset and that you are willing to learn. Along the way, look out for topics dealing with AI that will further deepen your analytics skills, which will be useful in implementing the CRM system. This is another parallel (and transferable) skill which you want to have in your toolbox. As you pursue this knowledge, do not be narrow-minded and assume that the skills are only applicable to your company; you are essentially learning about the implementation of a CRM system which is applicable to multiple industries — once you are proficient in implementing this software in your company, you can pivot to work as a consultant that specializes in CRM system implementation.

It is hoped that, through the above example, you can see how the linkages that you identify through your learning journey can help you identify opportunities in other industries as well. When you develop a polymathic mindset, through constant reading and learning, you will find it easy to identify linkages among the different fields of knowledge which you have gathered and you will start to see even more opportunities for your future development. This is the virtuous cycle of knowledge discovery that excites a polymath.

If, however, you feel that the previous example is not something that you will follow because you do not like the idea of not being paid more for the extra effort that you are putting in for the company, then, I think you fail to appreciate all that we have discussed so far; you are still stuck in the old economy with a single career arc. It is not uncommon for people to be rather calculative in the hours which they contribute to their company. However, this mentality is more suited if you are a factory worker in which your remuneration is based on the number of units produced by your position and by the hourly wage. If you are holding a white-collar job in an office, you need to transcend to the new knowledge economy model and learn to understand the difference between *a job* and *a career*. A job is what you are employed to do within your work description and for which you are paid a monthly salary. A career, however, is a collection of past job experiences that allows you to rise and take on more abstract and developmental jobs (with much higher salary) at the later stage of your career arc in the new knowledge economy. To get to this, you need to "learn through your work" — i.e., use your current work as a context to learn and gather related domains of knowledge. The future of work belongs to those with a polymathic mindset and who do not mind taking those extra hours to learn something that is related to their work. When the next senior position presents itself, these polymathic individuals will be more than ready to take it on compared to a calculative employee who did not put in the extra hours to prepare for it.

Final Comments

Before closing the chapter, it is important to reiterate that it is not my intention to help my readers become polymaths. The demands for becoming one are extremely high and those who manage to become polymaths are truly commendable. My intention is more down to earth and humble; I just hope that you are open to the idea of learning from fields that are related to your current profession and alleviate your fears and anxiety about the future of your work.

Our past education system was designed to produce a specialized workforce with goals based on a single career arc. We were told that "Jack of all trades, but master of none" is a bad thing. Hence, many of us were trained to be experts in just one profession. However, that reality has changed as we move into a new era of technological development.

As organizations beat the drum of lifelong learning and upskilling, I recognize the anxiety among working adults; it seems like they are sold a lie of specialization during their formal education years and now they fear being obsolete. This need not be the case. As discussed, polymathy does not emphasize specialization. This implies that you do not need to be an expert in the new fields which you are learning from, you only need to be proficient since you are already an expert in that one profession which you have been trained for. Hence, having a polymathic mindset now can help you become a "Jack of a few trades and master of one". I hope that this chapter has introduced you to the polymathic mindset and I wish you all the best in your future endeavors.

References

1. Macmillan Dictionary. Polymath. Available from https://www.macmillandictionary.com/dictionary/british/polymath.
2. Burke, P. (2020). *The Polymath: A Cultural History from Leonardo da Vinci to Susan Sontag*. Yale University Press, New Haven (CT).
3. Segen's Medical Dictionary. (2011). Leonardo da Vinci syndrome. Available from https://medical-dictionary.thefreedictionary.com/Leonardo+da+Vinci+syndrome.
4. Westerhoff, J. (2001). A world of signs: Baroque pansemioticism, the polyhistor and the early modern wunderkammer. *Journal for the History of Ideas*, *62*(4), 633–650.
5. Bastable, C. F. (1898). Adam Smith's lectures on "Jurisprudence". *Hermathena*, *10*(24), 200–211.
6. Taylor, F. W. (1911). *The Principles of Scientific Management*. Harper & Brothers, New York (NY).
7. Ahmed, W. (2018). *The Polymath: Unlocking the Power of Human Versatility*. Wiley, Chichester (UK).
8. Mann, A., & Harter, J. (2016). The worldwide employee engagement crisis. *Gallup Business Journal*, *7*(1), 1–5.
9. Simon, H. (1991). *Models of My Life*. Basic Books, New York, p. 170 .
10. Adams, S. (2007). Career advice. Available from https://dilbertblog.typepad.com/the_dilbert_blog/2007/07/career-advice.html.
11. McGowan, H. E. (2017). Preparing students to lose their jobs. Available from https://www.linkedin.com/pulse/preparing-students-lose-jobs-heather-mcgowan/?trackingId=QpmHDPwcbr0b%2BsgYFrHa%2FQ%3D%3D.
12. Cheong, S. (2013). Want to keep your job? "Be hungry, curious, persistent", says Thomas Friedman. Available from https://www.straitstimes.com/

singapore/want-to-keep-your-job-be-hungry-curious-persistent-says-thomas-friedman.

13. Friedman, T. L. (2013). It's P.Q. and C.Q. as much as I.Q. Available from https://www.nytimes.com/2013/01/30/opinion/friedman-its-pq-and-cq-as-much-as-iq.html.

14. Simmons, M. (2017). 5-Hour rule: If you're not spending 5 hours per week learning, you're being irresponsible. Available from https://medium.com/accelerated-intelligence/the-5-hour-rule-if-youre-not-spending-5-hours-per-week-learning-you-re-being-irresponsible-791c3f18f5e6.

Chapter 4

Delivering Service Innovation in a Digital World

Amy Wong Ooi Mei

Introduction

With the proliferation of technology and the intensified global competition, service innovation can be used as a strategic weapon for growth in organizations across industries and nations. This chapter discusses the importance of service innovation and its related principles. The chapter also covers the emerging technology trends for new products, services, and techniques, and examines the role of technology in transforming the customer experience through service innovation. Relevant suggestions for the effective implementation of service innovation are presented.

Service Innovation

In today's digital and connected world, service innovation is a critical predictor of competitive advantage and business success. A key aspect of service innovation is the manner in which the service is designed, communicated, and delivered to customers and the larger community of stakeholders. Unlike most other business functions and activities, there is no single widely accepted way to document service innovation success by using templates, frameworks, or even procedures as every single accomplishment of innovation is an exclusive achievement underpinned by sustained diligence and effort. Innovation is driven by an organization's investment in tangible resources such as infrastructure and fixed assets, or intangible ones such as organizational culture, hierarchy, and structure, as well as human capital and talent pipeline. These investments drive employee and stakeholder engagement in the organization's current and future innovative activities. Service organizations must not think of themselves as mere service entities, but as innovative, creative, and learning organizations which continuously strive toward the purpose of serving their customers as best as they can. As long as the organization is aligned and directed toward the generation of creative and innovative service solutions, positive customer attitudes and behaviors such as word-of-mouth and brand advocacy will result.

In recent years, some of the greatest opportunities for the fostering of service innovation are derived from the growth in digital disruption and widespread adoption of digital technology in worldwide digital environments which includes social media platforms, online programs and applications, multimedia channels, cloud computing technology, and robotic technology services. To truly innovate, organizations need to look beyond their existing service capabilities to understand their customers' real needs, including examining the jobs that customers are trying to achieve, or the "jobs-to-be-done". To do this, managers seeking to innovate their services can rely on a customer journey map, or a service blueprint. The customer journey map or service blueprint captures the service encounters and interactions between the customer and the front-line employees throughout the entire service process. With a holistic blueprint of the entire service process mapped out, managers can ascertain the specific questions they need to ask at each step and incorporate the different service innovation principles, as explained in what follows, to guide them along their service innovation journey.

Service Innovation Principles

Having presented an overview of service innovation, the following sections present some of the important service innovation principles, namely value co-creation, crowdsourcing, the DART framework, the four-step service innovation approach, and service design thinking.

Value co-creation

In our connected world, service innovation has become highly interactive and systematic as many service organizations are reliant on value chains that include suppliers, intermediaries, customers, and financial partners which combine their capabilities to build and create value-added processes. Vargo and Lusch[1] indicate that a great amount of business activities and functions have shifted much of the dominant logic away from the exchange of product-centered tangible goods toward intangible transactions such as skills and knowledge transfer. Not surprisingly, the participation and collaboration in value co-creation initiatives can provide several benefits to organizations, compared to the traditional practices of merely meeting the needs and demands of customers.

Value co-creation refers to the joint creation of value by the organization and its customers, which allows the customers to co-construct the service experience to suit their context.[2] Value co-creation is an essential tool for meeting customer expectations and improving organization performance. Co-creation brings the customer or user into contact with the producer or service provider. It provides a joint platform where feedback and perspectives can be exchanged. This open dialogue can occur in the form of information sharing, learning activities, or product/service testing and evaluation with the service provider and with other consumers.[3] By ensuring a high level of commitment to implement these activities, organizations can capitalize on the opportunity to listen to and communicate with their customers. The insights generated from these consumer-brand conversations can allow organizations to design innovative services with minimum viable standards that can meet the changing needs and rising expectations of their customers.

According to Ranjan and Read,[4] value co-creation comprises six elements that can be categorized into two stages, namely co-production and value-in-use. The three elements involved in co-production are: (1) the sharing of consumers' knowledge, expertise, and experience; (2) the empowerment of the consumer, and (3) the interaction between the organization and its customers as well as among the customers themselves. Once the "product" has been co-produced with the help of the participants, the second part, the value-in-use, comes into play. This part is made up of the experience that the customers encountered while taking part in the co-creation process, which ideally has been outstanding in terms of meeting customers' needs. Most often, the actual personalization of the product or service and the relationships formed between the parties involve a series of iterative processes. One notable example of value co-creation can be seen in the case of DHL, which conducted over 6,000 interactions and iterations with its customers to generate innovative ideas. In addition to customers, the organization encourages its staff to willingly co-operate and share information with customers to aid innovation.[4]

Value co-creation can also be seen as a market exchange process. To bring about service innovation, organizations need to start from the market exchange process (i.e., taking an outside-in approach) rather than concentrating on their products (i.e., taking an inside-out approach) and pay more attention to intangible resources such as knowledge and capabilities. Focusing on the market exchange process and individuals involved in the market exchange, organizations can adopt a systematic and dynamic perspective to value co-creation. A good example is how Netflix empowered its customers and other stakeholders in converting its value co-creation into a market exchange process through the use of its recommendation engine that is powered by artificial intelligence (AI) algorithm. In addition to creating their own original content for their subscribers, Netflix capitalizes extensively on AI to provide movies that customers like via their video-on-demand streaming services.

Moreover, value co-creation can be treated as a service delivery network. Adopting the network approach, value co-creation encompasses the activities centered around an individual or in collaboration with other stakeholders in the service delivery network including a customer's family, friends, other customers in the service environment, service providers, company employees, or representatives outside of the community. The customer can play several roles, for example, as a product conceptualizer, product designer, product tester, and product marketer in the co-creation process. By regular engagement of its employees, Lazada, an e-commerce platform, played a crucial role in shaping its service delivery culture. The organization's service delivery network is aimed at providing its customers with value-added guidance in all aspects of their interactions with their customers and business partners. At Lazada, the service delivery network involves third-party retailers and outsourced logistic suppliers such as NinjaVan and SingPost. The service delivery network is important as it fulfills the consumer's wants either directly through the Lazada platform or via its partner platforms through Lazmall. Another part of its service delivery network is Redmart, an online supermarket delivery business based in Singapore. Redmart provides customers with grocery ordering and delivery service through network links from the Lazada platform app. The groceries supplied by Redmart's external suppliers enable Lazada to build a highly interactive chain of service delivery network within its online business operational network.

Most of the time, value co-creation takes place within a service ecosystem. The concept of value co-creation has been discussed in terms of an adapting and evolving ecosystem which continuously improves the system's capabilities for responding to new opportunities.[1] Understanding the holistic aspects of a complex system requires a shift from an organization-centered perspective to focusing on the entire global setting. A good example is GrabPlatform, which adopted an open platform strategy in building the First Everyday Superapp with several partners co-creating and integrating their services with Grab. GrabFresh, the on-demand grocery delivery derived from a joint partnership between GrabPlatform and HappyFresh, is the number one grocery delivery provider in Southeast Asia. The partners in the Grab ecosystem share their resources in co-creation, with strong alignment in purpose and value proposition.

In addition, value co-creation can be observed in online communities. With the rapid growth of social media and digital disruptive technologies including reels and short videos, online communities such as Facebook fan pages have become popular platforms for fostering co-creation between the different stakeholders. The process of value co-creation occurs in online communities between customers or peers in a process commonly known as peer production, co-production, or social production. One example is the open innovation platform adopted by Starbucks. The organization's open innovation platform includes its website which operates like a forum where customers can provide ongoing suggestions to the company. When the company decided to remove breakfast items from its menu, the platform provided a space for customers to voice out their preference of having it back on the menu with healthier options. In response, Starbucks rolled out a suite of healthier breakfast products which became the company's best-selling items.

Crowdsourcing

These days, organizations are facing increasing pressure to innovate. To do this efficiently, companies are turning to crowdsourcing for new ideas, whether it is product or service introduction, redevelopment, or enhancement, or merely soliciting feedback. Crowdsourcing works independently from the internal creative team of an organization, and is different from co-creation, as it involves an open forum where the crowd is tasked with creating an idea. In the recent years, several crowdsourcing efforts have fallen short of expectations or have been abandoned at the last minute. For example, Amazon tried to crowdsource its film scripts, however, the scripts submission system was shut down as it did not attract globally appealing scripts. There is a common misunderstanding that there is only one best approach to crowdsourcing, which is to ask the crowds to address problems that the crowds might have no experience with or are poorly suited to solve. This often leads to crowdsourcing failures. To overcome crowdsourcing failures, the Smart Crowds Framework suggested by Riedl et al.[5] published in the MIT Sloan Management Review, can be relied on for tailoring selected crowdsourcing approaches to the complexity of the innovation challenge.

The Smart Crowds Framework details three major types of crowds, namely (1) search crowd, which generates high-value solutions to new problems through independent experimentation, (2) wired crowd, which explores problems that allow for learning and reuse across different problems, and (3) crowd teams, which tackle larger and highly complex problems that cannot be broken down into smaller tasks. Importantly, it is integral that organizations understand which type of crowdsourcing approaches to utilize for the different types of problems they seek to solve. Riedl et al.[5] recommend the use of search crowd for well-defined problems with low complexity and scope, as seen in examples such as crowdsourcing platforms (i.e., InnoCentive and 99designs). For moderately complex problems similar to those handled by Threadless (an e-commerce platform which supports a diverse, global community of artists) and Local Motors (an American motor vehicle manufacturing company focused on low-volume manufacturing of open-source motor vehicle designs using multiple micro-factories), wired crowd can be used as it has the capability to generate high quality solutions. Finally, crowd teams can be used to generate holistic solutions to highly complex and non-routine problems as seen in the Netflix Prize, an open competition for the best collaborative filtering algorithm to predict user ratings for films, which requires the effort of several individuals to come up with lengthy proofs of concept, detailed prototypes, and complicated algorithms.

The DART framework

Within the field of service innovation, Prahalad and Ramaswamy[2] analyzed co-creation as a critical development and provided four building blocks by which co-creation occurs: dialogue, access, transparency, and risk (DART). These building blocks are used as a starting point to explore the co-creation features between the customer and the organization to help organizations better engage customers.

Dialog refers to how knowledge is being shared through communication and ongoing discussion to boost interaction and engagement, bringing about the co-creation of experience between the customer and the organization.[6] Dialog allows customers to contribute their views for organizations to understand the emotional, cultural, and social aspect of their customers and allows the company to respond to the customers. One good example is Singapore Airlines, which frequently uses its social media accounts such as Twitter and Instagram to facilitate 24-hour engagement outside the normal working hours in Singapore. This facilitates ongoing two-way conversations and dialogs on the company's social media account. This engagement is undertaken as a joint-effort by many departments, and not just a small social media team. By facilitating interactive dialogs, Singapore Airlines can understand their customers better and act swiftly on their suggestions, which helps the organization create and maintain a loyal customer base.

The dialog element paves the way for access and transparency, as meaningful conversations and interactions cannot take place without accessibility.[7] Accessibility and dialog help in creating accountability and responsibility, giving rise to transparency. Easy access to information and tools is of utmost importance as it can allow dialogs to take place between the customer and the organization more effectively. In today's day and age, everyone has at least one social media account which means that the customers have easy access to a wide range of social media platforms, therefore organizations can participate jointly in online interactions via the co-creation process with their target audience. One good example is Ikea, which made its social media platforms accessible to their customers through its virtual Home Tour and YouTube Channel, both of which propel the company's agenda of conversations through dialog. To enhance the accessibility, Ikea invested in a user-friendly company website which displays general information about the furniture retailer as well as specific products and services offered. To increase the access to accurate information for its customers, the company enhanced its search engine optimization strategies by placing relevant keyword terminologies and phrases that suggest popular features related to the business at the top of the various search engine lists.

Dialog, access, and transparency can lead to a clear assessment by the customer in terms of the risks vs. benefits of a decision. Though opportunities arise with the use of social media sites such as communication channels, there is a risk of bad press or consumer boycott, which might be detrimental to the image of the organization as customers might leave inaccurate and unverified comments which might lead to misunderstanding or a misaligned brand image.[8] Comments from the public are unrestricted on social media, and negative comments can spread like wildfire. To mitigate the potential risks, organizations need to manage their social media accounts proactively and keep themselves updated on the latest happenings. As such, proper feedback channels and monitoring systems need to be in place to manage the feedback from the public.

The final DART building block, transparency, is important to customers as online information can be easily shared with the advancement of technology. If information that is purposely withheld from the customers is leaked online, it will create a negative image for the organization. When customers have access to the same information as the organization, the dialog can become more meaningful. Recognizing the importance of Airbnb hosts in scaling the platform globally, Airbnb incorporated a host community portal called the "Community Center", whereby existing hosts and prospects can share knowledge, get inspired, and network. As Airbnb users can easily access the website and start a conversation in the online community, the ease of access and transparency help promote active dialogs and connectedness, and mitigate information asymmetry. Evidently, the probability of risk with regards to accommodation booking is low as there are almost one million active users in the "Community Center", with some playing the role of moderators who proactively check and verify the information shared.

Service innovation approach

Organizations can embrace service innovation by adopting a structured approach to their innovation process. According to Bettencourt *et al.*[9] the approach to service innovation involves four major steps, namely,

(1) identifying the jobs that customers are trying to get done; (2) determining whether the jobs are part of a larger process; (3) examining the opportunities that exist to help customers get the jobs done, and (4) investing time, talent, and resources in value creation. For a better understanding, these four steps are illustrated in the following example that shows how Hewlett-Packard (HP) uncovered opportunities for its next-generation printers.

Step 1: Determine what job or jobs customers are trying to get done by using current services and support. For this step, HP assessed the following: which opportunities should be addressed with their products, which opportunities should be tackled with their services, and which opportunities might be addressed with both products and services.

Step 2: Determine whether the jobs for which customers are hiring current services are part of a larger process. For this step, HP examined the job from different perspectives: printing a document from a user perspective; maintaining a printer from the perspective of IT employees, and managing printing costs from the perspective of a purchaser. From this analysis, they found that the process of trouble shooting issues and resolving printer errors is a major concern for users and maintainers.

Step 3: Determine what opportunities exist to help customers get these jobs done. To address this area of opportunity, HP developed both product concepts such as enhanced sensor feedback within the printer as well as complementary service concepts such as automatic data transmission to HP regarding a printer error in order to provide guidance with technical support and automatic ordering of repair and/or replacement parts.

Step 4: Invest time, talent, and resources in value creation. Following the identification of new product and service concepts, HP invested additional resources into creating value in these areas, bringing about service innovation for the company.

Service design thinking

The process of design thinking can act as a structured framework for understanding the complexity involved in the pursuit of service innovation. The design thinking process offers a starting point for further service improvization. By applying a design thinking process to service design, organizations can generate suitable solutions to deliver personalized service experiences to their loyal customers. Specifically, design thinking starts with a deep understanding of customers' needs within the context of a service encounter or service experience. Applying the design thinking process, an organization can make sense of data and discover new insights, question alternative assumptions, explore different perspectives, reframe problems into opportunities, generate creative and innovative ideas, critique and choose the best possible ideas, test the ideas through prototyping and experimentation, refine relevant solutions, and finally implement the chosen service innovation. The design thinking process consists of five steps: empathy, definition, ideation, prototyping, and testing.

1. *Empathy*: The process starts with an empathetic understanding of the problem, typically through user-centric research and listening to users and finding out about how to help them move forward.
2. *Problem Definition*: Through the information accumulated and gathered, the observations are further analyzed and synthesized to define the core problems. A problem statement that adopts a human-centered perspective is defined.
3. *Ideate*: To create innovative ideas, assumptions are challenged, and the problems are viewed from "out of the box" perspectives.
4. *Prototyping*: This is an experimental phase which aims to identify the best solution possible.
5. *Testing*: The completed service is tested rigorously and refined through further iterations to rule out possible alternative solutions.

The five steps applied to a services context using Amazon Go as an example are as follows:

1. *Empathy*: Amazon Go empathized with its shoppers and understood their frustrations with the time-consuming task of queuing that is required to check out at the grocery store. At times, shoppers may need to wait for at least 15 minutes during peak hours.
2. *Define*: Amazon Go understood the entire customer journey experience and listed the specific details regarding what they hope to achieve for the Amazon Go shopping experience. The organization decided to focus on how efficient customers can grab their groceries and walk out without making payment at a store.
3. *Ideate*: Amazon Go brainstormed the possible options for customers to grab and walk out without paying. The retailer documented the technology required as well as the cost to be incurred.

4. *Prototyping*: The organization designed a proof of concept on how to capture all the items that each customer checks out of the store and how to ensure that the correct items and quantity are being captured.
5. *Testing*: Amazon Go tested the whole customer journey thoroughly to ensure all the details are captured efficiently with no technical glitches.

Using design thinking, Amazon Go is able to tackle customer pain points and design new innovative solutions that are tested within a short period. Eventually, a "Just Walk Out" technology was introduced, which includes a combination of sensors, in-store cameras, and machine learning algorithms that leverage on data from multiple sensors and cameras to track and charge for the items that customers pick up and walk out with, and all they need is a mobile phone and an app to complete the payment process. This innovative service, which was patented in 2015, was made possible with employees' active participation in the design thinking process as well as customers' proactive feedback.

As discussed, the service design thinking process, which is slightly different from the design thinking process, focuses on the customer's service experience to build and maintain customer perceived trust, customer satisfaction, and loyalty. The process relates to the activity of orchestrating people, infrastructure, communication, and material needed for a service to create value for all stakeholders involved. Service design thinking can be applied to develop or improve services, including interactions between a brand and a user, as a distinctive brand experience can be created, which can lead to maximized business potential. Service design thinking can work effectively in a collaborative and co-creative process grounded in engagement, dialog, and learning. With the active involvement of relevant stakeholders throughout the service design thinking process, an organization will have a greater chance of gaining commitment and buy-in for the service innovation. There are several important factors that need to be considered to ensure success in service design thinking implementation. These factors are as follows:

1. *Leadership*: Service design thinking initiatives should be integrated with the organization's strategic goals. The management should provide direction, resources, and commitment to show the organization's dedication to a design thinking culture.
2. *People*: Within the organization, it is important that management enable champions to lead the service design thinking projects.

The organization can focus on building up an internal design thinking community where best practices are shared.

3. *Process*: The service design thinking process can be used as a starting point for the organization, and relevant methods and tools that support the organization's objectives should be customized along the way.

4. *Environment*: To develop and create collaborative workspaces, the organization should co-innovate with all its stakeholders, including its customers and partners.

Emerging Technology Trends in Service Delivery

Against the backdrop of an increasingly uncertain global economy, service organizations need to keep abreast of the major emerging technology trends, or they will risk being disrupted. Understanding these trends will allow businesses to capitalize on opportunities through service innovations. Some of these trends, their implications for new products and services, as well as their role in transforming the customer experience are presented in the following.

Artificial intelligence (AI)

Artificial Intelligence (AI) is one of the most transformative technological evolutions during these times and most organizations have started to explore how they can use AI to improve the customer experience and to streamline their business operations. Organizations can tap into AI applications through service provider platforms such as Google Cloud Platform (GCP), Microsoft Azure, Tencent Cloud, and Amazon Web Services (AWS). These are cloud platforms that enable big data (i.e., huge amounts of data that are characterized by volume, variety, velocity, and variability that includes structured, unstructured, and semi-structured data) to be stored and processed in the cloud. The AI applications on these cloud platforms utilize algorithms and statistical models to help organizations make decisions that can lead to new opportunities, better marketing, improved customer services, and improved operational efficiency. For example, Amazon Web Services employs AI services to help businesses solve some of the toughest workplace challenges. Users can choose from pre-trained AI services for image recognition, language translation, product recommendations, predictive modeling, and statistical forecasting to build, train, and deploy machine learning models on a larger scale to solve business issues.

The usefulness of AI applications with big data can be seen in the example of UPS.[10] UPS uses GCP to deliver 21 million packages a day in 220 countries. Each driver makes about 120 pickup and drop off stops daily and each of these stops have several possible routes. In collaboration with GCP, UPS is able to design a routing software that directs each driver to the exact route for each delivery. More specifically, GCP's BigQuery is used to derive precise forecasts, which provides the capacity to run machine learning models across 1 billion data points per day, including package weight, shape and size, and facility capacity across the network. The insights from the data allow UPS to decide on how to load delivery vehicles, implement targeted operations adjustments, and minimize forecast uncertainty, especially around the peak holiday period.[10]

As AI applications deliver value to the business, the risk of the system being attacked by hackers remains a huge threat. To prevent this, organizations need to protect their AI applications, anticipate the different forms of cyberattacks, and beef up their cyber security to enhance the system. This is important as online platforms and AI applications may contain important customer information and personal data. If customer trust is being breached due to security lapses, they may lose trust in the AI systems, making it difficult for organizations to incorporate such technology in their service delivery.

Biometrics

Biometrics, which incorporate facial patterns, voice, fingerprint, and retina scans, are popular systems that have been adopted for authenticating and digitally identifying a person. This allows the individual to gain access to secured systems in an efficient manner. However, there are various concerns about fully depending on a single biometrics system as a standalone method for identification purposes. This is because hackers may be able to find flaws through this digital armor.[11] Moreover, fingerprint scanners and facial recognition tools can be easily duplicated by using a lifted fingerprint or a photograph of another person. Besides, at times, the biometrics system can be inaccurate. Nonetheless, the full potential of this technology is yet to be realized. The use of biometrics is still a highly favored security measure since human characteristics are distinctive, permanent, recordable, and measurable. In fact, by 2024, the worth of the biometrics industry is expected to grow to US$65.3 billion, with endless possibilities for the biometrics industry.[11] Moving forward, biometrics may replace an individual's identification card or paper documents for verification purposes. As these paper documents are easily misplaced, any person can utilize another person's identity. Further, as these documents are forgeable, fake licenses, identification cards, or passports can be easily accessed. To overcome the limitations of paper fraud, biometric technology can be adopted in the future for identification. To date, biometrics are being tried out in law enforcement and healthcare for fingerprint authentication, and in airports for security screening using retina scans.

Internet of things (IoT)

The internet of things, or IoT, is a system of interrelated computing devices, sensors, mechanical and digital machines, objects, animals, or people that are provided with unique identifiers. The elements of IoT can transfer data over a network without requiring human-to-human or human-to-computer interaction. In the healthcare industry, Gope and Hwang[12] reported the use of body sensor network technology where a patient undergoing healthcare treatment can have his/her health monitored using lightweight wireless sensors. The light wireless sensor can enhance user adoption of the sensor as it is an improvement over the wired heavy equipment that is traditionally used to monitor a patient's health. Further, human errors are easily eliminated as there is no need to manually collect and record data, leading to another positive benefit of the implementation of IoT as a sustainable service experience. The use of IoT can also allow the collection of large amounts of data over a period of time, which can lead to further savings in terms of operational costs.

The autonomous things (AuT)

The Autonomous Things (AuT) are devices such as robotics, vehicles, or drones that are capable of accomplishing specific tasks without human interaction due to their AI algorithms, sensors, and AI analytical software. For example, Tesla chief Elon Musk expects to create a truly "complete" autonomous vehicle by this year, and the number of vehicles capable of operating with lower degree of autonomy will become an increasingly common sight. In addition to this, other in-car systems not directly connected to driving, such as security and entertainment functions, will become increasingly automated and reliant on data capture and analytics. In years to come, the autonomous driving technology will expand into other modes of transport, such as air taxis, trucking, and shipping.

In addition, drones are becoming a popular vehicle with robotic automation that can be used with few geographical restrictions. Drones can be used in healthcare to deliver blood, medicine, and vaccine to remote places that are inaccessible or unsafe to travel physically. Using drones for delivery has vast potential for new market opportunities. For instance, Amazon has been a visionary leader in the delivery industry when it saw the potential of AuT and has been embarking on testing drone air delivery services via its "Amazon Prime Air". In 2013, Amazon first announced its plan to venture into an air delivery service, Prime Air Delivery, and today, Amazon has received the approval from the US Federal Aviation Administration, which allowed Amazon to efficiently deliver items to its customers.[13]

One can expect humans to be replaced by robots, and as technology capability improves, social acceptance grows, and regulations permit, autonomous things will increasingly be deployed in uncontrolled public spaces. An example of established robot technology can be seen in Amazon warehouses, which has established their automated robot picker in their warehouses to eliminate human manpower for the picker role. Amazon managed to reduce warehouse axle space as the robots can maneuver and complete their tasks within a much smaller space as compared to humans. This has improved efficiencies and added value to the organization, which has translated into increased productivity.

Service robots

Service robots are a type of robots that are seen specifically in the service industry, especially in frontline service delivery. Within the frontline service delivery context, service robots are referred to as system-based autonomous and adaptable interfaces that interact, communicate, and provide services to an organization's customers.[14] Empowered by AI and sensory technologies that can be connected to different internet related devices, smart systems, and sensors, service robots can "perform useful tasks for humans or equipment excluding industrial automation application".[15] These robots are often humanoids that share some human physical characteristics, for example, arms, a torso, and a head with some facial features.[16] Through a series of technologies that enable them to perceive, understand, react, and learn,[17] AI robots can interact with humans to deliver high-tech and high-touch services in frontline service environments.

Within the service industry, social robots are used in everyday settings including research platforms, offices, medical settings, hotel, kitchens, pet care settings, nursing homes, and therapeutic and rehabilitation centers. In addition, social robots can act as physical counterparts in remote spaces via the provision of telepresence. Examples include the use of "Pepper", the world's first social humanoid robot able to recognize faces and basic human emotions, by SoftBank Robotics in mobile phone stores, banks, shopping malls, and Nescafe coffee shops. Another notable example is the use of "Temi", a robot that interacts with humans while providing flawless autonomous navigation, dynamic audio/voice experiences, and advanced AI in hospitals, museums, libraries, student care centers, and unmanned retail stores in Singapore.

The benefits of social robots are tremendous, including addressing economic factors such as the increasing labor costs, and tackling social factors such as the need for social distancing due to the recent COVID-19 outbreak and the aging silver economy. Moreover, social robots can be used in frontline service delivery for productivity improvement through the deployment of fewer human employees to achieve efficiency via an accurate service process which reduces human errors, and to encourage consumer engagement through an interactive technology-enabled service experience.[18] In contrast, some of the limitations of social robots include possible anxiety, stress, and fear associated with using robots as well as the negative effects of robots, such as loss of jobs, intrusion into privacy, mistrust, dehumanization, malfunctions, and accidents.[19]

Extended reality (XR)

Extended Reality (XR) covers several new and emerging technologies being used to create more immersive digital experiences. It refers to virtual, augmented, and mixed reality. Virtual reality (VR) provides a fully immersive digital experience where individuals can enter a computer-generated world using headsets that blend out the real world. Augmented reality (AR) overlays digital objects onto the real world via smartphone screens or displays, while mixed reality (MR) is an extension of AR, where users can interact with digital objects placed in the real world (e.g., playing a holographic piano in a room via an AR headset). Businesses are increasingly exploring the possibilities offered by the current forms of VR, AR, and MR for training and simulation, as well as offering new ways to interact with customers. One good example can be seen in furniture retailers such as Ikea. With XR, customers can now view Ikea products at home and try out the hologram of the products before deciding if it is suitable. In addition, holograms can be made to scale, which means that customers who are seeking to purchase large items do not need to physically carry out the measurement of the products in-stores. Rather, they can try out furniture or large items via placing them in their homes at the actual location. This can help improve customer satisfaction as Ikea scales down on parts of their retail display space, which can help them save cost.

3D printing

3D printing offers a solution for the low volume manufacturing of complex parts, as well as fast production of difficult-to-find products. As 3D printing becomes more affordable, opportunities for this industry will continue to grow. A 3D printer is a computer-aided manufacturing device that can create objects in three dimensions. Compared to traditional manufacturing that uses materials such as metal, plastic, or wood, 3D printers can reduce waste and are thus more efficient.[20] 3D printers can be used to print products that are made of plastic and metal, leading to reduced transportation and storage cost. With 3D printing, more customizations can be allowed depending on individual customer needs. Further, immediate replacement of missing parts can be printed via a 3D printer when needed. More recently, companies such as General Electric, Lockheed Martin, and BMW are switching to 3D printing for industrial production at scale. More companies will follow as the range of printable materials continues to expand. Already widely available are basic plastics, photosensitive resins, ceramics, cement, glass, numerous metals, thermoplastic composites (some infused with carbon nanotubes and fibers), and even stem cells.

Hyperautomation

Hyperautomation is a new technology trend that provides the automation of tasks via a range of technologies such as Robotic Process Automation (RPA) and Process Mining.[21] Hyperautomation is done using a combination of tools which are meant to perform tasks at a powerful rate that can expand human capabilities and allow better measurement and monitoring. The goal of hyperautomation is to increase decision-making processes so that it can run without much human input.[22]

Hyperautomation is highly applicable in various document-based processes and it can be utilized in various service industries such as banking and insurance. The use of hyperautomation can allow work processes to be fully digitalized and completed in an efficient manner. For instance, in banks, one of the most important processes at the on-boarding stage is the Know-Your-Customer (KYC) process. In most traditional processes, it involves the due diligence process such as customer identity verification, gathering information of customer's particulars as well as screening of the customer, and details of his/her related family members prior to the bank account opening. With hyperautomation, the process can be seamless as the system can extract the required information from the document automatically and perform the due diligence. Compared to human data entry and checking, the system has lower error margin and higher accuracy, as the intelligent system is capable of verification and validation of the information. Hyperautomation can also be applied in the insurance industry. For instance, insurance companies can design the claim process to be fully automated with minimal or no input from humans. Due to the combination of technologies, the system can extract data from documents at a rapid rate and identify if the claim is within the policy guidelines and claim limit.

Conclusion

The current wave of digital disruption, triggered by advances in information and communications technology, is transforming the customer experience. This chapter discusses the importance of service innovation and its related principles. Relevant suggestions for the effective implementation of service innovation are presented. The chapter reviews the emerging technology trends that include AI, biometrics, IoT, AuT, service robots, extended reality, 3D printing, and hyperautomation, which will advance and boost service innovation.

References

1. Vargo, S. L., & Lusch, R. F. (2016). Institutions and axioms: An extension and update of service-dominant logic. *Journal of the Academy of Marketing Science, 44*, 5–23. Available from https://doi.org/10.1007/s11747-015-0456-3.
2. Prahalad, C. K., & Ramaswamy, V. (2004). Co-creation experiences: The next practice in value creation. *Journal of Interactive Marketing, 18*(3), 5–14.
3. Allen, S., Bailetti, T., & Tanev, S. (Nov, 2009). Components of co-creation. *Open Source Business Resource.* Available from https://timreview.ca/article/301#:~:text=This%20aspect%20of%20QCA%20was.
4. Ranjan, K., & Read, S. (Jan, 2017). The six faces of value co-creation: A field guide for executives. Available from https://www.researchgate.net/publication/316897074_The_Six_Faces_of_Value_Co-creation_A_Field_Guide_for_Executives.
5. Riedl, C., Seidel, V. P., Woolley, A. W., & Kane, G. C. (2020). Make Your Crowd Smart. *MIT Sloan Management Review.* Reprint #61324.
6. Solakis, K., Peña-Vinces, J. C., & Lopéz-Bonilla, J. M. (Sep 27, 2017). DART model from a customer's perspective: An exploratory study in the hospitality industry of Greece. Available from https://businessperspectives.org/images/pdf/applications/publishing/templates/article/assets/9168/PPM_2017_02SI_Solakis.pdf.
7. Yu, H., Liu, R., & Zheng, D. (2019). Interaction orientation based on value co-creation theory: Scale development and validation. *Journal of Contemporary Marketing Science, 2*(3), 298–322. Available from http://dx.doi.org/10.1108/JCMARS-08-2019-0027.
8. Davidsson, J., & Wallin, S. (2016). A case study of co-creation on Facebook. Available from https://www.diva-portal.org/smash/get/diva2:954511/FULLTEXT01.pdf.
9. Bettencourt, L. A., Brown, S. W., & Sirianni, N. J. (2013). The secret to true service innovation. *Business Horizons, 56*(1), 13–22.
10. Kurian, T. UPS uses Google Cloud to build the global smart logistics network of the future. Available from https://cloud.google.com/blog/topics/customers/ups-uses-google-cloud-to-build-the-global-smart-logistics-network-of-the-future.
11. Beck, P. (May 13, 2020). Biometrics: What the future holds for identity verification. *Readwrite, Data and Security.* Available from https://readwrite.com/biometrics-what-the-future-holds-for-identity-verification.
12. Gope, P., & Hwang, T. (2016). BSN-Care: A secure IoT-based modern healthcare system using body sensor network. *IEEE Sensors Journal.* Available from https://ieeexplore.ieee.org/abstract/document/7332745/authors#authors.

13. Palmer, A. (Aug 31, 2020). Amazon wins FAA approval for Prime Air drone delivery fleet. *CNBC News*. Available from https://cnb.cx/3eo9XTC.
14. Wirtz, J., Patterson, P. G., Kunz, W. H., Gruber, T., *et al.* (2018). Brave new world: Service robots in the frontline. *Journal of Service Management, 29*(5), 907–931.
15. International Federation of Robotics. (2022). Service robots. Available from https://ifr.org/service-robots.
16. Turja, T., Aaltonen, I., Taipale, S., *et al.* (2020). Robot acceptance model for care (RAM-care): A principled approach to the intention to use care robots. *Information and Management, 57*(5), 103220. Available from https://doi. org/10.1016/j.im.2019.103220.
17. Bowen, J., & Morosan, C. (2018). Beware hospitality industry: The robots are coming. *Worldwide Hospitality and Tourism Themes, 10*(6), 726–733.
18. Song, S. C., & Kim, Y. (Feb, 2022). The role of the human-robot interaction in consumers' acceptance of humanoid retail service robots. *Journal of Business Research, 146*, 489–503. Available from https://doi.org/10.1016/j. jbusres.2022.03.087.
19. Makarius, E. E., Mukherjee, D., Fox, J. D., & Fox, A. K. (2020). Rising with the machines: A sociotechnical framework for bringing artificial intelligence into the organization. *Journal of Business Research, 120*, 262–273.
20. Christensson, P. (Jan 2, 2014). 3D printer definition. Available from https:// techterms.com/definition/3d_printer.
21. Dilmegani, C. (Oct 20, 2020). What is hyperautomation? Technologies, benefits, challenges. Available from https://bit.ly/3890I8K.
22. Panetta, K. (Oct 21, 2019). Gartner top 10 strategic technology trends for 2020. Available from https://gtnr.it/2I7g4zY.

Chapter 5

Managing Customer Experiences through Digital Disruption

꧁꧂

Dianna Yan Li Chang

Customer Experience Management

Customer Experience Management (CEM) is a field of study that has drawn significant attention recently. Businesses exist for customers, and today's customers are changing. They are more informed, connected, knowledgeable, discerning, and demanding. They are often spoilt for choice and will easily walk away if they are unhappy. According to the 2022 Zendesk CX trends report,[1] 61 percent of customers will go to a competitor after encountering one bad experience. The number increases to 76 percent after two bad experiences. More importantly, customers value good experiences and are willing to pay a premium for extraordinary experiences which will mean happier customers and higher business and profit potential for the organization.

Organizations can enhance customer experiences (CX)s in intelligent ways through digital transformation by innovating their service offerings. Modern customers are used to exploring and finding creative solutions themselves. Businesses can improve CX and operational efficiencies by leveraging technologies and capitalizing on customers' digital capabilities. New technologies empower the CEM field, and CX transformations are integral to many organizations' digital transformation journey. Both technology giants and start-ups have joined forces to seize business opportunities in the CEM field, and the field is thriving with constant new developments and promising career prospects. The 2022 LinkedIn Jobs on the Rise List[2] identifies customer insights and CX related jobs as one of the top jobs in demand.

CX is a broad concept related to many functional areas within an organization. Good CEM requires a customer-centric corporate culture, support from the senior management, and investment. When CX is managed well, organizations often see rewarding outcomes from investments in CEM. This chapter discusses some critical issues in the CEM field. It aims to provide readers with an overview of the latest development in CEM and encourages readers to explore the different domains of CEM.

Introduction to CX

What is CX and why it matters?

> Customer Experience is the totality of an individual's interactions with a brand, over time.
>
> — Don Peppers[3]

In 1996, renowned strategists Michael Treacy and Fred Wiersema published an influential, best-selling book titled *The Discipline of Market Leaders*[4] after interviewing some top CEOs in the United States. The authors summarized three factors that lead to the success of big brands: (a) top quality products, (b) low prices enabled by operational excellence, and (c) best customer experiences. Here customer experiences, or "customer intimacy", as the original phrase used by the authors, refers to the strategy that an organization builds its success on the knowledge of the individual customers and their preferences without putting an excessive price tag on doing so.

To date, Treacy and Wiersema's work helps put CX into perspective. CX may not be the dominating strategy for all organizations, as product and price hugely matter; however, CX is a crucial success factor for most organizations. An increasing trend today suggests that even organizations that establish their successes based on product or cost leadership strategies, such as Wal-Mart, must adopt CX strategies for continued success.

In the past, face-to-face interactions with frontline service staff often played the most critical role in developing "customer intimacy". Today, the human factor is still essential, but digital channels play increasingly important parts in co-creating intimate customer experiences. Other non-human elements add to the overall effect, such as the design and function of both physical and virtual spaces where customers interact with brands and brand communications. The "totality" of experiences gives rise to the central idea of the CX concept, which essentially means everything matters. The CX definition also highlights the phrase "over time", which implies that it takes time to develop unique customer experiences and good customer experiences need to be long-term oriented and stand the test of time.

Customer experience vs. customer service

Customer service forms an essential component of customer experience. The totality of one's experience is made of individual experiences and interactions with brands. Whereas many of these interactions are related to customer service, such as making inquiries from sales agents, some customer experiences do not necessarily involve customer service, for example, browsing online content and using automatic machines or digital apps. It is necessary to replace customer service with customer experience because customer service is a narrow concept. In contrast, in the modern business world, everything counts in attracting and winning a customer's heart, including things brands have no control over, such as what other people say about the organization. When an organization monitors online channels such as social media, it can see that comments about the brand often come from different dimensions because they all form part of the customer's overall impressions or experiences. It is, therefore, necessary to design, manage, and monitor the various channels and touchpoints to create the ideal customer experiences, including but not limited to the traditional areas of customer service, which often center around service staff.

Examples of CX applications: Apple and Amazon

Apple is an excellent example of reinventing CX. Apple has created positive and unique customer experiences ("think different"), which explains the brand's success. Apple not only designs innovative and quality products but also follows design philosophies, such as simplicity and aesthetic excellence, to make their products physically and visually appealing. When Steven Jobs decided to open Apple stores in 2001, many people challenged the idea, and the mass media was suspicious, too. Today, over 500 Apple stores worldwide help Apple attract over 1 million visits daily. These stores generate outstanding sales per square foot that are even higher than recorded by successful luxury fashion brands such as Tiffany and Coach. Ironically, the stores' focus is not on sales and staff are not paid commissions. The concept of the stores is to provide customers with a chance to experience the Apple brand and help customers solve problems (i.e., the "Genius Bar"). These days, Apple stores are a huge success and many have become signature buildings and case studies for understanding retail design, such as the newly launched Apple store at Singapore's Marina Bay Sands. In addition to their stores, Apple also provides superior customer service and technical support via other offline and online channels.

Another example of excellence in CX is Amazon, although many people have never met a real person from Amazon, even after using their services for many years. Amazon offers an excellent e-commerce platform that is well-designed, easy to use, and fast. It provides a great variety of products at competitive prices. Further, Amazon pioneered many services that helped create superb customer experiences. For example, it invented the "one-click" technology to simplify payments and help customers save time. Despite being the world's largest e-commerce business provider, Amazon is good at personalizing services for each customer. It offers relevant and insightful recommendations based on extensive analytics and AI capabilities, which helps customers compare and select appropriate products, generating income for recommended sellers. The analytics capability allows the organization to understand its markets and create personalized experiences for both shoppers and sellers.

Touchpoints vs. overall experiences

The chain is only as strong as its weakest link.

— Thomas Reid

The CX concept highlights the importance of both individual touchpoints and overall experiences. Every single touchpoint and interaction are important because each can create a pain point for customers if mismanaged. The success of the whole customer experience requires the optimization of each touchpoint and the control of pain points along the whole customer journey. The CX team should investigate each touchpoint and try to improve its performance. For example, the following factors are critical in designing better web user experiences: the website loading time, consistency of look and feel, simplicity, flow, accessibility, and whether the site gives users the ability to use the site independently and efficiently, so they have a good sense of control. Meanwhile, customer touchpoints should not be developed in silos. Good CEM needs a holistic design of the overall customer experience, which may involve several different departments (not just sales and marketing).

Challenges of CEM

Despite its importance, CEM can be challenging for organizations for the following reasons:

The complexity and interdependencies of experiences. CEM involves a long and often complex process with several different touchpoints. These touchpoints and experiences are interdependent, as customers tend to view the brand holistically. A customer complaint may be associated with several interrelated issues involving different departments. Therefore, the Customer Blueprint and Customer Journey Mapping tools, which will be introduced later, are essential because these tools help provide a holistic overview of the customer journey. They demonstrate the interdependency and interconnectedness of possible customer problems and potential solutions.

Different ownerships of the touchpoints. From the management point of view, CEM faces the inherent problem of varying ownerships of the touchpoints. Whereas customers perceive information from all brand touchpoints as a unified voice from the same brand, there are different departmental ownerships of the touchpoints within the organization. For example, sales and after-sales services are provided by different departments. The separate ownership of channels and touchpoints means that various departments often view customer experiences in isolation.

Demanding customers. Businesses face a challenging task in serving today's demanding customers. It is good to put ourselves in the customers' shoes. What is also helpful is to put ourselves in the shoes of the frontline service staff. In Singapore, for example, many people find frontline service work challenging with growing customer expectations and demands. The issue of a shortage of service staff and, as a result, poorer customer service, intensified during the COVID-19 pandemic period in many countries. The wide adoption of technology, such as ordering apps and AI chatbots, can help alleviate the labor crisis and improve customer experience as customers are increasingly getting used to new technology and self-service.

CEM and digital transformation

Today's business leaders are often overwhelmed by requests for digital investments by different departments and functional areas. Each area seems essential, and they all fight for resources and priorities. CEM is a field that requests significant digital investment. Further, CX is not just related to sales and marketing. It often demands integrated systems that form part of an organization's overall IT strategy. CEM is related to the digitalization of operations, as organizations must improve overall efficiency to serve customers faster and better. CX also requires streamlined knowledge, information, and financial management systems, which may involve functions such as Finance and Human Resources. To summarize, the direct link to CEM is sales and marketing transformation. Still, efficient CEM implementation needs to be anchored upon a holistic review and redesign of an organization's overall digital solutions, involving digital transformation in IT systems, operations, and sales and marketing. Given the need for a holistic approach to digital transformation, improvements in CEM would require organizations to develop a customer-centric corporate culture, with CEM being one of the underpinning foundations of this overall strategy.

Case study: DBS Bank

DBS was founded in 1968 by the Singapore government and is rated as the leading bank in Southeast Asia. Although it has the largest retail network in Singapore, it has fewer branches in other ASEAN countries compared to its regional competitors. Realizing the exponential growth of internet users in the region and the need to connect with customers via alternative channels other than physical presence, DBS started a digital transformation journey led by a new Technology and Operation Division directly under the CEO. The bank wanted to build scalable platforms to uplift its IT and operation systems which can be used across countries. DBS decided to adopt a customer-centric approach in the design of these new systems. This requires the new systems to be flexible and scalable and easily integrated with updated applications and technologies to respond to an ever-changing market and customer demands.

Some key takeaways on CEM from DBS' digital transformation journey are as follows. First, the bank valued the importance of CX highly. Specialized CX teams that prioritize the CX function were formed in the formal reporting line. This instilled the idea that customers' digital experiences are critical to new banking experiences, and that excellence in customer experience should lead technology development. Second, DBS invested heavily in the development of digital technologies. The bank recognized the technology integration ability as a core competency of the organization and insisted that they "own" the competency by developing it in-house. Third, DBS leveraged technology to improve CEM. It developed well-designed websites and mobile apps to extend customer touchpoints, compensating for the lack of branches in some countries through better connection with young customers. It provided more functions at ATMs to offer convenience to customers. The bank also implemented voice recognition and analysis in 2012, which reduced customer waiting time, improved efficiency by directing calls to relevant teams, and enhanced customer satisfaction. Fourth, the bank applied design thinking in CEM and integrated physical experiences (branch and service pods) with digital experiences both within and outside of their branches. Fifth, DBS leveraged on big data analytics by partnering with IBM and Singapore's Agency for Science, Technology and Research (A*STAR) to develop advanced analytics abilities to better understand their customers' journeys with the bank. This allowed DBS to harness technology to collect feedback and utilize analytics to study customer pain points and formulate solutions. Indeed, DBS's investment in CEM and technology paid off with considerable growth in income, profit, and share prices. Adapted from Kien *et al.* (2015), Rewiring the enterprise for digital innovation: the case of DBS bank. Nanyang Business School, the Asian Business Case Center.[5]

CEM Tools: Blueprint and Customer Journey Mapping (CJM)

In the following section, two popular CEM tools, namely service blueprint and customer journey mapping (CJM), will be discussed. Both these tools are well recognized and widely used to help organizations improve their customer experience.

Service blueprint

What is a service blueprint?

A service blueprint uses a diagram to demonstrate the steps involved in service delivery and provides a graphical overview of the entire service process including backend support to customer interaction activities. A blueprint is a design or technical drawing that explains the overall details of a project. A building plan is a classic example of a blueprint. It provides a high-level graphic illustration of the whole building project with specific technical details. A service blueprint is an application of this blueprint concept. Like a building plan, a service blueprint uses a graphical or visual illustration to demonstrate the whole service process and helps bring all stakeholders on the same page. Figure 1 shows an example of a service blueprint of a hotel stay.

The service blueprint framework was first proposed by Lynn Shostack,[6] who worked for Citibank then. Shostack created the service

		Hotel Booking	Arrive at Hotel	Staying at the Hotel	Leaving the Hotel
Front Stage	PHYSICAL EVIDENCE Tangible evidence that consumers are exposed to that affect their quality perceptions	Hotel website and images	Hotel exterior and interior presentations	Comfort of beds	Availability of express service
	CUSTOMER ACTIONS What consumers do and experience before, during and after the service usage.	Make reservations	Check-in Deliver luggage to room Use valet parking	Use room and hotel facilities	Check-out Storage of luggage Transport to next destination
					--------Line of Interaction
	ONSTAGE EMPLOYEE ACTIONS Visible actions frontline employees take to deliver services	Service hotline	Greet customers	Concierge service	Send off customers
					--------Line of Visibility
Back Stage	BACKSTAGE EMPLOYEE ACTIONS Invisible actions backstage employees take to support service delivery	Ensure smooth operation of the system	Prepare for room	Clean the room	Arrange transportation, e.g., airport shuttle
					--------Line of Internal Interaction
	SUPPORT SYSTEM Systems companies use to support service deliveries	Reservation system	Facility management system	Facility management system	Suppliers for add-on services

Figure 1:　Key components of a service blueprint for a hotel stay.

blueprint to facilitate the design and control of the bank's service process. A service blueprint demonstrates both frontline deliverables at the customer interface and backend support that enables effective and pleasant interactions. For example, a smooth hotel check-in process needs frontline service staff and support from backend systems and teams. A typical service blueprint consists of the following components: physical evidence, customer actions, frontline (visible) staff actions, backend (invisible) staff actions, support processes, lines to separate components, and additional elements. Today, most backend support systems, such as logistics management and staffing management, are digitalized. The service blueprint tool demonstrates the importance of these support systems as they directly affect the performance of frontline service interactions.

Why use a service blueprint?

Whereas a service blueprint can serve many purposes, the critical objective of a service blueprint is to improve customer experience through service innovation. There is an old saying that it takes a village to raise a child. The same philosophy applies to service delivery. A seemingly simple task often involves tremendous behind-the-scene support which can be easily overlooked and it is easy to make mistakes when many steps are involved. The "totality" philosophy of CX suggests that every effort counts in the delivery of a service process and every component needs to be well developed and controlled. Shostack's service blueprint framework has significant influences on the quality of services. Specifically: (a) the process of developing a good service blueprint helps bring different stakeholders on the same page; (b) it demonstrates the importance of both frontline deliverables and backend support, without which, the former would not be possible; (c) it reveals insights about essential components of service quality and helps organizations prioritize their resources; and (d) it helps organizations re-design or streamline their service processes for greater customer experiences and cost-effectiveness.

How to create a service blueprint?

A Service Blueprint consists of the following components:

- **Physical Evidence** refers to the tangible evidence that customers are exposed to that affects their quality perceptions, for example, hotel exterior, lobby, hallways, rooms, staff uniforms, and hotel website.

- **Customer Actions** refer to what customers do and experience before, during, and after their usage of services; for example, customers make reservations, arrive at the hotel, check-in, go to the rooms and use facilities.
- **Onstage/Visible Employee Actions** refer to visible actions that front-line staff perform in service delivery, for example, greeting customers, processing registration, and serving food in the restaurant. The front-line staff are like actors with their actions planned according to scripts for role-playing.
- **Backstage/Invisible Employee Actions** refer to invisible actions that backend staff perform in service delivery, for example, arranging pickup services and preparing food.
- **Support Processes** refer to systems used for service delivery, for example, reservations systems and housekeeping systems.
- **Lines** are added to the service blueprint to denote different interactions and visibilities among the components. **The Line of Interaction** depicts whether direct interactions exist between the customer and the staff. **The Line of Visibility** shows whether the activities are visible to the customer. **The Line of Internal Interaction** depicts systems and activities carried out by staff who do not directly support customer interactions.
- **Additional Elements.** Other elements can be added to the service blueprint, such as arrows which are used to indicate sequences and relationships (one-way or two-way exchanges), time, regulations/policies (e.g., food regulations), emotions, and evaluation metrics.

How to craft a good service blueprint?

The following are some recommendations for developing and implementing the service blueprint successfully.

- Stay close to customers and use research to find out more about customers.
- Engage different departments and stakeholders and conduct service blueprint workshops that are productive and fun for all participants.
- Emphasize on the customer, not the process. Organizations should make frontline staff customer-centric leaders as they stay closest to customers.

- Identify areas of focus and highlight the most critical components.
- Translate service blueprints to practical execution plans for each functional area.
- Encourage flexible development and adaptions of the service blueprint to maximize its usage and benefits.
- As business and marketing evolve continuously, so does the service blueprint.

Customer journey mapping (CJM)

What is CJM?

Customer journey mapping (CJM) is a map or visualization that shows how customers interact with an organization across different channels and touchpoints so that the organization can develop strategies to improve customer experiences. Developing a CJM requires team effort and reflects a systematic approach to understanding customers' wants, needs, expectations, and interactions. The key to a good CJM is that all insights should come purely from a customer's perspective, not from the organization's. A CJM can lead to the development of new and improved services as well as underlying processes. Figure 2 shows an example of a CJM of a mother looking for a childcare center for her daughter.

Alice Lim

- Age: 38 years old
- Location: West Singapore
- Occupation: HR Manager
- Income Level: Middle Income
- Education: Degree

Motivation

 Family

 Career

Bio

Alice is a new mother with a 3-year-old daughter. As a working mother, she aims to balance her career and family well. She pays a lot of attention to her daughter's development. Despite the busy schedule, she spends time reading and playing with her daughter everyday.

Needs

The desired childcare centre should:
- Adopt adaptive curriculum
- Incorporate fun and interactive enrichment activities, e.g. speech and drama, sports and Math Olympiad
- Emphasize value and character
- Low teacher-student ratios
- Have no TV
- Be near home/workplace
- Charge reasonable fee ($1,000 - $1,200 per month; after subsidy)

"I am looking for a good childcare centre with adaptive curriculum that allows my daughter to drive her learning because she needs to fully unleash her potential."

Stage	Awareness	Consideration	Decision	Delivery & Use	Advocacy
Customer Activities	• Hear from friends • See online portal (e.g. Singapore Motherhood Forum and Stootpedia) and centre websites • Drive around neighbourhood/ workplace	• Compare options • Engage the selected childcare centres	• Shortlist 2-3 preferred options • Discuss with husband and daughter • Research more on the preferred options, through online portals • Clarify with preferred childcare centres, if necessary • Place deposit and purchase necessary items (e.g. uniform) from the selected childcare centre	• Prepare the daughter (e.g. explaining to her why she needs to go to centre, the dos and don'ts at the centre) • Accompany the daughter during the first few days • Engage the daughter on her experience (e.g. her emotions, activities, progress and interactions with teachers and students) • Engage the principals and teachers directly through communication app • Provide feedback if any	• Continue with the centre • Refer the centre to friends and family
Customer Goals	• Identify 3-5 feasible options		• Select the childcare centre	• Ensure the daughter adapts well to the centre • Provide feedback to the centre, if necessary	• Ensure the daughter grows well, both intellectually and emotionally • Share feeling and feedback
Touchpoints	• Word of mouth • Social media • Childcare centre website • Presence of childcare centre around neighbourhood/ workplace	• Physical visits • Engagement with principals and teachers • Class observation • Sighting of course material	• Word of mouth • Social media • Childcare centre website • Further engagement with principals and teachers	• Daughter • Observation at the centre during the few days • Engagement with principals and teachers before/ after class/ parent-teacher meetings • Centre-parent communication app	• Daughter • Engagement with principals and teachers before/ after class • Centre-parent communication book • Word of mouth • Social media • Childcare centre website
Experience	Lost, confused	Require effort	Excited	Observe some areas that require feedback — Happy	"I have to share this"
Business Goals	• Increase awareness and interest	• Align centre programme and the needs of parents and the daughter	• Sign up with the centre • Prepare the daughter and parents	• Ensure the daughter adapt well at the centre, together with the parents	• Ensure the daughter grow well at the centre, together with the parents • Have parents into advocate
KPIs	• Number of people reached	• Number of queries • Number of physical visits • Quality engagement with parents	• Conversion rate • Provision of necessary information (e.g. what to prepare and expect) for parents and daughter	• Graduation rate • Evaluation of parents/ daughter	• Referral rate • Evaluation of parents/ daughter
Organisational Activities	• Create content on online portals and centre website • Create prominent signs outside the centre • Create brochures to be placed outside/ all around the centre	• Provide clear and professional advice to the parents during/ after physical visits • Ensure parents may observe the class and course material without disrupting existing students • Develop adaptive curriculum, with mind-intriguing activities and healthy sports, which allows children to progress at their pace • Ensure the centre meets ECDA requirements, including subsidies	• Follow up with the parents • Provide information (e.g. centre-parent communication app and checklist) to prepare the daughter and parents • Understand the needs of the daughter and parents • Provide clarifications if necessary • Inform the teachers about the needs of the parents and daughter	• Ensure professional delivery of the curriculum • Engage the daughter and parents, through physical engagement and app, to share the emotional and intellectual progression of the daughter at the centre • Adapt curriculum for the daughter/ class based on feedback	• Provide referral discount • Engage the daughter and parents, through physical engagement and app, to understand the emotional and intellectual progression of the daughter

Figure 2: Customer Journey Map of a mother looking for a childcare center for her daughter.

Source: Provided by Tan Pei Boon who took the Customer Experience Management course at Singapore University of Social Sciences.

Why use customer journey mapping?

As another visual tool, CJM shares some common benefits with service blueprints. First, both tools encourage teamwork, often in the form of dedicated workshops involving representatives from different stakeholders, to make the final illustrations. These workshops can help bring together different owners of the various customer touchpoints and allow the team to hear different perspectives and enhance empathy. Second, both service blueprints and CJM serve as effective communication tools. Compared to words, visuals are more attractive and easier to understand. Visual tools such as service blueprint and CJM organize various highly useful information into a logical structure and present the information in a visually appealing format. As a result, the service blueprint and CJM help bring people on the same page and enhance internal communications within the organization.

Meanwhile, CJM also exhibits unique benefits as it focuses on customer interactions and emotions. Some of the benefits include the following:

- **Reveal hidden interactions and emotions.** CJM shows the entire customer experience over time, including processes that the organization lacks interactions with or has no control over. For example, it shows what happens before purchasing (e.g., customer reviews). CJM allows marketers to look at the steps in the purchase process that are often overlooked but highly impactful in the customer journey.
- **Identify critical experiences and pain points.** CJM helps identify critical customer experiences and pain points from the customers' perspectives. For example, the moment a customer steps into the hotel lobby is critical, as the experience forms the important first impression of the hotel. The queue time for consumers to check-in can be a potential pain point as most customers would be tired and impatient after traveling possibly long distances from elsewhere to the hotel.
- **Demonstrate ownership of touchpoints.** CJM shows which department(s) should take ownership of each specific part of the customer experience and who should be responsible for it.
- **Show links and dependencies of interactions.** CJM displays the associations and dependencies between different interactions and suggests necessary collaborations between internal teams.

As discussed above, CJM helps identify dependencies that happen both upstream and downstream. Creating and refining a CJM allows organizations to connect parts of the organization that are involved in the customer journey. It also facilitates mutual understanding with external teams. In many cases, CJM can demonstrate to the teams who believe they are disconnected from the customer experience just how pivotal they are.

How to create a CJM?

CJM are widely used these days, and organizations can utilize many great examples and resources from the internet. Some suggestions on how to create a CJM include the following:

1. **Create a customer persona.** A customer persona is a semi-fictional description of a person representing a distinct customer group. Customer personas can help marketers form a mental shortcut of their typical customers and bring customers to life. A good persona clarifies who an organization's target customers are, why they buy, and their relationships with the brand.
2. **Define stages.** Next, marketers need to identify key lifestyle stages that are essential to a customer's relationship with a product, service, or brand. For example, critical stages in choosing a degree course involve exploring options, researching, going to open houses, selecting schools and programs, submitting applications, paying, studying, graduating, and post-graduation engagements.
3. **Define needs.** At this stage, marketers usually start with a scenario. For example, the customer journey map for a flight begins with a scenario such as "I'm bringing my family on holiday in the summer". Then, establish the needs for each stage. The statements should start with the simple prefixes such as "I need to..." and include both tangible/functional and emotional needs. These statements should contain actions and should be kept brief.
4. **Define interactions.** Define high-level interactions that customers will have. During the CJM workshop, teams can write about the interactions and experiences in each stage on sticky notes. These statements can later be aggregated and reordered into a sequence. Marketers can highlight critical interactions. The numbers of items in each stage often indicate their importance. For example, if many items are generated in the early stages, it is clear that customer acquisition is essential for the business, as a typical customer journey starts from attracting customers to the brand. It is good to add emotions at

each stage. These emotions are critical in managing the customer experience. For example, customer delight should be achieved in the final stages, while customer anxiety should be allayed in the earlier stages of the customer journey.

5. **Define ownership of touchpoints.** This step will reveal deeper learning and the organization's actual control over the touchpoints. The organization should revisit each stage and answer the following questions:

6. (a) do I own this interaction? (if it is essential yet I don't own it, I may want to have it); (b) which departments are responsible for this interaction? And (c) which department should take up the responsibility for the performance of the interaction?

How to facilitate a good CJM?

- **A learning attitude.** First, start with a learning attitude for the whole team: try to understand and learn from the CJM experience.
- **Do the homework first.** Prepare for the CJM workshop. Collect as much information as possible before the workshop. Share existing learnings about key customer groups by utilizing existing data and optimizing the power of market research.
- **Capture everything from the customers' perspectives.** CJM workshop participants need to put themselves in their customers' shoes and allow themselves to immerse in the customer experience. The organization should start with the most significant customer segment to create the base CJM, then create variations or subsets of CJM for different customer segments thereafter.
- **Capture meaningful experiences.** Participants need to consider the type of life and experience that is truly meaningful to customers so that businesses and their frontline service staff can provide true-to-life information and recommendations. Pay special attention to critical experiences (i.e., experiences that matter more than others). Consider peak or top experiences (i.e., experiences that are the most unforgettable) and how the organization can make these experiences more memorable for customers. Think about creating first and last impressions, as they are more important and lasting.
- **Make the map appealing to attract more people to read and use it.** Organizations should take time to explore various forms in which the customer journey can be presented and find the form that will work

best for their target audience. It is advisable to apply story-telling and visual design techniques to make the maps more appealing.

- **Think about follow-ups and find inspirations.** Ask how the organization can design a better customer journey experience that meets growing customer expectations. Remember, the sole purpose of investing in a CJM is to improve customer experience.

Service blueprint vs. CJM

These two CEM tools complement each other. CJM is usually the first step to understanding customer experience. A CJM displays a customer persona's interactions from the first interaction to the last post-sales interaction. In CJMs, different scenarios are listed, and customers' actions and thoughts are included from start to end. A service blueprint is a comprehensive diagram that visualizes the relationships between different service components — people, props (physical or digital evidence), and processes directly tied to touchpoints in a specific CJM. Service blueprints are then used after the CJM as a deep dive to gather evidence of the customer experience, as seen in relevant frontline actions, backend actions, and support processes.

Different focuses. CJM focuses on the customer action component of the service blueprint. The service blueprint contains far more information than the CJM, including customer actions and experiences, as well as activities undertaken by frontline and backend staff and the organization's support system.

CX Measurement

Why measure customer experiences?

First, what gets measured gets done. This saying points to the importance of setting up a metric to measure customer experience. Measuring customer experiences in systematic ways helps an organization identify issues arising from their customers' experiences.

Second, CX measurements help to reveal customer preferences and form a better understanding of the customers. As data are the fuel of the modern digital economy, they offer insights that are cheap (sometimes free). Making data-driven decisions is a hallmark of leading organizations. In the digital economy, the growth of customer data within businesses is substantial. These data are valuable assets to any organization, as they reveal patterns and insights about customer preferences that can suggest strategies to improve business operations. CX-related data are the most crucial component of an organization's analytics functions, as these data could be leveraged on to directly improve sales and profits.

The most widely used CX self-report measures: NPS, CSAT, & CES

The following three self-report measures are commonly used in CX measurement: net promoter score (NPS), customer satisfaction score (CSAT), and customer effort score (CES). Nowadays, most of these self-report measures are collected digitally, forming an essential part of the CEM system. Many CEM vendors provide services to collect these measures.

Net promoter score (NPS)

The Net Promoter Score (NPS) was developed by Bain and Company, Satmetrix and Fred Reichheld.[7] It is a simple measure based on one question: "On a scale of 0 to 10, how likely are you to recommend us to a friend or colleague?" Based on this score, customers are divided into three groups: those scoring 9 or 10 are referred to as Promoters, 7 or 8 as Passives, and 0 to 6 as Detractors. Generally, an organization calculates the NPS score by subtracting the percentage of Detractors from the percentage of Promoters.

The NPS is often referred to as a "broad level" brand or relationship metric. It measures not just customer experience but also customer loyalty, as recommendations are often based on accumulated experiences. The NPS can be followed up with an open-ended question such as "Care to tell us why?" This question will enable rich qualitative feedback that can guide organizational improvement efforts.

Customer satisfaction score (CSAT)

The Customer Satisfaction Score (CSAT) asks a customer to give a rating based on how satisfied they are with a recent interaction. Similar to the open-ended follow-up question for the NPS, marketers can add an open-ended question that allows customers to elaborate on specific causes of satisfying or dissatisfying experiences. Marketers can use icons such as emojis of smiling and sad faces to spice up the survey and improve engagement.

The CSAT is widely used in CX research. It is a valuable tool to identify issues with support staff and provide interventions, such as training. The learnings from the open-ended qualitative question can provide helpful insights into other KPIs for CX. For a healthcare service provider, customers may mention certain factors more frequently than others, such as waiting time, quality of consultations, and the comfort in waiting rooms. These factors can then be integrated into the CX measurement matrix, given their importance to customers.

The CSAT can be embedded into mobile apps for users to provide context-specific feedback to help product design and service delivery improvements. For example, customers can be prompted to answer "how satisfied are you with this feature" during the usage of that feature.

Customer effort score (CES)

The Customer Effort Score (CES) measures the ease of use of products and services with the following question: "How much effort did you have to expend to handle your request?" In improving customer loyalty, improvements on existing strengths may only offer a marginal increase in utility, whereas improvements on weaknesses may prove to be more effective (for more information, please refer to the Prospect Theory[8]). The CES can identify obstacles and problems for organizations. If customers are expending much effort in product usage, then the organization can focus on solving product-related issues that matter most to customers. The CES is especially valuable to Software as a Service (SaaS) businesses. SaaS organizations use CES as early as during the installation or onboarding experience, which is critical for SaaS businesses, as a user's first experience is vital.

Customer analytics

In today's data-driven economy, the development of market intelligence through the utilization of customer analytics technology is vital for customer relationships management and an organization's long-term success. Customer analytics refers to the analysis of customer behavior after collecting data from various offline and online sources such as retail sales, online sales, mobile apps, and social media. Customer analytics is part of market research and is an effective way to accumulate knowledge about customer preferences.

The growing importance of customer analytics makes CX one of the fastest developing fields in recent years, even during the pandemic. The field has attracted significant attention from consulting organizations, software developers, and marketing agencies. The booming field means excellent business and career opportunities. Many organizations have also formed dedicated internal analytics teams who either work independently or collaborate with third-party suppliers to enhance the collection and utilization of valuable data across channels.

Google Analytics

Modern businesses often engage in various digital platforms for sales and communications. Many platforms, such as Facebook, offer free or paid analytics as part of their services. Some of them also provide free resources and training materials to encourage better usage of their platforms. One of them is Google Analytics, a service provided by Google to help organizations track web usage.

In Google Analytics, users are requested to create a Google Analytics account and add a small piece of JavaScript tracking code to the webpages that require tracking. Each time a user visits a website, the tracking code will collect anonymous information about how that user interacts with the webpage. Google Analytics collects information about a user's hardware and activities, including the browser, the device used, and the operating system, as well as the originating traffic source (e.g., a search engine, an advertisement the user clicks, an email link, or another website). After collecting the information, Google Analytics will package the data and compile it into customized reports. Users can then further customize the reports according to their individual needs.

CX research and measurement good practices

CX measurement scorecard/index

Organizations can collect and use different CX metrics to assess performance. For example, the following can be used to evaluate the performance of a mobile app: average time to make a purchase, number of clicks before hitting the "Submit" button, the success rate of application completion, average ease-of-use rating for creating an account, the eight-week retention rate for a mobile app, and usage rate. The KPIs for an e-commerce site may include click rate, loss rate, and conversion rate.

It is recommended that organizations create a CX Measurement Scorecard/Index, which includes the following:

- Objectives: list the areas of focus that they want to improve, e.g., customer acquisition
- Measure: list specific metrics for each touchpoint
- Targets: define their goals in quantitative terms, e.g., First Call Resolution (FCR) >50 percent
- Key business KPIs: list KPIs that will enable the organization to realize the objectives

Using CX metrics together

CX metrics focus on different aspects of customer experiences. The NPS gauges customer loyalty and relationship over time, the CSAT and CES focus on each transaction and provide real-time performance measurements at each touchpoint. All measurements can be customized flexibly. For example, the CSAT can be used to measure overall satisfaction on several attributes that are meaningful to customers. The CES usually focuses on one specific feature, especially those likely to be problematic.

Modern technology enables instant tracking of customer experiences along the customer journey. CX software allows omni-access and flexible adaptation of customer analytics. Natural language processing and machine learning enable auto-categorization of textual responses to open-ended questions that can be done in real time. All these developments would allow businesses to identify issues quickly, prioritize solutions, and improve customer experiences.

Organizations' business models differ. Some are business-to-business (B2B), some are business-to-customer (B2C), and some adopt a mixed model. Each industry demonstrates industry-specific characteristics. Each organization may define their customer experiences differently, so the CX metric must be customized to respond to each organization's individual needs.

Businesses can use tools such as CJM to suggest touchpoints that truly matter to customers and focus their limited resources on them.

Organizations need to develop customized measurements for each touch-point and collect data on a regular basis. Disjointed measurement costs more money and leads to confusing conclusions. Hence, it is crucial to have a holistic view of the customer experience and all the touchpoints and design the system of data collection accordingly.

How to improve CX research and measurement?

The following guidelines are recommended for organizations that are keen to improve their CX measurement:

- CX metrics should be linked to CJM closely and interactions that matter the most to customers should be prioritized.
- Apply the balanced scorecard concept and do not just measure sales-related performance. The balanced scorecard[9] concept proposes that organizations adopt broader, more diversified indicators in measuring business performance, taking into consideration the long-term business growth.
- The quality of the data are highly essential. Otherwise, it will be "garbage in and garbage out."
- Storytell the data! It is vital to find meanings in numbers and create stories to help the audience connect the dots.

Emerging Trends in CEM

Focusing on what's next in CX, the field will witness the following emerging trends:

Growing awareness, regulations, and good practices in customer data protection. One significant direction is data privacy since more and more customer experiences are now online, accelerated by the COVID-19 pandemic. Organizations in Singapore must strictly comply with the Personal Data Protection Act (PDPA)[10] as it regulates the collection, use, disclosure, and care of personal data in Singapore. Data use should be supervised by the staff or department responsible for customer data management. It is advisable to formally include customer data protection in the functions of those staff and departments that access and use customer data. Actions should be taken to encrypt customer identifiers and ensure that anonymized customer data are used in most applications. Organizations must practice compliance with the PDPA and have regular risk reviews.

The continuous rising of digital channels. Organizations should realize that going digital is no longer an option but a must for survival and growth. Digital channels will play critical roles in e-commerce, payments, and communications in the future.

Greater channel integrations. Omnichannel marketing will become the norm, as seen in the seamless coordination of offline and online services. For example, Singtel, one of the largest telecommunication operators in Singapore, launched 24/7 unmanned popup stores named Unboxed in Singapore, where consumers can touch and try actual products, chat with live agents at video-assisted kiosks, and make purchases. The hybrid retail model provides consumers with richer experiences enhanced through both physical and digital channels.

Fast adoption of state-of-the-art technologies. The CX field has always been at the forefront of technology development. In the future, there will be more applications of the newest technologies, such as augmented reality (AR) and metaverse, artificial intelligence (AI), and chatbots. Metaverse is an online virtual world that incorporates AR, video, 3D technologies, and other emerging technologies to create immersive and enhanced customer experiences. Chatbots, widely used in online customer services, are software applications that mimic humans to engage in customer conversations automatically. In the future, chatbots will become more intelligent and human-like. The use of chatbots and broader robotic technology can help organizations address the issue of staff shortages, increase operational efficiency, and reduce costs.

More personalized CX experiences. Organizations' analytical capabilities will grow with accelerating technology development. Analytics will be used more widely in customer recommendations and predicting customer behaviors. Organizations will be able to more accurately identify prospective customers, provide better recommendations, and estimate the potential lifetime value of customers so that organizations can allocate resources to focal areas accordingly. Customers will increasingly demand more customized products and services, and analytics, coupled with AI, will facilitate greater personalization of CX.

More convenient and secure experiences. The broad penetration of omnichannel marketing and easier payments will give consumers more peace of mind. There will be more extensive use of cryptocurrencies in payment experiences. In its current form, cryptocurrency operates more like a distinct type of digital asset than real currencies. Cryptocurrency adopts peer-to-peer data verification abilities from blockchain technology, and will likely enable more accurate and efficient identification of customers and more convenient and secure payment options.

Continuous growth and development of CX software. The CX software will be more widely adopted, and its functions will be more intelligent, scalable, and flexible. Currently, CX software helps to empower agents to verify and identify customers, make instant decisions, and solve customer pain points more efficiently. It will become a vital intermediary and focal point to bridge customers, staff, suppliers, data, and systems and benefit organizations and customers.

Summary: CX is about People

A customer's experience, by its very nature, is based on humanity

D. Peppers (2016, forward session)[3]

Putting everything together, CX or CEM is about people. Everyone is a customer. CX is about how organizations should respect their customers, not just treat them like cash cows, but as individuals in particular purchase situations with emotional ups and downs, and strong desires for a better life. CX or CEM is also about how organizations develop and design measurements to improve work processes and product offerings and prevent service failures from happening in the future. Finally, CX or CEM is about how organizations design and implement CX systems to make their staff and customers' lives happier without invading their privacy. Indeed, CX is an exciting field that involves people, technology, and innovation.

References

1. Zendesk. (2022). Zendesk CX trends 2022, p. 14. Available from https://www.zendesk.com/sg/customer-experience-trends/.
2. Linkedin. (Jan, 2022). LinkedIn jobs on the rise 2022: The 20 Southeast Asia roles that are growing in demand. Available from https://www.linkedin.com/pulse/linkedin-jobs-rise-2022-20-southeast-asia-roles-growing-/.
3. Peppers D. Customer Experience: What, How and Why Now. Bookbaby, Portland, Oregon, United States, 2016.
4. Wiersema, F., & Treacy, M. (1995). *The Discipline of Market Leaders: Choose Your Customers, Narrow Your Focus, Dominate Your Market.* Addison-Wesley, Cambridge (MA).
5. Kien, S. S., Soh, C., Weill, P., *et al.* (2015). Rewiring the enterprise for digital innovation: The case of DBS Bank. Nanyang Business School, the Asian Business Case Center.
6. Shostack, G. L. (Jan-Feb, 1984). Designing services that deliver. *Harvard Business Review, 62*(1), 133–139.
7. Reichheld, F. F. (Dec, 2003). One number you need to grow. *Harvard Business Review, 81*(12), 46–54, 124. PMID 14712543.
8. Kahneman, D., & Tversky, D. (1979). Prospect theory: An analysis of decision under risk. *Econometrica, 47* (2), 263–291.
9. Kaplan, R. S., & Norton, D. P. (1996). *The Balanced Score Card: Translating Strategy into Action.* Harvard Business School Press, Boston, MA.
10. Privacy Data Protection Commission. PDPA Overview. Available from https://www.pdpc.gov.sg/Overview-of-PDPA/The-Legislation/Personal-Data-Protection-Act.

PART III

ENHANCING BUSINESS REVENUES THROUGH DIGITAL VENTURES

Chapter 6

Analytics in the Age of Disruption

———⛭———

James Tan and Priyanka Gupta

Introduction

In a VUCA (volatile, uncertain, complex, and ambiguous) world, organizations must be adaptive to change, inventive in conducting businesses, and perceptive when spotting risks and opportunities. This chapter presents several use cases to demonstrate how analytics has been used to help organizations make better decisions and improve outcomes in the age of disruption.

Background

The COVID-19 pandemic has resulted in social, economic, and technological disruptions in the world. In particular, the accelerated growth of online businesses, digital consumers, logistics, and delivery services will continue to drive demand for data- and analytics-related services. According to the latest employment projections by the United States Bureau of Labor Statistics,[1] data- and analytics-related occupations will grow by more than 31 percent from 2020 to 2030. Similarly, Valuates Reports[2] highlighted that the global big data and analytics market size, valued at US\$198.08 billion in 2020, is projected to hit US\$684.12

billion by 2030, with an estimated CAGR of 13.5 percent increase from 2021 to 2030. Indeed, data management and analytics can help organizations find critically useful information in the midst of massive volumes of data which otherwise may remain hidden and cost them to lose their competitive advantage

By 2030, the Southeast Asian (SEA) region is predicted to become a US$1 trillion digital economy,[3] entering a so-called *Digital Decade*. It is also forecasted that there will be a year-on-year increase of 40 million internet users within the SEA region. According to the Ministry of Manpower Jobs Situation Report,[4] analytics and artificial intelligence (AI) are identified as among the key frontier technologies in Singapore.

With a thriving digital economy in the region, Singapore is uniquely positioned as a hub for data storage and processing, especially since the increasing demand for data- and analytics-related services is greater than ever, both locally and regionally. Within Asia-Pacific, Singapore is the fourth-largest market[5] for Internet data centers, after Japan, China, and India.

Among the tech giants, Facebook, for example, is currently building a US$1.4 billion data center in Singapore, creating data- and analytics-related jobs.[6] The rising demand for analytics-related services spans across a wide range of industries, such as healthcare, hospitality, marketing, finance, and logistics. The strong demand for analytics services within Singapore is also reflected in job demands. For example, the number of job postings which contained "data analytics" as keywords on jobstreet.com.sg increased from 2,086 to 9,402 within a month from May 2020 to June 2022.

The preceding information suggests the crucial need for the application of analytics in organizations, especially in a world of digital disruption. Analytics is key to helping organizations thrive, and not just survive. Thus, the aim of this chapter is to showcase how analytics can be applied to uncover actionable information for improving business performance.

The rest of this chapter is organized as follows. The next section presents Mind-mapping for Analytics Projects (MAP), a development methodology that can be used to manage analytics projects. Unlike many existing analytics project development methodologies that assume a sequential flow of project development stages, the framework focuses on time-independent, high-level elements that can be considered when one is planning and executing an analytics project. In the remaining sections, the framework is applied in three different areas, namely data visualizations, customer segmentation, and predictive analytics.

Mind-Mapping for Analytics Projects

Most of the analytics projects involve answering the following three basic questions. First, what is the business problem to be addressed? Second, what data are required to provide information for addressing the problem? Third, what kind of analytics technique is required to generate the required information from the data?

Answering these three questions will help analysts better conceptualize ideas and guide the planning and execution of analytics projects. Three key aspects, namely Business, Data, and Analytics (BDA), form the backbone of the mind-mapping approach for Analytics Projects (MAP). In short, the mind-mapping approach is known as BDA-MAP.

Using the BDA-MAP

In project management, it is useful to think of any project as a series of tasks that are to be executed one after another. In analytics projects, an example of a process-oriented methodology is the Cross Industry Standard Process for Data Mining (CRISP-DM) proposed by Chapman *et al.*[7] which consists of six largely sequential stages. Another example is SEMMA,[8] which stands for a list of sequential phases, namely Sample, Explore, Modify, Model, and Assess. Unfortunately, real-world analytics projects are rarely executed in a sequential fashion. There is always a need to go back and forth between stages to fix issues that were previously overlooked. As such, a process-oriented methodology tends to be rigid if an analyst were to follow it strictly.

For many years, software engineering has well evolved from a waterfall (i.e., sequential) model to one that is more agile, such as prototyping, to support the need for iterative refinements in application development. In the same vein, analysts should shift their focus from processes to three core aspects that cover (1) Business requirements, (2) Data requirements, and (3) Analytics techniques. This way of planning and executing analytics projects allows analysts to be more agile, rather than following a rigid process-oriented approach.

Over the past years, the idea of mind mapping[9] has become a widely popular tool for ideation. The nimble approach to penning down ideas and organizing them through iterative refinements fit the very purpose of planning an analytics project with high level of flexibility.

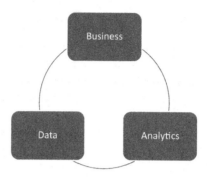

Figure 1:   The BDA project development framework.

In BDA-MAP, BDA is adopted as an initial framework for project planning, which is extended when new ideas and questions are added using a mind map. Figure 1 depicts the BDA Framework. Firstly, the Business Aspect involves defining the business problem that can be addressed using an analytics approach. In practice, this would involve an elaborate and focused discussion between the analyst and the stakeholders. The objective is to identify the right business problem and articulate it precisely. It is crucial to ask a series of clarification questions about the business problem to be solved. This can ensure that both the business problem owner and the analyst have a common understanding of the business problem to be addressed.

In practice, many real-world business problems can only be solved partially, and some business problems are better solved using non-analytics approaches. Thus, it is important to determine the extent to which a business problem can be solved using analytics. Basic questions on project feasibility include the following:

- Is the business problem addressable using analytics?
- Is there an alternative non-analytics solution to the business problem?
- What kind of information is required to solve the business problem?
- Is the data available with the chosen analytics technique able to generate the required information?
- What are the costs and benefits of solving the business problem?

If analytics is considered a promising approach to address the business problem, the next step is to examine the data aspect by specifying the information requirements which can be used to identify the raw data required to produce such information. This step requires higher order cognitive skills on the part of the analyst, who is expected to conjure up a mental picture of mapping the raw data into the required information needed for problem solving. This conceptual mapping step requires prior knowledge and experience in producing useful information for decision-making. For example, if the objective is to reduce customer attrition, the information required could be the list of churned customers that the company wants to engage. In this case, the raw data must contain customer contact information as well as behavioral data (e.g., date of last purchase made) which indicates customer recency.

Once the raw data are specified, they have to be collected and examined for availability, quality as well as sufficiency. Some examples of data quality problems include erroneous entries, missing values, outliers, etc. From the data quality assessment, treatments of these quality issues are then performed.

For example, if it is found that there is insufficient quality data available to produce the required information, more data should be collected. If the additional data cannot be collected, the problem may be deemed unsolvable using analytics and other approaches should be considered.

When sufficient good quality data are available, the next step is to identify an appropriate analytics technique to convert the raw data into the required information. This aspect covers the evaluation of various analytics techniques that can be used to derive patterns and insights from the data. Note that this step may require the analyst to revisit the data preparation step. For example, a chosen analytics technique usually prescribes a specific data format. Since the raw data format may not be compatible with the prescribed format, it will need to be converted into a format that can be processed by that analytics technique.

Once the required information is generated by that analytics technique, it should be looped back to the business aspect for final evaluation and solution implementation. At this stage, the generated information is compared against the information requirements identified in the initial stage of the project, and differences (if any) will be evaluated to assess the usefulness of the generated information. If the generated information is deemed useful, the next stage is solution implementation. Examples of implementation include deploying a model to make predictions, or simply using the knowledge generated to design a new workflow. For example, in the case of reducing customer attrition, the implementation involves inviting the list of churned customers for company engagement events.

In summary, the three aspects, (1) Business requirements, (2) Data requirements, and (3) Analytics techniques, involve the following key activities:

1. Formulate a business problem clearly after communicating with stakeholders
2. Assess the feasibility of the analytics project
3. Define information requirements for solving the business problem
4. Examine data for quality issues
5. Treatments of data based on results from the data quality assessment
6. Assess the appropriateness of analytics techniques to generate the required information or insights
7. Identify the gap between the raw data and the format required by the chosen analytics technique
8. Prepare the data in a form that is suitable for the chosen analytics technique
9. Construct analytics models using appropriate software
10. Evaluate the results of the analytics models
11. Recommend the best course of action based on the results.

Note that the main objective of having this methodological framework is to help analysts manage a wide array of analytics projects in a consistent manner. The three aspects have to be well-defined individually, yet well complemented and aligned with one another to produce meaningful outcomes. Importantly, every analytics project should start with this framework, where details can be elaborated using a mind map, so that all three aspects are well understood and aligned to produce a solution.

The final BDA-mind map (Figure 2) shows a general version of the BDA framework, which includes all the intermediary stages in the entire analytics process. The work starts with defining a **Business** problem, which is then used to identify the *information required* to solve the problem. To generate the required information, the *raw **Data*** must be mapped (conceptually) to the *required information*. This data mapping information is then used to select an appropriate **Analytics** technique. In return, the analytics technique dictates the data format required. In addition, the raw data are treated for any inherent data quality problems (such as missing values, outliers, etc.) and then further prepared to meet the data format requirements of the analytics technique. Finally, the prepared data and the analytics technique are used to generate the *information* to solve the identified business problem.

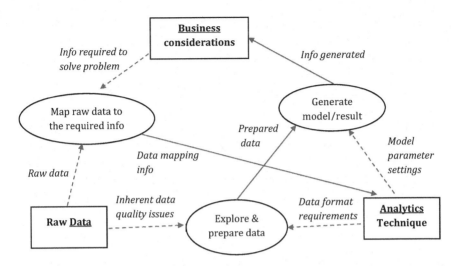

Figure 2:   A general version of BDA-mind map.

There are three important skills needed to plan, design, and execute an analytics project, as follows:

1. *Conceptual skills*: One must be able to define a business problem clearly and express how relevant data should be analyzed to address the problem.
2. *Technical skills*: One must be able to use software and tools to assess data quality, treat data quality issues, and prepare data for mining and analysis. Similarly, one must be familiar with software and tools for analyzing data, so as to derive the underlying patterns in the data, and interpret the results through a business lens.
3. *Soft skills*: The ability to communicate and liaise with business users and information technology colleagues in order to achieve the best possible outcomes for an analytics project.

Use Cases of Analytics Applications

This section presents three analytics projects to demonstrate the application of the BDA-MAP. The first project is on call center analytics. This project uses visual analytics to diagnose the underlying root cause that impacted the service level performance of a call center. Being able to pinpoint the exact problem and then resolving it has helped the call center improve its service level above the target given by its management.

The second project is on reducing customer attrition. This project uses sales transaction data to discover different groups of customers with different purchasing patterns and behaviors. From the results, specific customer retention programs were implemented to engage the churned customers.

The third project uses predictive modeling to better understand important factors that affect customer recommendations. The results help management to prioritize initiatives for improving customer recommendations as well as define realistic and meaningful targets for more effective performance management.

Project 1: Visual analytics — call center performance analysis

A call center is a department that handles large volumes of telephone requests from customers. Most call centers have systems that capture call-related information, such as details of the callers, name of the call agents, call waiting time, call length, etc. With such details, it is possible to derive a wide range of indicators to measure various aspects of the call center performance.

One of the more useful performance indicators is known as the service level, which is a customer experience metric that is computed from the proportion of incoming phone calls promptly answered within a specified time period (e.g., 30 seconds). For example, if a call center receives 110 incoming calls within an hour, and the number of promptly answered calls is 80, then, the Service Level for the hour is computed as 80/110, or 72.7 percent. Since a typical service level performance target is 80 percent, the call center is deemed to have performed below this target for that hour.

Background

In this project, the business objective is to improve the service level of a call center that has been found to be performing below its given target. From the outset, it was unclear what has caused the service level to be below the target. Is it related to the performance of some call agents? Is it related to certain categories of requests made by the customers? Is it related to the high call volumes at certain time of the day, week, or month? While the process of finding the root cause of the problem may not be straightforward, a diagnostic analytics approach seems to be a good way to start. Furthermore, the call center system has a data logging function that captures all the call-related information over a three-year period. This call log captures most of the call details and offers a lot of opportunities for developing a successful diagnostic analytics solution.

The call log attributes are described in more detail in Table 1.

It can be seen that the data provided offers a number of possibilities for deriving various performance measures that can be used to character-ize the operating performance of the call center. For example, the "Time Waited" numeric attribute can be used to compute the service level of the call center over a specified period. This is done by computing the propor-tion of calls with Time Waited $\leq$ 30 seconds, out of all the received phone calls during a given period (e.g., an hour). Another example is the "Problem Resolved?" binary attribute, which is calculated based on the proportion of customer issues being resolved within a given time period (e.g., a week). This leads to the First Contact Resolution measure, an

Table 1: Structure of the call log.

Attribute Name	Description	Data Format
Call_Log ID	Unique identifier for the phone call	String
Call_Agent ID	Employee ID of the call agent	String
Date	Date of the incoming call	In DD:MM:YYYY format
Time	Time of the incoming call	In HH:MM:SS format
Caller ID	Phone number of the caller	String
Services Selected	Examples of Services include "Operating hours enquiry", "Change appointment", etc.	Categorical
Time Waited	Duration (in seconds) that the caller waited before a call is answered	Integer
Call Length	Duration (in seconds) that the conversation lasted	Integer
Call Abandoned?	Whether the caller hung up before the phone was answered by a call agent	Binary: {Yes, No}
Problem Resolved?	Was the problem successfully resolved?	Binary: {Yes, No}

important part of customer-focused measures. Similarly, the "Call Abandoned?" binary attribute provides a sense of the Call Abandon Rate, which is a measure of the percentage of callers who hung up when their calls were not answered.

Note that the above-mentioned measures can also be better analyzed under certain meaningful contexts. For example, the First Contact Resolution can be measured for each of the call agents over a period of time. Another example is computing the average call length for each category of "Services Selected", and this would suggest the time and efforts needed to address each type of customer requests.

Visual analytics software

Since there are a wide variety of questions that can be posed during the diagnostic process, an analytics software that could help answer these questions with a high level of flexibility is needed. A natural choice is to use a visual analytics software that comes with user friendly functions for slicing, dicing, and drilling the data to help identify the root cause of the problem.

Unlike traditional database queries and reporting, visual analytics enables non-technical end-users to formulate data query through the use of simple graphical user interface (e.g., using a filter, rather than writing a code in Structured Query Language). Similarly, results can be returned using graphical plots, rather than rows and columns of data in a tabular format. This interactive-cum-graphical approach to querying and retrieving data facilitates the analysis of complex data such as those observed in a call center.

Figure 3 illustrates a typical visual analytics engine and shows how it can be used to bridge the gap between traditional database query and reporting, which is enclosed in a dashed box. The key components of the visual analytics engine include a Visual Query Processor (VQP) and a Graphical Output Processor (GOP).

The VQP allows users to specify the kind of data required. This is done through a graphical user interface (e.g., Microsoft Power BI® filter), using actions such as drag, drop, point, and click, to select the data attributes, state the conditions under which the data should be retrieved, specify the subsets of records required, or define groups of records to be aggregated. The VQP then converts the data requirements into a form of database query statement (e.g., a Structured Query Language statement), which is sent to the database for data retrieval.

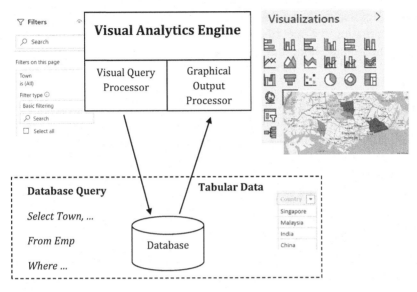

Figure 3:   The structure of a typical visual analytics software.

The GOP is a component that allows users to visually create the graphical charts needed based on the available or generated data attributes. When data are retrieved from the database, they are in a tabular format that will need to be converted into a graphical format that is defined by the user.

VQP and GOP, respectively, allow users to develop complex database queries without having to worry about language syntax, and to visualize query results using intuitive graphical charts. This is made possible by hiding all the lower-level details of database query and retrieval (enclosed within the dashed box in Figure 3) from the end-users, thereby reducing the cognitive loads in the entire process.

Although a visual analytics software is a great tool for diagnosing the call center performance issues, it does not take away the careful work needed to inspect, audit, and prepare the data so that good and relevant data can be made available for visualization and analysis.

In this case, the preliminary analysis found the data to be complete and accurate. A subtle but important decision made was to combine the Date and Time attributes and convert them into a single numeric variable called "Time Elapsed". This attribute stores the number of seconds that have elapsed after a reference time point. With details of each call now being captured to the nearest second, relevant measures can be computed by aggregating the records based on any higher time resolutions, such as by the minute, hour, day, week, etc.

Results

After going through a number of questions in the investigations, it was eventually found that there were time periods in which the call center was unable to keep up with the volumes of incoming calls. To better examine this irregularity, an overall map can be developed. Figure 4 shows a time-table heatmap that plots the service level performance for each hour over a five-day workweek. The colors and intensities show the variations in service level of the call center.

Figure 4 shows that the busiest times of the day are mornings and lunchtimes. Lunchtimes have slightly lower call volumes compared to the mornings; but lunchtimes tend to have lower service level performance because half of the teams are away for lunch-breaks. Another interesting observation is that Monday mornings appear to be the busiest time of a typical week. This is largely due to the closure of the call center over weekends, and issues accumulated over weekends would begin to surface on Mondays.

Solutions

With the insights gained, a multi-pronged approach with three comple-mentary solutions was considered. The first solution was to introduce a new staggered lunchtime system of three rotating teams instead of two. This improved lunchtime staff availability from 50 percent to 67 percent. Although this solution appears to be simple, the implementations required

Day\Time	8am	9am	10am	11am	12nn	1pm	2pm	3pm	4pm	5pm
Monday	0.4	0.68	0.85	0.86	0.57	0.5	0.74	0.85	0.81	0.89
Tuesday	0.52	0.61	0.74	0.8	0.48	0.5	0.83	0.95	0.86	0.85
Wednesday	0.55	0.55	0.75	0.87	0.53	0.59	0.76	0.87	0.92	0.82
Thursday	0.57	0.68	0.82	0.85	0.44	0.55	0.8	0.81	0.89	0.86
Friday	0.53	0.71	0.81	0.86	0.52	0.48	0.81	0.86	0.92	0.82

	Below	Meet	Good	Exceed
Service Level	0.1	0.4	0.6	0.8

Figure 4: (Color version available online) A heatmap showing the service level perfor-mance of a call center.

careful change management. Because the call agents had to follow a more drastic change in lunch schedules, proper communication sessions were conducted to explain the rationale and benefits of doing so. This solution was expected to relieve the stress and anxiety of the call center staff during lunchtimes. Feedback from staff was also sought and addressed so that the final solution was more well-considered and sustainable.

The second solution was to offer alternative touch points when the call volume was high. For example, callers have the option of requesting a call back, or contacting the call center via email. These options allowed the call center to get back to the callers during off-peak periods, thereby balancing the workload between peak and off-peak periods. To ensure the feasibility of this solution, a further check was needed to ensure that the workload transferred to the off-peak periods was reasonable. This ensured that the call center staff had time to take a break, and were not constantly under pressure to clear the backlog. Another issue to be addressed with this approach is the need to make changes to the call center system. For example, the interactive voice response system needs to capture a user's contact number when a call back is requested.

The third solution was to cross-train staff from other departments so that they could be mobilized to help attend to calls during peak periods. These staff members can be given basic training to help them answer simple queries such as questions related to operating hours or location. When a query is too complicated, they can obtain the query details and arrange a call back. This added human touch was crucial to improve customer experience. As this solution required careful collaboration with other departments, senior management support was required to make this happen. This consequently benefited other departments as they would have fewer outstanding cases from the call center for them to follow up on.

In this project, a simple timetable heatmap was used to identify the time periods in which service performance target was not met, and appropriate solutions were explored to fix the manpower issues. After some refinements to the proposed solutions, the call center was finally able to meet its service performance target six months after the root cause was found.

This case study shows the importance of using analytics to understand call center problems rather than relying on mere speculation. It adopts an agile, BDA mind map approach to develop an analytics solution for the call center (Figure 5). First, analysis of the business problem led to the

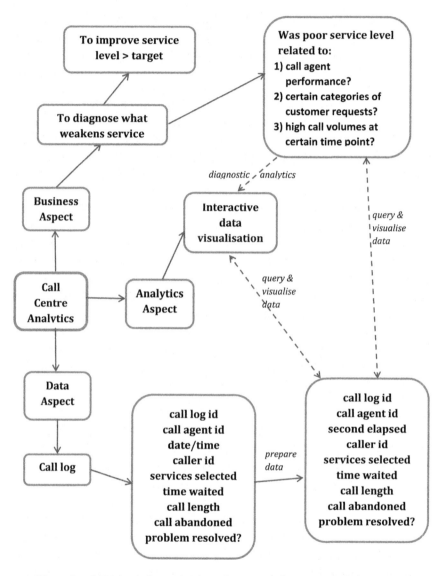

Figure 5: A BDA mind map for the call center performance analytics project.

decision to adopt a diagnostic analytics approach. The diagnostic process was facilitated by using visual analytics to query various aspects of the call log data, which were readily available for analysis. The implementation stage involved making changes to their existing technology (e.g., routing of customer calls to other departments) to enable workflow change, redesigning staff roster, and getting buy-in from the call agents as well as engaging in cross-departmental collaborations to support one another to improve customer satisfaction.

Project 2: RFM and cluster analysis — reducing customer attrition rate

The project pertains to a multinational women's lingerie company that has several retail outlets. The company wants to understand its customer attrition rates and how it can improve its customer engagement levels.

The company has a customer loyalty program that tracks the sales transactions of each member. The sales transaction data are retrieved from the point-of-sales system. The data attributes include Customer ID, the Date and Time when a customer visited a store, the details of the store visited, the products purchased, the quantity of product bought, and the amount spent. The records were collected over a period of four years, which is sufficient for the purpose of this project. For women's lingerie business, a four-year period would allow them to identify return customers.

Customer profiling

In general, the analysis is divided into two stages. In the first stage, the purchasing profile of each customer is derived from the sales transaction data. This profile has three features: (i) Recency (R), obtained by computing how recently a customer has made a purchase; (ii) Frequency (F), obtained by counting how many times a customer made purchases over the four-year period; and (iii) Monetary (M), the average amount of money spent over the four years.

Each of the Recency, Frequency, and Monetary (R, F, M) features has a range of values, from 1 to 5. Here, a 1 means the least recent, lowest frequency, and lowest monetary amount spent for R, F, and M, respectively. A 5 reflects the other end of the spectrum (i.e., the most recent, the highest frequency, and the highest monetary amount spent for R, F, and M, respectively).

Considering the permutations, we would end up with 125 (5R × 5F × 5M) types of customers. Hence, it is necessary to reduce the number of customer types. For example, natural customer groupings can be created by simply discretizing each of the (R, F, M) scores into two

Table 2:   Eight possible groups of customers using dichotomized RFM features.

RFM Profile			
R	F	M	Customer Type
High	High	High	High-value and frequent customers
High	Low	High	*Prospective high-value customers*
High	High	Low	Regular shoppers
High	Low	Low	New customers
Low	Low	Low	Inactive customers
Low	High	High	*Churned*
Low	Low	High	High-value customers who may have churned
Low	High	Low	Regular shoppers who have churned

categories: "High" for scores in the range of 3–5; and "Low" for scores in the range of 1–2. This reduces the number of customer clusters to eight groups as shown in Table 2.

While the above approach makes sense, it does not consider the actual distribution of the scores within each feature to decide the High and Low categories. For example, if a feature has majority of scores with values 1, 2, and 5 as shown in Figure 6, it would be more appropriate to define 1–3 as Low, and 4 and 5 as high. Recent research[10] suggested that clustering on a single feature can perform this type of discretization more meaningfully.

Another major advantage of using clustering is the ability to generate different sets of clustering solutions based on different number of clusters specified by the user.[11] This capability allows users to explore different sets of solutions and choose the one that best fits the current business requirements.

For this project, clustering is used to find natural customer segments based on their RFM profiles. Essentially, customers with very similar RFM scores are grouped into the same cluster, such that the RFM profiles of customers within the same cluster are similar yet different from the RFM profiles of customers in the other clusters. Figure 7 provides a simple illustration.

After cluster analysis has been applied on the RFM profiles of customers, eight groups of customers similar to that of Table 2 are also found. However, the memberships of records in their respective clusters are different from those in Table 2. This is because of the more refined

Frequency Distribution of Recency

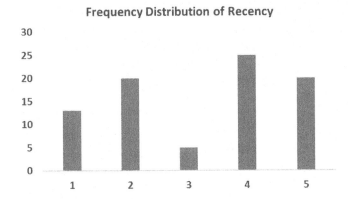

Figure 6: A natural way to discretize this distribution is classifying interval [1, 3] as "Low", and [4, 5] as "High".

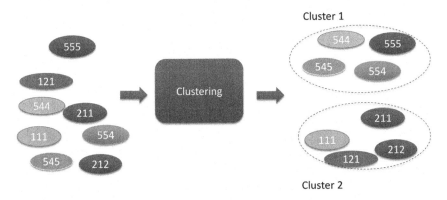

Figure 7: An illustration of two customers groups found by clustering their RFM features.

assignments of records to clusters achieved by clustering. Of the eight groups generated, two groups of customers are of high interest to the company. The first group comprises the high-value customers, with very high recency and monetary scores, though their frequency scores are low. This suggests that these customers are either newly acquired, or they are customers who spend a lot whenever they visit a store. Hence, this group of customers must be managed carefully and given more personalized attention and services.

The second group is the churned customers, who are customers who have stopped purchasing from the company. This can be seen by their very low recency scores which suggests that these customers have not returned to make purchases for a long period of time. For this group of customers, the company can implement customer retention programs to reduce its customer churn rate. To follow up on this, the company invited these customers for special product events. Interestingly, some of the customers who attended the events started making purchases again.

Finally, the BDA mind map used to conceptualize the entire project is given in Figure 8.

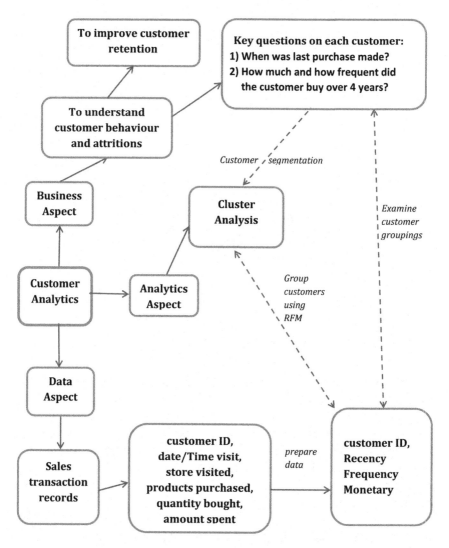

Figure 8:   A BDA mind map for customer analytics using RFM clustering.

Project 3: Predictive modeling — factors affecting airline recommendations

This project involves the use of predictive modeling to understand factors affecting airline recommendations. To understand the concept of predictive modeling, consider a simple spreadsheet with two columns as shown in Figure 9. The first column relates to salary, while the second column pertains to purchase decision. A simple predictive model that includes salary as input and purchase decision (YES, NO) as the target is created. The assumption here is that the salary figures help explain the purchase decision of a product. Using the data shown on the left, a predictive model in the form of a decision tree can be built to explain the relationship between the input and the output (aka target).

The decision tree first checks whether a customer record has a salary entry of more than US$2,000 or not. If the answer is Yes, the decision tree will predict that this customer is likely to make a purchase; otherwise, the customer is unlikely to make a purchase. This simple decision tree model therefore predicts customers' purchase decisions based on their salaries.

Predictive modeling of intention to recommend

This project examines how service ratings for an airline affect customer recommendation. The structure of the airline review data is given in Table 3. The service rating records were collected from airline passengers who provided online reviews after their flight. Each review consists of a series of ratings given to different aspects such as seat comfort, value for money, cabin staff, food and beverages, inflight entertainment, ground

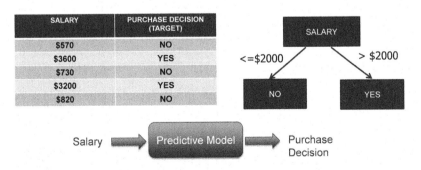

Figure 9: An example showing how a predictive model is generated.

Table 3:   Structure of the airline review data.

Attribute Name	Description	Role	Data Format
Seat comfort	Review rating measured from 1	Input	Numeric
Value for money	(i.e., most dissatisfied) to 5		
Cabin staff	(i.e., most satisfied).		
Food and beverages			
Inflight entertainment			
Ground service			
Wi-Fi connectivity			
Recommendation	Yes for recommend; No for do not recommend	Target	Binary

service, and Wi-Fi connectivity. Each rating is measured from 1 (i.e., most dissatisfied) to 5 (i.e., most satisfied).

In addition, each passenger was asked to rate their overall travel experience with the airline on an overall rating scale (of 1–10), as well as a recommendation outcome, assessed via either a 'Yes' or a 'No'.

To understand how the service-related ratings are associated with the recommendation outcome, predictive modeling, which explains how a set of input data attributes affect the response of an output attribute, is applied. Here, the inputs include the various service ratings, while the output is the recommendation outcome (Figure 10). This is a logical prediction as the airline would like to understand how the various input ratings affect a customer's recommendation.

The overall rating attribute was intentionally excluded as the objective is to understand how the specific service-related inputs are associated with the recommendation outcome.

Predictive model for airline data

Turning to the results of the predictive model based on the airline review data, Figure 11 shows the important ratings that are found to affect the recommendation outcomes.

The results show that *value for money* is the most important rating, followed by seat comfort, then food and beverages. This means that variations in these ratings could swing the recommendation rating from Yes

Figure 10:   Predictive modeling setup for the airline review data.

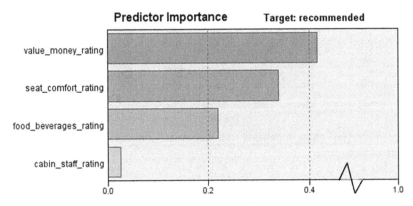

Figure 11: This chart highlights the important predictors associated with the recommendation target.

to No or vice versa. Common sense suggests that the higher these ratings, the better the chance of receiving a Yes recommendation.

The ranking of rating importance allows management to prioritize which aspects of their service they would like to improve on, given the limited resources. In this case, the first rating should be value for money, followed by seat comfort, and then food and beverages.

A plot of the *value for money* rating distribution in Figure 12 shows that most customers will not recommend the airline if this rating is less than 4. For performance management, it is then sensible to set performance target for this rating to be 4 and above.

It is interesting to note that cabin staff is deemed the least important as compared to the other ratings. Note that this does not imply that cabin staff performance is not important. Rather, this means that cabin staff as a factor may not have exhibited sufficient variations to affect significant changes in the recommendation outcomes. Throughout the predictive modeling process, domain knowledge plays an important role.

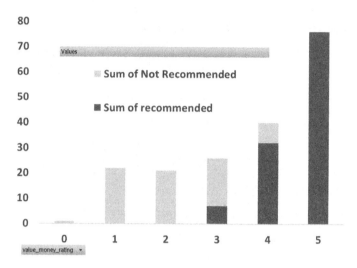

Figure 12: This chart highlights the important predictors associated with the recommendation target.

For example, the staff involved in the project must identify the inputs and outcome in order to generate a meaningful model.

Finally, the BDA mind map for conceptualizing this project is given in Figure 13.

Conclusion

According to a survey by IBM,[12] 95 percent of 1,226 respondents stated that "big data and analytics capabilities are now necessary to stay on par with competitors or required to outpace them." They attributed this necessity to the rise of digitized ecosystems; radical technological transformation; and greater capability to know rather than speculate about the future. This survey suggests a general consensus that analytics is no longer an option for organizational survival in a VUCA world. The natural question is how then should an organization leverage on analytics to their best advantage. The methodology and use cases presented in the chapter help address this question.

This chapter outlines several ways by which data can be converted into organizational assets. The first case study on call center analytics shows that visual analytics can facilitate querying a database and

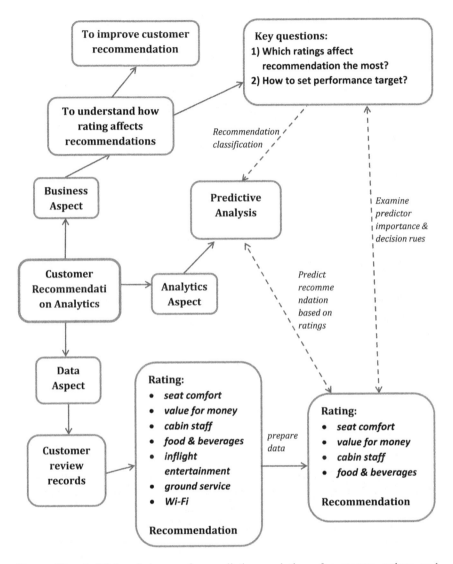

Figure 13: A BDA mind map for predictive analytics of customer ratings and recommendation.

generating useful information to spot operation anomalies and help address business problems.

The second case study conducted in a lingerie multinational corporation shows how analytics methods such as clustering can help uncover hidden patterns (e.g., churned customers) that are otherwise not easy to obtain through simple query of data.

The third case study on airline customer review ratings highlights how predictive analytics can offer an innovative way to study how a set of factors can be related to an outcome of interest to the organization.

Last but not least, we have presented the BDA mind map approach to showcase how analytics projects can be iteratively conceptualized, planned, and executed in a dynamic business environment.

References

1. U.S. Bureau of Labor Statistics (Sep 8, 2022). Fastest growing occupations. Available from https://www.bls.gov/emp/tables/fastest-growing-occupations.htm.
2. Valuates Reports (Feb 11, 2020). Global big data & business analytics market size, share & forecast, 2021–2030. Available from https://reports.valuates.com/market-reports/ALLI-Manu-3K13/global-big-data-and-business-analytics.
3. Baijal, A., Cannarsi, A., Hoppe, F., Chang, W., Davis, S., & Sipahimalani, R. (Nov 10, 2021). e-Conomy SEA 2021 — The digital decade: Southeast Asia's internet economy resurgence is fueling growth across the region. Available from https://www.bain.com/insights/e-conomy-sea-2021/.
4. Ministry of Manpower, Singapore (Nov 24, 2020). Jobs situation report 14th edition — infocomm technology. Available from https://www.mom.gov.sg/newsroom/press-releases/2020/1124-jobs-situation-report.
5. SimpliLearn (2022). Hot jobs: Why are data analysts in demand and how to be one. Available from https://content.mycareersfuture.gov.sg/rising-demand-data-analytics-professionals-singapore/.
6. Cheok, J. (Sep 7, 2018). Facebook to build S$1.4b data centre in Singapore — its first in Asia. Available from https://www.businesstimes.com.sg/garage/news/facebook-to-build-s14b-data-centre-in-singapore-its-first-in-asia.
7. Chapman, P., Clinton, J., Kerber, R., Khabaza, T., Reinartz, T., Shearer, C., & Wirth, R. (2000). CRISP-DM 1.0 Step-by-step data mining guide. Available from https://www.researchgate.net/publication/225070403_CRISP-DM_1.0_Step-by-Step_Data_Mining_Guide.
8. Azevedo, A., & Santos, M. (2008). KDD, SEMMA and CRISP-DM: A parallel overview. *IADIS European Conference Data Mining*, pp. 182–185. Available from http://recipp.ipp.pt/handle/10400.22/136.
9. Buzan, T., & Griffiths, C. (2014). *Mind Maps for Business: Using the Ultimate Thinking Tool to Revolutionise How You Work*, 2nd edn. Pearson, Harlow (GB).

10. Tan, S. C. (2018). Improving association rule mining using clustering-based discretization of numerical data. *International Conference on Intelligent and Innovative Computing Applications (ICONIC)*, pp. 1–5. IEEE. Available from https://doi.org/10.1109/ICONIC.2018.8601291.
11. Anitha, P., & Patil, M. (2022). RFM model for customer purchase behavior using K-Means algorithm. *Journal of King Saud University — Computer and Information Sciences*, *34*(5), 1785–1792. Available from https://doi.org/10.1016/j.jksuci.2019.12.011.
12. Finch, G., Davidson, S., Haren, P., Kurtz, J., & Shockley, R. (2015). Analytics: The upside of disruption. The IBM Institute for Business Value. Available from https://www.ibm.com/thought-leadership/institute-business-value/report/2015analytics.

Chapter 7

Opportunities from Blockchain Solutions

Poh Ling Neo

Introduction — The Collision of Two Worlds

Bitcoin has its origins in the cypherpunk movement. The cypherpunks are a group of privacy advocates who want to make use of cryptography for anonymous transactions. They wanted privacy in an increasingly digital age, and they can only rely on themselves because they "cannot expect … large, faceless organizations to grant … privacy out of their beneficence". In their manifesto published in 1993, it is stated that they wanted to write code to build autonomous systems and make the code freely available so that the "software can't be destroyed, and a widely dispersed system can't be shut down".[1] To have a privacy-first society in this digital age, one of the most important pillars is to have an anonymous electronic money system where monetary value can be transferred without the oversight and monitoring of the government. This therefore motivates their discussion for an implementation of an anonymous payment system.

In 1998, Dai Wei published the concept of B-Money, which discussed the use of cryptography to hide the identities of parties in a payment instruction and the use of periodic fines/rewards to ensure that servers are honest for the proper tracking of the distribution of money.[2] His concept included the use of a distributed system to track the distribution of money. In the same year, Nick Szabo wrote about Bit Gold[3] where he suggested the use of cryptographic hashing and mining to create a new unit of gold in his decentralized monetary system. Both discussions were acknowledged by the creator of Bitcoin for laying the groundwork for the successful implementation of Bitcoin, a decade later.

The motivation behind electronic money was to eliminate "large, faceless organizations" so that a choice could be made to hide identities in transactions, and in 2009, it became a reality through Bitcoin and its blockchain technology. The development of blockchain reached a perhaps surprising twist when J.P. Morgan co-opted it to say that "blockchain technology is a game changer"[4] and it has the potential to revolutionize the way businesses are carried out. How did the interest of a niche group of privacy advocates go mainstream such that words such as "decentralization" and "blockchain" are now part of the lexicology of businesses and governments? What can the blockchain technology offer to businesses that they are studying and experimenting with it within their businesses?

In this chapter, the rise of blockchain technology will be discussed, by understanding the working principles behind the first blockchain application, i.e., Bitcoin. Through Bitcoin, it will be realized that blockchain technology can be the infrastructure to deliver services without the need for trusted intermediaries , such as lawyers in a business transaction. This has led to a proliferation of new businesses seeking to use blockchain technology to create distributed services, leading to the multiple phenomena of DeFi, NFT, and web3 that are being witnessed now. The discussion will also examine how businesses are using blockchains and distributed ledger technologies (DLT) to deliver cost-effective and cross-business solutions to entire markets and industries. Finally, the meaning, ethos, and philosophy behind blockchain in the current social climate will be examined. It is a technology that provides a decentralized means of providing services to the people, by the people, ushering an online world where privacy, wealth, and power would go back to the people.

The First Digital Asset, Bitcoin

Today (2022), there are more than 20,000 cryptocurrencies[5] and it all began with Bitcoin, which was created more than a decade ago. Bitcoin is the oldest cryptocurrency (13 years), with a market capitalization of US$390 billion, and it is worth more than some of the established brands and companies such as Walmart (50 years) or Exxon Mobil (102 years).

Since its inception Bitcoin has gathered a raucous following and, despite its storied history, less than 1 in 10 Americans truly understand it,[6] even though 9 in 10 Americans have heard about it.[7] The lack of understanding is perplexing especially when we consider the total transparency about its creation,[8] implementation,[9] and usage.[10]

In this section, Bitcoin will be demystified by explaining how it works. The technology behind Bitcoin will be examined — blockchain — and how it functions as a payment system without a trusted intermediary to check and inspect on the validity of transactions. This understanding is important, because it will allow debate on how meaningful it is to quantify the intrinsic value of the cryptocurrency and, hence, decide whether Bitcoin has a place in society. At the moment, for every Bitcoin evangelist who believes Bitcoin is "one of the most important inventions in the history of mankind,"[11] one can find another who thinks that Bitcoin is rat poison squared.[12] This is perhaps the reason why Satoshi Nakamoto, the creator of Bitcoin, had chosen to keep his identity secret initially, for he had the foresight to predict the dichotomy that Bitcoin will bring forth as it enters the mainstream market.

Participants in the Bitcoin network

Bitcoin is designed to be a payment system where value can be "transferred from one party to another without going through a financial institution". The concept behind Bitcoin was published by Satoshi Nakamoto in a white paper titled "A peer to peer payment system" in 2007. In the paper, Satoshi has laid out his clear intentions that he wanted the payment system to be operated by the participants of the system, and anyone is welcome to leave and rejoin the network at will. There are various roles in the network and an entity (or node, in Bitcoin's parlance) can join the network in the following roles:

- Users
  A user is a node who transfers their Bitcoin from one wallet to another and this movement of Bitcoin has happened because an individual would like to use Bitcoin to pay for the services he has acquired. The first real-world use of Bitcoin was made on 22 May 2010 where ฿10,000 was used to pay for the purchase of two Papa John's pizzas, which cost about US$40 then. This transaction has been immortalized in the history of Bitcoin[13] and 22 May is now known as Bitcoin Pizza Day. The two persons involved in the transaction, Laszlo Hanyecz and

Jeremy Sturdivant, were developers who wanted the bragging rights to be the first in the world to use Bitcoin to facilitate a real-world transaction. Indeed, their first transaction is especially poignant now because the ₿10,000 is worth about US$200 million today.

Nakamoto has intended Bitcoin to be a means of payment, but with the meteoric rise in Bitcoin's price, many people are now holding Bitcoin for future price appreciation, resulting in Bitcoin being widely regarded as a store of value now, just like gold. A notable example of Bitcoin user and enthusiast who is acquiring it as a store of value is Michael Saylor of MicroStrategy. He is reputed to have 130,000 Bitcoins[14] because he believes that Bitcoin has enormous potential that is in an early stage of development and poorly understood.[15] Whether he is right about the *use* of Bitcoin as a good store of value, only time will tell.

- Core developers
Bitcoin Core is the name of the code base of Bitcoin, and it documents the entire protocol of the cryptocurrency. For example, it is known that only 21 million units of Bitcoin will be available in the payment system and Figure 1 documents the five lines of code where the 21 million limit is imposed in Bitcoin Core.

Bitcoin Core is designed to be an open-source project because Nakamoto wanted the development of the code base to be entirely democratized. Any developer is welcome to join the project, and any changes or implementation can be viewed by all, and discussion can take place to filter out clearly bad implementation.

Nakamoto was the person who created the code base, and he is the first Bitcoin core developer. The role of core developer is to ensure that

```
1153    CAmount GetBlockSubsidy(int nHeight, const Consensus::Params& consensusParams)
1154    {
1155        int halvings = nHeight / consensusParams.nSubsidyHalvingInterval;
1156        // Force block reward to zero when right shift is undefined.
1157        if (halvings >= 64)
1158            return 0;
1159
1160        CAmount nSubsidy = 50 * COIN;
1161        // Subsidy is cut in half every 210,000 blocks which will occur approximately every 4 years.
1162        nSubsidy >>= halvings;
1163        return nSubsidy;
1164    }
```

Figure 1: A screenshot of Bitcoin Core where a 21M BTC limit is implied.

Bitcoin Core gets updated continuously, with new features and improvements that were agreed by the Bitcoin community. Proposed improvements to be made to Bitcoin are done through the use of Bitcoin Improvement Proposals (BIPs) where the community will debate about the merits of the proposals. Some of the most important BIPs, such as BIP141, allow the Segregated Witness (SegWit) protocol to "increase the block size"[16] for faster transaction capacities. This proposal went through a long period of discussion before consensus was achieved.

In the early days of Bitcoin, core developers tend to be Bitcoin enthusiasts who maintain the code base out of interest. Today, the work of core developers is funded by grants, NGOs, and crypto companies who have stakes in the continued success of Bitcoin.

- Miners

The primary role of miners is to provide security in the payment system so that the distribution of Bitcoins in the network can only be changed with valid transactions. Miners are responsible for checking the validity of transactions whenever users post *unconfirmed transactions* into the network. No one can claim that he has ฿10,000 unless the *community* of miners has endorsed it. What this means is that if one wanted to create Bitcoins out of thin air or try to spend the same amount of Bitcoins twice (double-spent transaction), the amount of processing power, i.e., the hash rate, that needs to be possessed must be greater than the collective hash rate in the community of (benevolent) miners in the network. With more miners in the network, the cumulative hash rate is higher, and this implies a higher hurdle rate for a bad player, translating to a more secure payment system. The collective efforts of all the miners, rather than a single miner, secure the entire Bitcoin payment system.

Individual miners enhance the security of Bitcoin by contributing its hash rate to the network, and when they do so, they will incur electrical charges. Therefore, miners must be enticed economically to join the network, and this is where the mining rewards come into the picture. The rewards are the creation of new units of Bitcoin (hence, it is called "mining") which is given to a single successful miner. The probability that a miner will be awarded is proportional to the hash rate he contributes to the overall network. Due to the meteoric rise of Bitcoin's prices, there are organized mining pools that locate themselves in cold places with cheap electricity to mine for Bitcoins. Some of these mining pools, such as Antpool, are responsible for more than a tenth of the total hash rate in the Bitcoin network and because of the level of security provided by them, the executives of these mining pools are influential individuals in the Bitcoin community. For the BIPs mentioned earlier to pass, these mining executives must support them before they can be widely deployed in the Bitcoin network.

Nakamoto has designed the mining reward with a high initial value of 50 Bitcoins to be awarded every 10 minutes in the Bitcoin protocol. The rationale for a high mining reward is to attract new miners into the nascent Bitcoin network when Bitcoin is young and does not have any market value. With the increased adoption of Bitcoin as a payment method, there will be more users and, hence, a greater demand and market value for Bitcoin. With this increase in market value, the number of Bitcoins for the mining rewards should be adjusted downwards accordingly. Hence, in Bitcoin Core as documented in Line 1161 of Figure 1, there is a systematic halving of mining rewards happening approximately every 4 years. The next halving of mining rewards is expected to happen in 2024. Past halving of miner rewards in 2016, 2020, etc., have been accompanied with a spike in Bitcoin's prices, as

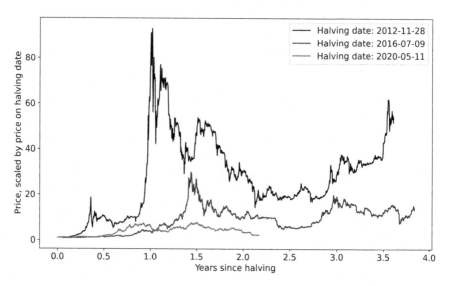

Figure 2:   (Color version available online) Bitcoin price trend after a halving event.

shown in Figure 2. Some Bitcoin price commentators have rationalized that this is due to a smaller circulating supply of Bitcoins.

For Bitcoin to succeed in the long run, either as a means of payment or as a store of value, it is important that these three roles must work closely together to ensure the steady growth in the use, demand, and market value of Bitcoin. There must be a growing number of users who want to use or hold Bitcoin. Only with this demand would the price of Bitcoin appreciate, and this would entice core developers and miners into the Bitcoin network. With core developers in the network, Bitcoin will be further improved through the implementation of good BIPs, and with more miners, the security of the Bitcoin network is enhanced, resulting in greater confidence in Bitcoin, either as a means of payment or a store of value. A more secure Bitcoin will entice greater confidence in its legitimacy, drawing more users into the Bitcoin network, creating a virtuous cycle, as shown in Figure 3, where each round of technical and security improvements brings forth more users, core developers, and miners, allowing the network effects to ensure the long-term success of Bitcoin.

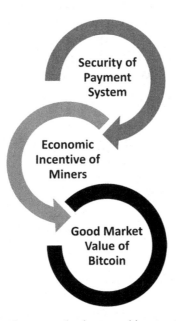

Figure 3:   Users, core developers, and miners working together to increase the uses, demand, and market values of Bitcoin.

Features of Bitcoin network

Depending on how one wants to contribute to the success of Bitcoin, either as a user or miner, a key feature of the Bitcoin network is that once one joins it, the interactions with other network participants will be governed by the Bitcoin protocol. For example, if a user wants to spend his Bitcoin wealth in a transaction, he must pay a transaction fee and set up his transaction in a stipulated format. If a miner wants to mine for new units of Bitcoin, he must compete with other miners, following the proof-of-work algorithm. The details of the mining competition and the algorithm are all stipulated in the Bitcoin protocol.

The second feature of Bitcoin is that there is no centralized authority responsible for making decisions in the network. It is designed to be a decentralized network, as shown in Figure 4. Even though there are rules established in the protocol, there are still many decisions that have to be made in the network in real-time. As discussed in the earlier section, the protocol states that miners have the responsibility to check on the validity of unconfirmed transactions. But with many miners in the network, who does the network listen to if different miners have different conclusions about the validity of a transaction? This conundrum is further complicated if there are malicious miners whose intention is to destroy the network. Without an authority, how does Bitcoin achieve a state of consensus so that there is an agreement on the distribution of Bitcoin in the network? The tracking of Bitcoin distribution is a prerequisite for a payment

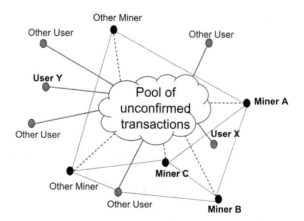

Figure 4:   A distributed network of nodes in Bitcoin.

system. Without it, Bitcoin ceases to function effectively as a payment system.

Decisions in the Bitcoin network are made through independent verification and consensuses. Miners are first equipped with all the agreed valid transactions that have ever happened in the entire history of Bitcoin. These records are contained in the *blockchain* of Bitcoin. With this information, miners are able to follow the instructions in the Bitcoin protocol to examine if an unconfirmed transaction is valid. For example, a miner can go through the blockchain to inspect the source of Bitcoin in an unconfirmed transaction. If the miner is able to trace the source in the history of Bitcoin, the source of wealth in transaction is valid because the Bitcoin that a user is spending is valid and not created out of thin air.

All the miners will carry out these checks independently, using the Bitcoin protocol and the blockchain. If there is consensus and the miners agree on the validity of the transactions, they will then update the records in the blockchain, by adding a new block to it. After a new block is appended to the blockchain, the records cannot be changed due to the use of cryptography to secure the updates in the blockchain. As dictated in the protocol, a new block is appended to the blockchain every 10 minutes, i.e., the distribution of Bitcoin in the network is updated every 10 minutes. Independent verification and consensus are therefore the mechanisms that allow decisions to be made in the distributed Bitcoin network. Because decisions are made by each miner checking on the validity themselves using the Bitcoin protocol and the blockchain, without relying on what other miners have told him, the Bitcoin network is often described to be a *trustless* network. If a miner is malicious and said that a double-spent transaction is valid, his version of truth will not prevail in the network, as long as > 51 percent of the miners are benevolent. This is commonly known as the "51 percent attack".

To put together the discussion of the roles of Bitcoin participants and the main features of Bitcoin network, let's examine a hypothetical transaction, where user X wishes to pay ฿1 for a service that he has acquired from user Y. X will set up his payment instruction, i.e., a Bitcoin transaction using his mobile wallet, with Y providing X with his wallet address. This unconfirmed transaction will be added to the pool of unconfirmed transactions in the network (as shown in Figure 4) and miners in X's proximity, Miners A, B, and C, will see it first.

Miners A, B, and C will follow the Bitcoin protocol and examine the validity of X's transaction, by referring back to the blockchain. Suppose

X's transaction is valid, which miner will be awarded with the mining rewards since they have all done the work to inspect the transaction? Recall that there is no one to make decisions in the network. This question is resolved through the use of the proof-of-work algorithm, which is documented in the Bitcoin protocol. The proof-of-work algorithm will ask miners to compete and solve a cryptographic puzzle, and the puzzle is constructed using the inspected transactions and the blockchain. All the miners will compete and suppose that B solves the puzzle first, he will be awarded the new units of Bitcoin. However, B will not be awarded the newly mined Bitcoin unless the other miners in the network have checked on all the (new) claims that are made by Miner B, i.e.,

- He said he has solved the puzzle and the answer to the puzzle is 123.
- He said transaction between X and Y is valid.

Recall that Bitcoin is a trustless network, hence all the other miners will not trust what B has claimed and they will carry out their own verifications. Hence, the other miners will go to the pool of unconfirmed transactions to pick up the details of X's transaction and they will carry out their own validity checks, using the instructions given in the Bitcoin protocol and the transaction history recorded in the blockchain. In addition, they will also verify that 123 can be used to solve the cryptographic puzzle constructed by B by building the puzzle themselves and testing it with 123. If a miner is satisfied that all the new claims made by B are indeed valid, he will update his blockchain with a new block, as illustrated in Figure 5. The new block will record X's transaction and also the Coinbase transaction of Miner B. The Coinbase transaction is a transaction made by the network crediting the wallet of a successful miner with the miner's reward.

All these checks are repeated by the entirety of miners in the network. By the process of diffusion, this new information will permeate the entire Bitcoin network, allowing a new distribution of Bitcoin to prevail in the network. Now that X's transaction is no longer unconfirmed, and there is an updated version of the blockchain, miners will resume their competition by choosing new unconfirmed transactions from the pool using the updated blockchain as the new reference for valid transactions. This competition will run continuously, with the results of the competition known every 10 minutes. The competition will keep the pool of unconfirmed

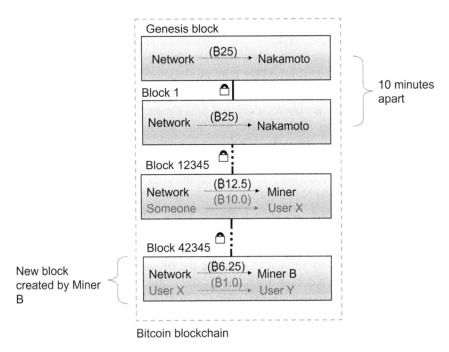

Bitcoin blockchain

Figure 5: A chain of blocks, where a previous block shows that X's Bitcoin wealth originated in a previous transaction that happened in Block 12345. The current transaction between X and Y is recorded in Block 42345, allowing Y to spend it in the future. Miner B's Bitcoin is also recorded in Block 43455. Each subsequent block is spaced, on average 10 minutes apart, and each block is secured to the preceding block by cryptography. The block cannot be changed once it is part of the Bitcoin blockchain.

transactions and blockchain updated every 10 minutes and all these are achieved through the use of the Bitcoin protocol, supported by the agreed history recorded in the blockchain. The independent verification process therefore allows Bitcoin to function as a payment system without the use of trusted intermediaries.

What's next, after Bitcoin?

It is worthwhile to reiterate that the verification of transactions is done with the help of the blockchain which contains an agreed record of all valid transactions. The blockchain can therefore be thought of as an append-only database tracking the provenance history of Bitcoin as it moves from one wallet to another, where users spend their Bitcoin wealth through valid transactions. The Bitcoin blockchain is updated every 10 minutes and because of the rate of updating the blockchain and the 1 MB block size limit, it has been calculated that the number of Bitcoin transactions is capped at a maximum of 7 transactions per second,[17] which is significantly lower than the 1,700 transactions per second limit that is supported by the Visa network.[18] The low transaction throughput of Bitcoin therefore hinders its ability to function as a large-scale payment system *if* this is what Nakamoto had envisioned.

To overcome the transaction limits, there were a lot of technical enhancements and developments that were made to make Bitcoin scalable. Some of the work that Bitcoin core developers worked on were the Lighting network and SegWit to increase the block size and to allow off-chain transactions. Another approach to solve the transactional limits of Bitcoin was to create new cryptocurrencies which involve design considerations that address the scalability problem from day one. For example, one of the earliest competing cryptocurrencies, Litecoin, used the code of Bitcoin and made changes to the protocol such as updating the block every 2.5 minutes, instead of 10 minutes to increase the transaction limits by a factor of 4 easily.[19] From this example, it can be seen that that it is not difficult to create new cryptocurrencies because Bitcoin Core is an open-source project.

In addition to the technical work addressing the scalability problem, there are also two main threads of developments that started to explore the use of blockchains for other purposes, beyond payments, by exploiting the cannot-be-changed, i.e., immutable, secure, trustless, and distributed properties of the technology. One area of exploration uses the fact that blockchain technology is able to provide transaction immutability and security despite the absence of a trusted gatekeeper to organize and filter faulty records and to keep malicious players away. Blockchain technology provides an avenue to pivot away from the current mode of services delivery, where a dedicated service provider is replaced by the peers in the network. The participants in the network can deliver the required services and they are kept honest through the clever use of economic incentives and the network protocol. With blockchain technology, one can democratize the delivery of services, by allowing anyone with the means to deliver the services, hence allowing a participant to either use or provide the intended services in the distributed network. This therefore allows services to be delivered in a distributed manner. This thinking has led to the development of Ethereum, which became an infrastructure for the delivery of distributed services and resulted in the tokenization phenomena.

The second area of exploration was to recognize that blockchain technology provides a means of sharing a single source of truth (database of records) with privacy features. This provides a way for the same ledger to be used by different participants, with each participant only seeing the records they need. This has the potential to revolutionize business practices among businesses and has led to the development of distributed ledger technologies (DLT) or enterprise blockchains.

The broad categorization of these two developments is differentiated through the use of public and private blockchains in their applications. In the delivery of distributed services, the blockchain tends to be public, i.e., anyone can join the network, and everyone can see all the records. In a public blockchain, due to the absence of an administrator, the consensus algorithm is very important to prevent faulty records by malicious players to be appended to the blockchain. In DLT, the blockchain tends to be private and this means that there tends to be an administrator who will decide which participants can join the blockchain. These participants are trusted parties and, hence, the consensus algorithm is not the most important feature in the blockchain. A private blockchain is sometimes known as a permissioned blockchain and its main strength is to have a common database for all participants for the ease of record reconciliation.

Nevertheless, the essence of these two threads of developments is to move away from a centralized setup to a decentralized setup. A centralized setup has a node — which can be a service provider, an institution, or a computer terminal — that carries significant responsibilities in the service or computer network. The failure of this node will result in the failure of the entire network. This node in a centralized set-up is therefore a single point of failure and to mitigate the failure of this node, administrators, such as regulators, will have to

- raise the threshold of failure in the node by imposing stringent requirements. If one is referring to a computer network, the node must be set up using robust and hence expensive hardware. If one is referring to a service provider, there must be high quality thresholds and design buffers in place to prevent catastrophic failure. All these measures will lead to a higher cost of service. This way of risk management can help to

Table 1:   Comparison between a centralized vs. decentralized network.

Centralized Networks	Decentralized Networks
Nodes in the network have different levels of importance and roles.	All nodes have the same importance and role.
Single points of failures exist in the network.	Fault tolerance and collusion resistance.
New information propagates quickly through the network.	New information takes time to disseminate across the entire network.
Management of network is simpler.	Suitability of consensus algorithms is needed to achieve equilibrium.

reduce the probability of failure, but it does not remove the single point of failure entirely.
• introduce redundancy by duplicating the services of the node. This is the foolproof way to remove the single point of failure, and if one is to pursue this course of action, a distributed network like blockchain is a good solution because it is designed to be highly fault-tolerant.

Table 1 summarizes the key differences between a centralized and decentralized network.

Using a distributed network therefore has the natural advantage of eliminating the single point of failure, and if it is the way forward, improvements in blockchain technology must continue so that it can be used for large-scale deployment, without compromising on performance and security.

Ethereum, a Distributed Computing Resource

Bitcoin was the first successful application of the blockchain technology. Vitalik Buterin noted that the power of blockchain can be further extended by using the community to gather distributed computing power to (1) execute code, (2) achieve consensus about the outcome of code execution, and (3) record the outcome in the blockchain. This is the idea of Ethereum (Bitcoin), where the blockchain is used to record the results of code execution (list of valid transactions). Table 2 summarizes the main features of Bitcoin and Ethereum.

Table 2: Summary of main features of Bitcoin and Ethereum.

	Bitcoin	Ethereum
Purpose	A payment system	A distributed computer, providing data storage and processing powers.
Types of records	Transactions recording the transfer of Bitcoin from one wallet to another wallet	Three kinds of records: 1. Transfer of Ether from one wallet to another 2. Keep a smart contract in an address 3. Execute a smart contract stored in an address with relevant data inputs
Supply	A limit of 21M Bitcoin	Unlimited supply of Ether
Frequency of blockchain update	Every 10 minutes	Every 15 seconds
Competitors	Litecoin, Bitcoin Cash	Cardano, Solana, Polkadot

The extension proposed in Ethereum was documented in the original white paper, published in 2014,[20] 6 years after the creation of Bitcoin. The extension was to have "a built-in Turing-complete programming language, allowing anyone to write smart contracts and decentralized applications". Ethereum enhanced the capability of Bitcoin by having a programming language such that any real-world business transaction can be coded up, with the coded version of the transactions termed as "smart contracts". These smart contracts can be stored in the Ethereum blockchain and users of Ethereum can access and execute them with their own inputs using the distributed computing powers in the network. Miners of the Ethereum network will execute the contracts independently and compete to record the outcome of the code execution in the blockchain.

The ability of having smart contracts in Ethereum has significant business and legal applications. First, any real-world transaction can be coded up into a smart contract and stored in the Ethereum network. A collection of such smart contracts will become a business application and this same set of smart contracts can be executed repeatedly with different inputs, signifying different clients using the same services provided by a business, as illustrated in Figure 6. With the proper implementation of the smart contracts and external data sources (oracles), the smart contract automates the monitoring of the terms and conditions in the transaction using the processing powers in the Ethereum network. When the

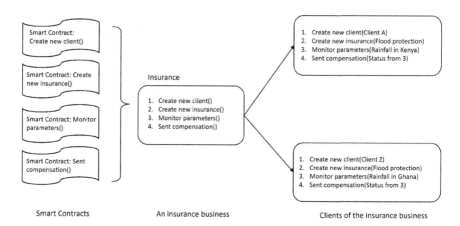

Figure 6: A collection of smart contracts is a business. The smart contracts store the business logic and automate business processes.

conditions of the contract are fulfilled, all the miners will verify the fulfillment of the conditions and compete to record it permanently in the Ethereum blockchain if there is consensus among the miners. The act of the miners verifying the outcome of the smart contract execution plays the role of trusted third parties (lawyers, banks) that is required in a typical transaction. Recording the result of the code execution in the blockchain has the effect of reaching a certainty and finality in the transaction, since the outcome is recorded permanently once it is appended into the blockchain. The use of Ethereum network with smart contracts allows automation and removes the need for expensive intermediaries. This can reduce the cost of business.

Using the lexicology of Ethereum, an Ethereum virtual machine (EVM) is the decentralized network of computing resources, where users pay to execute distributed applications (dApps) and miners record the outcome of the execution onto the blockchain. Similarly to Bitcoin, miners need to be enticed economically to provide hash rate to the network, hence, Ether is the fuel used in Ethereum to execute smart contracts in the network. Because of the versatility of the smart contracts, there has been a flurry of new blockchain businesses using Ethereum as a platform for delivering their services.

Ethereum therefore provides the platform and infrastructure needed to host, build, and run distributed services. One of the first uses of Ethereum was to create other tokens, where these tokens are used to access services provided by new blockchain businesses. The creation of tokens has led to the initial coin offerings (ICO) phenomenon in 2016–2019. Many entrepreneurs issue their own version of tokens using Ethereum ERC20 standard, which provides "the guideline for creating tokens on the blockchain… monitoring supply, balances, or transactions".[21] This means that all the smart contracts required to create and monitor the supply of a new token are already available in Ethereum and all that is required is to create a name and "use case" for the token. A genuine and valid use case will drive a demand for the associated token, and this will translate to a real-world fiat price for the token, creating tangible wealth for the token creators and holders. The ability to create ERC20 tokens easily has led to a proliferation of ideas and excitement among technology evangelists because they realized that a lot of existing real-world transactions can be moved onto the blockchain, where services are provided in a distributed manner, thereby making services cheaper and more accessible to everyone.

During the ICO craze in 2016, many entrepreneurs, made use of white papers to discuss and broadcast their use cases to raise funds to start their blockchain-based businesses. Those funds are required to recruit blockchain developers to code up the bespoke smart contracts needed for their use case. Investors are enticed to exchange their fiat money for tokens on these new businesses and indeed, many investors did this and record sums of money were raised in a few hours. For example, the token EOS raised US$4 billion in 2018.[22] The use case of EOS was to provide a blockchain platform to make it easy to create dApps. EOS seeks to do the same things as Ethereum, except that it promises to be faster and more powerful.

ICO does not give ownership rights to the new blockchain company. Instead, the tokens give access to the services/user case of the business and ICO investors are keen to acquire these tokens, because some of them believe that they will be the *users* of these services. But for most of the ICO investors, they believe the world will demand for these services and hence the price of these tokens will increase. Hence, they are acquiring these tokens for the capital gains. For example, one of the earliest ICOs was Ethereum, in July 2014, where a sum of US$17.23 million was raised from the sale of 50 million Ether.[23] These 50 million Ether are worth more than US$60 billion today (June 2022). Many participate in ICOs because of the fear of missing out (FOMO), especially after they had missed the initial huge price appreciation in Bitcoin and Ethereum.

Today, with the benefit of hindsight, many of the ICOs have turned out to be failures, with more than 90 percent of ICOs having failed. Some of the ICOs turned out to be outright scams while the progress of some ICOs has stalled due to technological challenges. In short, many of the claims made in the white paper were simply too grand and deadlines were missed, and key personnel left when the pressures to deliver were too great. These developments have therefore tampered the expectation of investors and led to a general cool down in fund-raising through ICO. Financial regulators also stepped in to regulate the ICO phenomenon and some regulators, such as the Chinese and Korean regulators, banned the sales of tokens in their countries to protect their people. Nonetheless, it is worthwhile to note many of the ICOs, i.e., fund raising, took place on the Ethereum blockchain and the mechanics of fund-raising took place without the involvement of investment bankers or lawyers. Anyone who believes in the founder and/or the use case of a business, are welcomed to invest in it, unlike the traditional fund-raising activities where shares were typically offered to institutional/sophisticated investors. With ICO, anyone can participate — *caveat emptor*, let the buyer beware, or as long as they are willing. The use of the Ethereum to carry out ICOs proved the idea that it is possible to carry out real-world business transactions, in this case, fund raising, without intermediaries and a blockchain was used to record the outcomes of the exercise.

DeFi phenomenon

With the blockchain architecture in place, many entrepreneurs are seeking to build the distributed versions of many financial transactions that are facilitated by middlemen. This group of financial applications are collectively known as DeFi, which stands for distributed finance in short. Proponents of DeFi believe that the use of blockchains to deliver, execute, and record financial transactions will make finance more inclusive and safe. Blockchains remove the need for large financial intermediaries in a typical transaction and these financial intermediaries need to be compensated because they need to fund their staff and the IT infrastructure they maintain for their businesses. By replacing these intermediaries with a blockchain, it can reduce the cost of the delivery of the financial services, reduce the minimum transaction amount, and thereby allow more people to be serviced.

An interesting case study of a DeFi application is the services offered by Uniswap which is a decentralized exchange of crypto assets. Uniswap was created by Hayden Adams after he was laid off by Siemens AG. His initial work was funded with a US$100,000 grant from the Ethereum Foundation in 2018,[24] and subsequently, there were multiple successful rounds of fund raising, with the latest being a Series A funding where a sum of US$11 million was raised from venture capital firms including Andreessen Horowitz in 2020. This is now a trend, where institutional investors and venture capitalists are funding the growth of DeFi and dApps.

Uniswap is a decentralized exchange (DEX) where users can exchange a crypto asset for another crypto asset by paying a fixed fee of 0.3 percent. For example, a user can go to the Uniswap web interface to exchange Ether for Bitcoins at the prevailing market rate. The user needs to pay a fee because he is getting the services from Uniswap and this is similar to how a typical centralized exchange works, where clients have to pay a trading fee to buy stock. In a centralized exchange, the trading fee is used to fund the daily operation of the exchange and any excess will be the profits of the business which is shared among the shareholders.

This is, however, where the similarity ends, because it is possible to earn income from Uniswap, by providing liquidity for the exchange services. This type of Uniswap participant is known as "liquidity providers". Liquidity providers make the entire swap transaction possible, by providing the pool of assets that users demand. Hence, liquidity providers are given an income for being the counterparties to the swap and the income that is due to a liquidity provider is dependent on his contribution in relation to the overall pool. The income is tracked using "liquidity tokens" and this is recorded in the Ethereum blockchain. Uniswap therefore enables participants to take either side of a swap operation, i.e., providing or taking liquidity and allows this kind of financial transaction to be provided in a peer-to-peer manner.

The role of Uniswap in the entire swap operation is to provide the protocol required to adjust the exchange rate between the two crypto assets algorithmically. The working of the decentralized exchange is enshrined in the Uniswap protocol — "A suite of ... smart contracts that ... creates an automated market maker ... on the Ethereum blockchain"[25] which will provide all the business logic for the automated exchange to work. As Uniswap provides and maintains the protocol, they are also entitled to a small share of the fees (protocol fee) paid by the users. At the time of writing, this proposed protocol fee of 0.05 percent has not been implemented. When it is implemented, the 0.3 percent fee will be split two ways, with 0.25 percent going to the liquidity providers and 0.05 percent going to Uniswap.[26]

The Uniswap protocol is therefore very important to the business as it determines the clearing prices of the swap operation. Hence, any changes to the protocol must be rectified by the community and a governance token, UNI, is used to decide who can make changes to the protocol and to track the level of support for a proposed change to the Uniswap protocol. UNI holders who have > 1 percent total UNI supply can submit development proposals while any UNI holder can vote on these proposals. An example of the change that can be made to the protocol is to decide when to turn on the protocol fee. The use case of the UNI token is to give the holder the right to influence development on the Uniswap protocol and it will ensure that decisions are made collectively by the Uniswap community.

As Uniswap is built upon the Ethereum blockchain, a user needs to have sufficient Ether to use Uniswap services and there have been instances where the cost to use Uniswap services has been expensive, due to a congested Ethereum blockchain, because it hosts a multitude of other services. Hence, there are many technical developments underway to enhance the Uniswap protocol so that DEX services can be delivered cheaply. An example of current development is to make Uniswap services run on multiple blockchain platforms.

Since inception, Uniswap has facilitated more than US$1 trillion in trade and the total users' fees have grown to the range of millions[27] in a single day.[28] There are now a community of app developers who are developing more products and applications upon the open source Uniswap protocol.[29] It is worthwhile to note that Uniswap protocol is open source and, hence, theoretically, it is not difficult to create another DEX using the codebase of Uniswap. However, this has not happened because it is difficult to rebuild the markets, the community of users, and liquidity providers, i.e., network effects that Uniswap has gathered.

With the growing numbers of investors holding crypto assets, the demand for DeFi applications is projected to grow as it will address the demands of crypto holders (or "hodlers") deriving incomes from their assets. A metric of measure for tracking the growth of DeFi is the total value of assets locked (TVL) in liquidity and funding pools of DeFi applications. The value of TVL has grown together with the burgeoning crypto markets and the value of TVL in 2022 is reportedly in the range of billions.[30] However, *caveat emptor*, again when it comes to involvement in

DeFi applications. It will take time to know if the algorithmic protocols or DeFi products are able to function as intended in various market conditions.

Tokenization

The DeFi phenomenon is a move of financial applications onto the block-chain. There is also interest in moving real-world, physical assets onto the blockchain by the process of tokenization. Tokenization, as defined by BaFin, is "the digital reproduction of an asset or value".[31] By moving the real-world objects, such as real estate and art works, onto the blockchain, it has the potential to facilitate tradability.[32]

An interesting use case of tokenization is to use multiple fungible tokens to represent a single, expensive asset, such as an artwork. The tokens confer fractional ownership rights to the artwork allowing a single artwork to be sold to multiple investors. The high price of the artwork is reduced proportionally by the number of tokens issued and the lowered (token) price increases the investor base, making once-illiquid assets liquid. For example, a Picasso masterpiece, *Fillette au beret*, was tokenized in 2021 and co-owned by more than 50 investors.[33] A total of 4,000 tokens, each selling for 1,000 Swiss Francs was issued and made available to professional and institutional investors.[34] The ownership rights of token holders are fully recognized under Swiss law and the tokens can be transferred to other holders, by trading it in the secondary markets. The tokens were traded at a price of 1,100 Swiss Franc[35] in June 2022, a few months after acquiring the tokens, and this demonstrates the ease of trading of a once-illiquid artwork. The effect of tokenization therefore has the potential to open up asset classes which were once limited to institutional investors to a broad range of new investors.

Even though the tokenization of physical assets has been demonstrated in Switzerland, taxation, regulatory, and legal issues have to be addressed before tokenization of physical assets can take place easily. For example, in many counties, US included, there are still on-going debates on the definition of a digital asset, and it is still not clear which regulatory agency has the purview over the regulation of such digital assets. Without clear regulatory guidance, the tokenization of assets is a wild market, and indeed, this is currently observed in the market of non-fungible tokens (NFTs).

NFTs are tokens mostly used to represent digital artwork and it is extremely easy to tokenize the artwork by using the ERC-721 protocol.[36] The protocol creates a *single* non-fungible token for the entire digital asset and because it is one unique token for a piece of work, the token is *non-fungible*. The NFT is then recorded as a transaction on the Ethereum blockchain. It is worthwhile to highlight that ownership of NFT does not confer the automatic transfer of copyright or intellectual property to the NFT holder, since in the eyes of law, copyright is conferred to the original creator of the work. Hence, unless there is an understanding between the creator and the NFT holder, the NFT is a mere transactional record of the existence of NFT of the digital artwork on the blockchain.

Despite the legal and licensing uncertainties surrounding NFTs, artistes and companies have capitalized on the NFT phenomenon. For example, the British auction house Christie's sold a piece of digital art by Beeple for US$69.3M[37] and the NFT buyer has earned the bragging rights to record such a momentous moment[38] onto the Ethereum blockchain forever. The US$69.3M image can be viewed by anyone by accessing the Ethereum blockchain for the image URL.[39] The speculation of NFTs has reached a maniac phase where the sales of the Bored Ape Yacht Club (BAYC) — computer generated images of apes — NFTs has reached a total of US$1 billion in 2022. Investors sought to capitalize on the craze by flipping NFTs, but not all were successful. For example, the first tweet made by Twitter's co-founder, Jack Dorsey, was sold for US$2.9M[40] when it was turned into an NFT, and when it was put up in an auction a few months later, the highest bid was US$280.[41] Whether NFT is a legitimate means to tokenize digital arts is a subject for further discussion among legislators, regulators, and businesses. In the meanwhile, whether NFT is a viable asset for investment, *caveat emptor*, again.

Financial inclusion with blockchains

It is worthwhile to mention that the tokenization of assets has also reached the developing countries to assist in financial inclusion. There are social entrepreneurs who are using blockchain technology to assist people in countries such as Kenya to build greater financial resilience in their lives. Blockchain technology is used to provides access to basic financial services, such as savings, payments, credit, and insurance services that can be relied upon to smooth out consumption/income shocks in their lives.

For example, the blockchain project Grassroots Economics helps low-income families who do not have cash for their daily lives and have difficulties in securing the goods and services they need. However, they have tangible goods and skills, such as crops, or carpentry services, if they are carpenters, that can be monetized. By making use of tokenization and blockchain technology, their goods and skills are tokenized and traded as currencies. These currencies are backed by the future revenues of the goods and skills, and they serve as a means of exchange in the community, replacing the need for the national currency. These currencies, known as community inclusion currencies (CIC), operate within a barter system in the community, facilitating the exchange of goods and services. The use of blockchain technology allows the transfer of CIC to be recorded securely and cheaply. Communities that have used CIC observed a five times increase in local trade within 2 months of implementation and there are communities who have used it for more than a decade.[42]

Blockchain technology is also used to provide flood-related insurance services in Kenya. The use of clear compensation criteria encoded in smart contracts automates the claim processing. For example, in 2021, 17,000 farmers were compensated automatically if it rained 5 inches in 24 hours. The digital wallets of farmers were credited with the insurance payout and this speeds up the claim processes, allowing the farmers to recover quickly from the damage. The use of automation and clear compensation criteria increases transparency and trust, removing the need for financial intermediaries and reducing the costs of businesses.[43] Blockchain technology therefore makes the insurance premiums affordable for everyone in the ecosystem.

Enterprise Blockchains

The discussion on blockchain technology so far has been on providing services in a distributed manner using public blockchains such as Ethereum. There is, however, a version of blockchain that is used exclusively by enterprises. These enterprise blockchains form part of their IT infrastructure and enterprises develop suitable applications for their businesses on these blockchains. Some examples of enterprise blockchain providers are Condra by R3, Hyperledger by IBM, and Quorum by ConsenSys. Enterprise blockchains are also commonly known as distributed ledger technologies (DLT).

Enterprise blockchain provides the technology for the use of a single shared record of information by a group of entities which typically rely on their own in-house databases to record the same deals or transactions. The vision of DLT is to move away from IT infrastructure that are developed at the level of individual companies and optimized at the level of markets and industries, as pictured in Figure 7. The ultimate aim is to have a global database maintained by the market where firms and individuals will inter-act with the distributed ledgers to obtain the data they need as they move to different phases of a deal. The use of cryptography will ensure data privacy such that only deals that are relevant to a party can be observed and the use of distributed systems to host the ledgers will remove single points of failure. The updating of the status of a deal is automated and described using computer code, negating the need to do manual reconcili-ation across different in-house databases. DLTs have the potential to reduce IT cost, speed up settlement of transaction, and improve the relia-bility of the infrastructure. Many businesses and industries are therefore investigating into the different use cases that are offered by DLTs. For example, J.P. Morgan has established a dedicated blockchain business unit, Onyx, with more than a hundred employees exploring the applica-tions of DLT. They have developed Link, which is a cross-border payment system that allows the status of the fund transfer to be known real-time. This application is particularly useful for currency transfer that has long transaction chains.[44] The banking behemoth is therefore spearheading the creation of shared infrastructure, and as of September 2021, it was reported that 25 world leading banks, and more than 400 leading

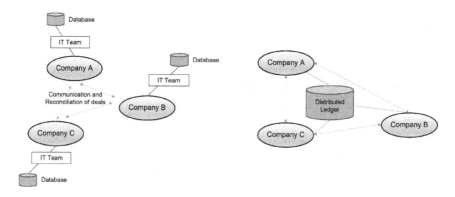

Figure 7:   In-house databases and a single global database.

institutions, have signed letters of intent to join, and more than 38 countries have joined Link.[45]

It is worthwhile to note that to realize the purported benefits of DLT, the single global database must be adopted and used by most, if not all, companies in the industries. This will mean standardization of workflow processes and adopting new data and message formats. Therefore, if companies have already spent resources to build up their existing IT infrastructure and clients are used to the existing processes and performances, it can be difficult to justify the returns and risks from using the new technology.

The adoption of DLT is best illustrated by the experience of Australia Stock Exchange (ASX) when it announced in 2017 that it will use DLT for its next generation security settlement system called the Clearing House Electronic Subregister System (CHESS). ASX will therefore be the first in the world to use DLT to build an actual industry-scale database to be shared among market participants. In their consultation with stakeholders, ASX has to provide sufficient latitude in their design because not all parties are willing to use DLT. In their implementation, they recognized that "users may choose to connect and transact by sending and receiving messages in a similar way as today or they may choose to take a DLT node and interact directly".[46] To justify the risks for using the DLT, stakeholders have stated clearly that they wanted to benefit from day one, rather than the enhanced performance coming from phased upgrades down the development timeline. ASX mentioned in their report that "We do not underestimate the challenge to replace CHESS and transition the market to the new system".[47]

Using a new technology is already fraught with operational risks and to use a new technology that needs the buy-in of all stakeholders, where they need to adhere to the same and yet unproven workflow processes, greatly magnifies the challenges of deploying in the real world. Hence, for the use of DLT to be successful, it must be steered and championed by existing important market players, such as regulators, and important institutions, who need to coordinate with all stakeholders to communicate, design, document, and standardize practices.

Conclusion

The first block of Bitcoin was mined on 3-January-2009 and it came with a quote referencing the headline from *The Times,* "Chancellor on brink of

Script Signature in genesis block:
04ffff001d010445
5468652054696d65
732030332f4a616e
2f32303039204368
616e63656c6c6f72
206f6e206272696e
6b206f6620736563
6f6e64206261696c6c
6f7574206f6666220
62616e6b73
B'\x04\xff\xff\x00\x1d\x01\x04EThe Times 03/Jan/2009 Chancellor on brink of second bailout for banks'

Figure 8:   Genesis block of Bitcoin. The 50 Bitcoins in the genesis block has not been spent till date. It is worth about US$1 million in the market.

second bailout for banks" as decoded in Figure 8. We do not know the intention of Satoshi Nakamoto for including the headlines. Did he use the headline to document the birth of Bitcoin on 3-January-2009 or was it to register his disdain with the then financial giants? Perhaps, both? Nevertheless, the beginning of blockchains coincides with the Global Financial Crisis (GFC) in 2008 when the world witnessed the near failure of large, centralized financial institutions.

The GFC nearly brought "the world's strongest financial system to come to the brink of collapse"[48] and it was a culmination of risk management failures by "the captains of finance and public stewards of the financial systems". Their failures resulted in more than 26 million Americans being out of work and US$11 trillion in household wealth that includes retirement and life savings completely wiped out. Large amounts of public money were used to bail out bankers and their institutions because they were "too big to fail". As the embers of the crisis died down, there was a period of banker bashing and an anti-establishment movement, culminating in the Occupy Wall Street Movement protesting against economic inequality and the influence of large financial institutions on the government and daily lives. The slogan of the movement "We are the 99 percent" reflects their opinion that the 99 percent are paying the price of the mistakes made by the tiny majority. This is a somber reflection that one is living in a highly centralized world where the financial well-being of the public is held ransom by a few large financial institutions.

This scenario continues to play out today, but with technology companies being the antagonists now. As one is increasingly online, the daily interactions are captured by a select group of technology companies. They provide "free" services in exchange for personal data and privacy. These companies then exploit these data through the use of algorithms to deliver relevant and highly personalized services. As lives get more entrenched with these companies, and with more and more people coming onboard, this network effect makes it difficult for one to leave this ecosystem of "free" services. Again, the result is that there is a highly centralized setup in society, where these financial and technology companies become an important part of everyone's lives.

A highly centralized setup has the problem of having single points of failures. The disruption of their services will affect the functioning of daily activities. Or perhaps, an *abuse* of the services they provide, as in the case of Facebook/Cambridge Analytica affairs, showed that they can affect the world view of matters and unduly influence the choices being made. These companies therefore need significant oversight from regulators because their failure to do good will affect the whole of society, or repeating the words of financial regulators, they are "too big to fail". There seems to be no easy way to exit this centralized setup, except in the emergence of Bitcoin, blockchain, and the associated technologies.

Bitcoin drew its power from its anti-establishment roots and blockchains provide a decentralized means of providing services to the people, by the people, ushering in an online world where power would go back to the people. Blockchains allow services to be provided by a community, using agreed rules that are coded up, allowing no deviation from the rules, and giving total transparency on how decisions and consensuses are achieved. Instead of a single institution monopolizing all data on their platform and getting rent out of it, blockchain technology is inclusive and it allows a redistribution of data, wealth, and power to the community. Understandably, such ethos have garnered a lot of following, leading to the crypto, DeFi, and now, the growing web3[a] phenomenon.

The ethos representing blockchain suits the social climate today, but the protocols and technology remain woefully under-tested to replace the existing services offered by the aforementioned institutions. Even among the experts,[49] they are concerned about the hyped-up promise of blockchains made by its advocates. There are still significant technical hurdles that must be overcome before the promises of blockchain technology can be fully realized. Solving the scalability problem, without compromising

---

[a] Web 1.0 is a library of static web pages and Web 2.0 is the web of applications which is curated by the big tech companies. The web3 phenomena is about building the third iteration of web services, where services provided by tech behemoths are replaced by a distributed equivalence.

on security and performance, is the number one technical issue that must be overcome for a chance of large-scale deployment. The business protocols in applications need to be tested for robustness and reliability in the real world. As these developments are underway, they will significantly impact the delivery, long-term success, and sustainability of new blockchain-based businesses.

These new blockchain based businesses are the underdogs today. It is hoped that they can deliver their promise of using blockchain technology to deliver services in a fair, inclusive, and transparent manner. As of today, their businesses have not grown to a scale that is comparable to the incumbents, and perhaps, given time they will deliver on their promises. Many of the crypto assets have not been used for their intended use cases, except for speculation in the market. In some cases, they were outright scams.[50] Again, hopefully, given ample time, the bad will be weeded out as the crypto markets go through some rounds of crashes and burns. Amidst these uncertainties, a pragmatic approach to take, whether as a developer, investor, or user of these new blockchain-based businesses, is that most of these new businesses/assets will fail. Therefore, keeping one's financial, and technological literacies up to date is extremely important if one seeks to be involved in this discussion. It is also important to note that, at the end of the day, regardless of the ethos/superiority of the technology, for blockchain or any crypto asset to have a long-term future, it must be a solution to a real-world problem.

References

1. Hughes, E. (Mar 9, 1993). A cypherpunk's manifesto. Available from https://nakamotoinstitute.org/static/docs/cypherpunk-manifesto.txt.
2. Wei, D. B-money. Available from http://www.weidai.com/bmoney.txt.
3. Szabo, N. (Dec 29, 2005). Bit gold. Available from https://nakamotoinstitute.org/bit-gold/.
4. This $12 billion tech investment could disrupt banking. Available from https://www.jpmorganchase.com/news-stories/tech-investment-could-disrupt-banking.
5. Available from https://coinmarketcap.com/.
6. Available from https://cryptoliteracy.org/.
7. Perrin, A. (Nov 11, 2021). 16% of Americans say they have ever invested in, traded or used cryptocurrency. Available from https://www.pewresearch.org/fact-tank/2021/11/11/16-of-americans-say-they-have-ever-invested-in-traded-or-used-cryptocurrency/.

8. Nakamoto, S. Bitcoin: A peer-to-peer electronic cash system. Available from https://bitcoin.org/bitcoin.pdf.

9. Available from https://github.com/bitcoin/bitcoin.

10. Available from https://www.blockchain.com/explorer/assets/btc.

11. Roger Ver. Available from https://www.rogerver.com/bio/.

12. Kim, T. (May 5, 2018). Warren Buffett says Bitcoin is 'probably rat poison squared'. Available from https://www.cnbc.com/2018/05/05/warren-buffett-says-bitcoin-is-probably-rat-poison-squared.html.

13. Pizza for Bitcoins? Available from https://bitcointalk.org/index.php?topic= 137.msg1141#msg1141.

14. Turner, M. (Jun 14, 2022). MicroStrategy's losses on its Bitcoin bet near $1 billon. Available from https://www.bloomberg.com/news/articles/2022-06-13/microstrategy-s-bitcoin-bet-backfires-as-losses-near-1-billion#xj 4y7vzkg.

15. Waters, R. (Jun 25, 2022). Michael Saylor: MicroStrategy's Bitcoin true believer. *Financial Times*. Available from https://www.ft.com/content/ 53880cca-910a-4e31-96b7-de6e7776ab9b.

16. Available from https://github.com/bitcoin/bips/blob/master/bip-0091. mediawiki.

17. Croman, K., Decker, C., Eyal, I., Gencer, A. E., Juels, A., Kosba, A., *et al.* (2016). On scaling decentralized blockchains. *Financial Cryptography and Data Science*. Lecture Notes in Computer Science, Vol. 9604, pp. 106–125.

18. Visa acceptance for retailers. Available from https://usa.visa.com/run-your-business/small-business-tools/retail.html.

19. Lee, C. (Mar 22, 2022). Litecoin (LTC): The silver to Bitcoin's gold. Available from https://www.gemini.com/cryptopedia/litecoin-vs-bitcoin-blockchain#section-origins-of-litecoin.

20. Ethereum Whitepaper. Available from https://ethereum.org/en/whitepaper/.

21. ERC20 Token Standard. Available from https://www.indexuniverse.eu/ erc20-token-standard/.

22. Rooney, K. (Jun 1, 2018). A blockchain start-up just raised $4 billion without a live product. *CNBC*. Available from https://www.cnbc.com/2018/05/31/a-blockchain-start-up-just-raised-4-billion-without-a-live-product.html.

23. Ethereum and the ICO boom. (Mar 11, 2022). Available from https://www. gemini.com/cryptopedia/initial-coin-offering-explained-ethereum-ico# section-ethereums-role-in-the-ico-boom.

24. Ethereum Foundation Grants Update — Wave III. (Aug 17, 2018). Available from https://blog.ethereum.org/2018/08/17/ethereum-foundation-grants-update-wave-3.

25. What is uniswap? Available from https://docs.uniswap.org/protocol/ introduction.

26. Uniswap V2 overview. (Mar 23, 2020). Available from https://uniswap.org/blog/uniswap-v2#path-to-sustainability.
27. Crypto fees. Available from https://cryptofees.info/.
28. Kharif, O. (Jun 24, 2022). Crypto exchange Uniswap overtakes Ethereum in user fees. *Bloomberg*. Available from https://www.bloomberg.com/news/articles/2022-06-23/crypto-exchange-uniswap-overtakes-ethereum-in-user-fees.
29. Uniswap v3-core. Available from https://github.com/Uniswap/v3-core/blob/main/LICENSE.
30. DeFi pulse. Available from https://www.defipulse.com/.
31. Tokenisation. (May 20, 2019). *BaFin*. Available from https://www.bafin.de/SharedDocs/Veroeffentlichungen/EN/Fachartikel/2019/fa_bj_1904_Tokenisierung_en.html.
32. Tokenization: Opening illiquid assets to investors. (Jun, 2019). Available from https://www.bnymellon.com/us/en/insights/all-insights/tokenization-opening-illiquid-assets-to-investors.html.
33. Picasso's Fillette au beret painting now co-owned by more than 50 investors. (Nov 4, 2021). Available from https://www.insights.sygnum.com/post/picasso-s-fillette-au-b%C3%A9ret-painting-now-co-owned-by-more-than-50-investors.
34. Sygnum bank and Artemundi tokenize a Picasso on the blockchain. (Jul 15, 2021). Available from https://www.insights.sygnum.com/post/sygnum-bank-and-artemundi-tokenize-a-picasso-on-the-blockchain.
35. Asset Pablo Picasso Fillette au beret. Available from https://www.sygnum.com/sygnex/trade-history/?asset=PIC1-DCHF.
36. EIP-721 Non-fungible token standard. Available from https://eips.ethereum.org/EIPS/eip-721#simple-summary.
37. Beeple the first 5000 days. *Christie's*. Available from https://onlineonly.christies.com/s/beeple-first-5000-days/beeple-b-1981-1/112924.
38. The first 5000 days sold for $69,346,250 to Metakovan, founder of Metapurse. (Mar 12, 2021) Christie's, Singapore. Available from https://www.christies.com/about-us/press-archive/details?PressReleaseID=9971&lid=1.
39. Available from https://ipfs.io/ipfs/QmPAg1mjxcEQPPtqsLoEcauVedaeMH81WXDPvPx3VC5zUz.
40. Available from https://opensea.io/assets/matic/0x28009881f0ffe85c90725b8b02be55773647c64a/20.
41. Kauflin, J. (Apr 14, 2022). Why Jack Dorsey's first-tweet NFT plummeted 99% in value in a year. *Forbes*. Available from https://www.forbes.com/sites/jeffkauflin/2022/04/14/why-jack-dorseys-first-tweet-nft-plummeted-99-in-value-in-a-year/?sh=108f9da765cb.

42. Grassroots economics: Integrating an emergency response platform for stakeholders to access digital payments. Available from https://www.unicefinnovationfund.org/broadcast/updates/grassroots-economics-integrating-emergency-response-platform-stakeholders-access.

43. Etherisc update: Etherisc and Acre Africa announce first payouts through blockchain based platform with over 17,000 Kenyan farmers insured during first season. (Aug 16, 2021). Available from https://blog.etherisc.com/etherisc-update-etherisc-and-acre-africa-announce-first-payouts-through-blockchain-based-platform-a0c5194214f4.

44. Cross-border payments. *Bank of England*. Available from https://www.bankofengland.co.uk/payment-and-settlement/cross-border-payments.

45. Transforming how payment-related information moves. Available from https://www.jpmorgan.com/onyx/liink.htm#_ftn1.

46. CHESS replacement: New scope and implementation plan. Available from https://www2.asx.com.au/content/dam/asx/participants/clearing-and-settlement/chess-replacement/chess-replacement-new-scope-and-implementation-plan.pdf.

47. CHESS replacement: New scope and implementation plan Response to consultation feedback. Available from https://www2.asx.com.au/content/dam/asx/participants/clearing-and-settlement/chess-replacement/response-to-chess-replacement-consultation-feedback.pdf.

48. The financial crisis inquiry report. (Feb 25, 2011). US. Available from https://www.govinfo.gov/content/pkg/GPO-FCIC/pdf/GPO-FCIC.pdf.

49. Chipolina, S. (Jun 1, 2022). Tech experts urge Washington to resist crypto industry's influence. *Financial Times*. Available from https://www.ft.com/content/f4b2fa1a-4057-4b10-9f3b-efa57e6bcbac.

50. Sands, L. (Jul 1, 2022). Missing cryptoqueen FBI adds Ruja Ignatova to top ten most wanted. *BBC*. Available from https://www.bbc.com/news/world-us-canada-62005066.

PART IV

FOSTERING SUSTAINABILITY IN THE DISRUPTIVE ENVIRONMENT

Chapter 8

Corporate Social Responsibility (CSR) in the Digital Age

Huong Ha and Peter Chuah

Introduction

Corporate social responsibility (CSR) is not a new concept. CSR has been practiced by organizations for decades given the benefits that CSR practices can produce. Given the general consent that CSR matters to organizations and stakeholders' demand for more responsibility, many organizations have implemented CSR initiatives.[1] Specifically, many studies have found a positive relationship between CSR and organizations' financial performance.[2,3] However, some organizations question whether such efforts are merely "public relations stunts or corporate image-building activities"[4] or a waste of resources that conflict with an organization's responsibility to its shareholders.[5] Several studies reveal the inverse relationship between CSR and financial performance.[6–8]

Traditionally, CSR is defined as activities that organizations practice to give back to society and support communities. Apart from profit maximization, organizations need to go beyond what is required by law as discussed by Carroll.[9,10] Common CSR initiatives include supporting community and development projects, providing scholarships to needy students, sponsoring sports events, organizing campaigns to enhance awareness of environmental protection, and so on. Yet, these are more relevant to the physical environment.

In today's volatile, uncertain, complex, and ambiguous (VUCA) business world, the rapid development of technologies (e.g., artificial intelligence (AI), big data, social media, etc.) and new ways of doing business (e.g., sharing economy models) have forced organizations to find novel approaches to fulfill their social responsibility.[11] Organizations are expected to do more to protect stakeholders in the digital era. Apart from implementing traditional CSR activities and complying with legal requirements, organizations need to discharge their new CSR in terms of technology adoption, protection of customers and their privacy in the online market, protection of stakeholders' data, security, and privacy.[12] During and after situations like the pandemics, organizations need to provide business/service continuation to ensure their business sustainability. Other responsibilities include how organizations should adopt and manage AI and related technologies to create social impact, and how they should produce, distribute, and control digital goods/services.[12] In this context, a new subset of CSR, i.e., corporate digital responsibility (CDR), has emerged in the operations and business strategies of many organizations given the need to achieve sustainability in today's business.[13] However, new forms of CSR in the digital era are still under-researched and are areas for further investigation.

Thus, this chapter aims to (i) revisit CSR concepts in the context of a digital economy, and (ii) examine new practices of CSR in the digital age and how organizations adopt digital-related technologies to fulfill their social responsibility. The chapter also recommends nudging as a novel approach to promote CSR in the technology era.

Overall, this chapter will provide a better understanding of how organizations can apply various digital tools to perform CSR activities that can address social challenges. This chapter is significant as it is interdisciplinary in nature, incorporating change management theories, CSR concepts, and environmental sustainability. This chapter will serve as a pilot test for further research on CSR, environmental sustainability, and financial performance in other industries in Singapore and other neighboring countries.

Revisiting Corporate Social Responsibility (CSR)

The discussions on social responsibility have become a popular topic since the 1950s,[10] but until the late 1970s, CSR continued to be ridiculed as a joke.[14] By the late 1990s, CSR became one of the essential elements in organizations and businesses[14] when the concept of CSR began to be backed by research, practice, and theories.[15] Over the years a list of related concepts emerged from the CSR literature: corporate social performance, corporate sustainability, creating shared value, stakeholder theory/management, stakeholder engagement, and strategic CSR (refer to Camilleri[16] for a non-exhaustive list of citations).

In the past, improving customer service and maximizing profit for shareholders were the main goals of many large organizations and businesses.[5,9] However, in recent years, more leaders have begun to recognize (a) the need to measure success beyond the economic and legal duties, (b) the responsibility to act for the greater good, and (c) the action and impact of their organizations and businesses on people, the environment, and society at large. Despite the long history and ample research on CSR, there is a lack of conceptual consensus on a definition of CSR[17,18] partly due to the interpretations and applications of the CSR construct in both academia and practice.[19,20]

Over the years, there have been numerous attempts to study and understand the conceptions of CSR.[14,20–22] The term corporate social responsibility (CSR) is a concept that means something to someone — e.g., prosocial behavior, charitable contribution, carbon footprint reduction, purchase of fair-trade products, "environmental, social, and governance" (ESG), etc. — but not always the same thing to everyone.[22,23] In essence, CSR has been understood as the balanced achievement of economic, environmental, and social imperatives while simultaneously addressing the expectations of shareholders and stakeholders as depicted in Figure 1.[24]

In addition, it has also been conceptualized as how organizations and businesses integrate social and environmental concerns and issues in their operations and interactions with their stakeholders voluntarily.[25] Such voluntary integration and interactions are believed to have a positive impact on financial performance and sustainable growth.[2,3,16,26] Consequently, more organizations and businesses have begun to embrace CSR as a differentiation factor and marketing tool to position themselves favorably in the eyes of shareholders and stakeholders.[27–30] The increasing awareness of corporate practice and reputation in the consumers' purchase decisions, and employee motivation and retention, have made organizations and businesses act more ethically and responsibly.[26,31,32]

Figure 1: The three CSR imperatives: Economic, environmental, and social issues.
Source: Adapted from United Nations Industrial Development Organization.[24]

Levels and types of CSR

In the CSR literature, perhaps a more commonly known attempt to understand CSR is Carroll[9] CSR pyramid (refer to Figure 2), or the four kinds of social responsibilities that are expected and required of organizations and businesses by society, specifically, (1) economic or make a profit, (2) legal or obey the law, (3) ethical or do what is right and fair, and (4) philanthropic or be a good corporate citizen. While the responsibilities might have been metaphorically depicted as a pyramid — such depiction might have given the impression that economic performance is the

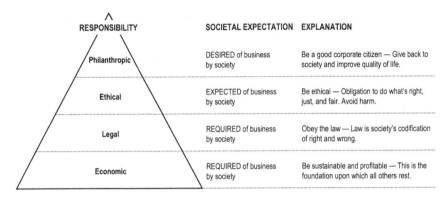

Figure 2:   The CSR Pyramid: Responsibilities, societal expectation, and explanation.

Source: Adapted from Carroll[9,10]; Carroll, Brown, and Buchholtz.[33]

foundational building block and organizations and businesses should hierarchically approach CSR to fulfill each responsibility in sequential order, i.e., starting from the bottom and gradually moving to the top — Carroll[10] points out that all four responsibilities should be considered and fulfilled simultaneously and holistically as each type of responsibility will impact different stakeholder groups. Table 1 identifies the potential stakeholder groups that could be impacted by the social responsibilities.

Besides the different levels of CSR, and from the perspective of CSR practices and practitioners, organizations can engage in the common types of CSR to become more socially responsible,[34–38] including, but not limited to the following:

Corporate philanthropy: Refers to an organization's collective efforts to contribute to a cause or non-profit's mission. The contribution could include monetary donations, non-monetary or in-kind donations, gift matching or matching the donations, community grants, and corporate sponsorships and scholarships.

Corporate volunteerism: Refers to workplace-supported efforts that give support and assistance to employees who wish to volunteer and participate in the local community activities, including direct service, "pro-bono" service, mentorship and expertise, team volunteering, field or on-site volunteering, crowdfunding, and employee internship at a non-profit organization.

Environmental leadership: Refers to organization-wide or small group efforts to work on sustainability-themed issues to make change happen.

Examples of environmental issues that groups could work on include the promotion of "no meat day", waste segregation, and eco-living and/or reduction of energy consumption, paper waste, and food waste.

Ethical and sustainable work practices: Refers to an organization's efforts to examine the internal operations to ensure fair and decent treatment of workers and provide a safe and welcoming working environment. Examples of such practices could include the provision of competitive salaries, compensation packages, parental leaves, and career development and training.

Impact of CSR

Today, as the public has become more aware and educated on social issues — such as health and disease, low income/vulnerable groups, global warming, aging population, malnutrition, poverty and hunger, and unethical labor practices — they expect organizations to practice and establish clear and effective CSR strategies that benefit and improve the society rather than just the organization's bottom line. As a result, meaningful CSR activities and programs are becoming more important for organizations to gain better recognition in the eyes of socially conscious investors and stakeholders.

Furthermore, it is believed that CSR can provide many benefits including customer satisfaction, customer trust, brand loyalty, financial returns, corporate reputation, attractive company culture, and employee retention, engagement, and organizational commitment.[1,39–46]

In addition, the rise of social media including YouTube, blogs, and social network sites and platforms can easily expose an organization's unethical business conducts and practices — such as false advertising (e.g., inappropriate product claims and deceptive sales practices), poor environmental practices (e.g., fast fashion where cheap and trendy clothing gets produced in the shortest time at a lower possible cost, which are worn possibly only for a short period of time without considering the impact on the environment and the use of natural resources, food waste, animal captivity, and forest destruction), mistreating employees (e.g., poor working conditions, deliberate classifying of full-time employees as freelancers or independent contractors for tax and legal purposes, and workers' rights violations), etc. — within seconds or minutes. Not only do the social media created outlets for virtual whistle-blowing bypass the

Table 1: How do social responsibilities impact different stakeholder groups?

Type of CSR	Impact on Stakeholders	Explanation/Rationale
Economic	Current and future employees and shareholders	If a business is not financially viable, the employees and shareholders will be significantly affected.
Legal	Owners, employees, consumers, and/or customers	The threat of litigation against businesses will mostly affect the owners. Still, the outcome could impact the employees, consumers, or customers who filed the case against the organization or business.
Ethical	All stakeholder groups	The ethical issues businesses face today — e.g., harassment, workplace health and safety, discrimination, privacy practices, etc. — typically impact the owners, employees, consumers, and customers.
Philanthropic	Employees, shareholders, investors, consumers, the community, and non-profit organizations and businesses	The philanthropic involvement not only impacts the community and non-profit organizations and businesses, but also employees' morale and engagement, and the perception of shareholders, investors, and consumers.

Source: Adapted from Carroll.[10]

internal channels to expose wrongdoing,[47] but they could also threaten an organization's reputation easily through posting fake news, inaccurate rumors, and negative remarks. Having said that, an accurate or unintentional post can cause problems or damage to an organization, too.[48]

Corporate Social Responsibility in the Digital Age

In today's business world, organizations have been operating in an external environment where volatility and constant changes are the norms. In addition, the digital economy has blurred the boundaries among markets and enabled stakeholders to collect information, communicate with one another, and scrutinize organizations' behavior.[49] There have been challenges for organizations to meet stakeholders' requirements in terms of performing CSR. At the same time, the digital economy does offer some opportunities for organizations to embark on the digital CSR journey. Thus, two main trends shape the way CSR has been perceived and performed by organizations.

First, today's business world is digitally connected. Organizations cannot function as closed systems as they have been affected by changes in both local and global markets as well as physical and online marketplaces. The expansion of globalization has compelled organizations to be more proactive in terms of practicing CSR because many stakeholders, who can powerfully influence how organizations operate, consider CSR as a better approach to monitor organizations' business behavior.[49–51]

It is noted that governments in different countries have encountered difficulty in terms of regulating organizations, especially multinational corporations (MNCs) which have many branches, factories, and offices in different countries all over the world. It is not feasible for local regulators, using local legal systems, to monitor and control organizations' behavior in other jurisdictions or other countries.[51] Also, many organizations have outsourced their business activities and processes to other business entities around the world, and these include e-suppliers who may operate only in the online marketplace. Governments of the home countries, where organizations' headquarters operate, are unable to ensure that organizations' subsidiaries or suppliers comply with the regulatory frameworks of the respective host countries. Thus, regulations may not be the best instruments to monitor every organization's behavior. Therefore, practicing CSR is one of the approaches that can help organizations be self-regulated.[16]

Second, the components of CSR should evolve to include activities that benefit not only stakeholders in the physical market, but also the online marketplace. In this aspect, there are two emerging subsets of CSR, namely (i) CSR activities that adopt digital technologies (e.g., AI, big data, machine learning, etc.) to deliver CSR activities, and (ii) digital CSR that refers to organizations' social responsibilities in the online market.

Corporate digital responsibility (*CDR*)

Like Carroll[9] who introduced the four levels of CSR in the physical market, Wade[13] proposes the four categories of CDR, including social, economic, technological, and environmental responsibilities, in the online environment.

Social DR

Social DR refers to organizations' responsibility to protect stakeholders' privacy and security in the online environment.[13]

Organizations also need to promote digital inclusion and digital diversity. Digital inclusion is defined as an initiative that enables people to access and use the internet as well as enjoy the benefits that digital technologies offer.[52] The UK government identifies four challenges that deter people from going online, i.e., access, skills, motivation, and trust, and thus digital diversity and digital inclusion aim to address these challenges.[53] In Singapore, the IDMA has introduced various programs to promote digital inclusion. For examples, "the Silver Infocomm Initiative, NEU PC Plus Program, Home Access Program, and Enable IT Program"[54] have been launched to assist the elderly, students who are in need, households with low income as well as people with disabilities (PWD) so that they can go online. Such programs have enabled Singapore to be ranked first in terms of digital inclusiveness in the Southeast Asian region.[55]

Organizations should provide protection for stakeholders' data privacy, and train employees to have good technical practice concerning cybersecurity protection. Organizations should encourage employees to comply with copyright law when using information online, or not access and use online information without owners' permission.

Economic DR

Economic DR refers to responsibilities that organizations should take when using robots and automation for jobs that need to be done by humans. Organizations should be responsible when engaging gig workers for outsourcing work.[13] Organizations should share benefits that they can gain from participating in the economy in terms of fair prices and tax contribution. In addition, organizations should respect the intellectual property rights in online marketing, i.e., avoid plagiarism and piracy.

Technological DR

Technological DR refers to responsibilities that organizations should take when adopting AI in making decisions.[13] Organizations should avoid producing digital products and technologies that can harm society.

Technological DR also refers to the adoption of ethical practices in the online environment. For instance, well-known companies, such as Microsoft and Google, have developed their standards and code of ethics for the adoption of AI.[56] Lobschat *et al.*[57] explain that when big data, machine learning, and AI are used to make decisions, users should exercise some form of ethics and responsibility to prevent biases and discrimination caused by digital technologies.

Organizations should go beyond what is required by the legal framework to collect, save, use, retrieve, and dispose of data responsibly. In Singapore, Infocomm Media Development Authority of Singapore (IMDA) and Personal Data Protection Commission (PDPC)[58] have introduced the Trusted Data Sharing Framework which guides organizations on the advantages of data sharing, how to share data, and the challenges associated with data sharing. The Credit Bureau Singapore (CBS), a partnership between the Association of Banks in Singapore (ABS) and Infocredit Holding Pte. Ltd., is a good example of how organizations can exercise their technological DR via responsibly participating in data sharing. Banks, financial institutions, and credit providers which are CBS members can obtain credit-related information about their customers from CBS with customers' consent. CBS collects relevant credit information about customers and shares it with banks and credit providers so that these organizations can make quick and fair lending decisions.[58]

Environmental DR

Environmental DR refers to responsibilities that organizations should adopt to recycle and dispose of digital technologies and devices. Organizations should also produce digital products that can promote green energy consumption. Supermarkets and companies like Best Denki, Courts, and Harvey Norman do provide free e-waste disposal services to their customers.[60] Canon and Epson have their programs to gather used toner and ink cartridges for recycling.[61] Seagate has also initiated a recycling program (called "Seagate Product Take Back Program") to encourage customers to exchange its used products for shopping vouchers so that it can extend the life cycle of its products to achieve sustainability.

Digital technologies and CSR

Technological and digital development has changed the ways that CSR is implemented and communicated with stakeholders. This section discusses three main contemporary topics of CSR in the digital age: digital communication, artificial intelligence, and digital nudging.

Digital communication and CSR

Organizations have adopted several digital platforms and communication channels to reach the intended recipients. For example, organizations use emails, SMS, and Cloud storage to send, receive, and store CSR-related information. This has helped organizations reduce paper usage and paper waste and allow stakeholders to access information easier.[62] Meetings via Zoom and video conferences can help organizations save manpower and transport costs as employees do not need to take flights to attend business meetings.

By doing so, organizations can achieve the following objectives, namely (i) cost-effectively delivering their CSR initiatives, (ii) reducing costs, time, and resources, and (iii) improving transparency, convenience, and speed of message delivery.

Montiel et al.[63] explain that schools and organizations have also used several technologies, for example, mobile apps, simulations, and Web 2.0, to teach students and educate employees about environmental protection to achieve sustainability, the complicated issues of sustainable development, and how to balance between economic development and triple the bottom line. Such technologies are also used for communication in schools and organizations.

Artificial intelligence and CSR

Many organizations have embarked on digital transformation and AI-focused initiatives and are faced with challenges associated with AI-based decision-making and AI governance. Governance of AI is an issue that many countries have been trying to address, using both regulatory and non-regulatory approaches. Hence, the ethical use of AI should be part of organizations' CSR efforts as legal frameworks may not be able to resolve all issues associated with the unethical use of AI. Organizations should formulate AI strategies together with their business strategies within the CSR framework to be accountable to all groups of stakeholders.

Theoretically, Elliott et al.[64] discuss Digital Responsibility Code (DRC) for AI/FinTech-enabled financial services. This DRC focuses on purpose and trust, enhancing societal well-being, providing fair and equal access for all (digital inclusion), improving economic transparency, investing in the new economy (e.g., circular economy), and reducing the technological impact on the environment as well as promoting sustainability. Elliott *et al.*[64] and Pasquale[65] further explain that the DRC has strong linkages to the concepts of green finance and green technology that are consistent with the United Nations' Sustainable Development Goals (SDGs) stated in the United Nations' *Resolution 70/1* on "Transforming our world: The 2030 Agenda for Sustainable Development".[67] The resolution provides guidelines and directions for countries to develop and implement their action plans to achieve sustainable development. This document includes 17 Sustainable Development Goals (SDGs) that aim to alleviate poverty, improve health and well-being via economic growth, embark on green finance, adopt green technology, provide education to all, improve gender equality and equality in education and job opportunities, develop infrastructure, encourage innovation, achieve responsible consumption, investment, and production, etc.

In practice, international organizations and MNCs have tried to address the ethical challenge of AI adoption via the introduction of AI principles, AI code of conduct, etc. At the international level, in May 2019, the Organization for Economic Co-operation and Development (OECD) adopted a set of AI principles that aim to encourage countries and organizations to use AI responsibly, i.e., to promote innovation, trust, and respect for human rights. The OECD's five AI principles include "(i) inclusive growth, sustainable development, and well-being, (ii) human-centered values and fairness, (iii) transparency and explainability, (iv) robustness, security, and safety, and (v) accountability".[66] These principles are aligned with the SDG3 (Good health and well-being), SDG9 (Industry, Innovation, and Infrastructure), SDG10 (Reduced inequalities in terms of AI access and use), and SDG12 (Responsible consumption and production).[67]

At the national level, IMDA and PDPC have published Singapore's Model AI Governance Framework.[59] This framework is not mandatory, and it provides directions to organizations on two main AI principles and how AI should be implemented. The first AI principle is "explainable, transparent, and fair", i.e., organizations that adopt AI-based decision-making should make sure that the AI-based decision-making process is reasonable, understandable, transparent, and fair to all stakeholders. The second AI principle is "human-centric", i.e., AI systems and solutions should be designed, developed, and deployed in a manner that can protect human beings' interests and promote their well-being and safety.[59]

At the corporate level, many MNCs do promote responsible AI usage, i.e., AI should be adopted in an equitable, non-biased manner; and AI systems should be clear and understandable, and safe for users. In a nutshell, AI adoption should generate benefits for humankind.[68] Partnership on AI (PAI) is a not-for-profit organization that brings together corporates, academics, civil society organizations, industry partners, media partners, etc., to promote AI for social good among other objectives. One of its functions is to guide users to mitigate the harmful effects of AI and machine learning adoption.[69] Its corporate funders include Adobe, Amazon, Apple, IBM, Intel, McKinsey, Samsung, and Sony.[69] Well-known MNCs do take initiatives to introduce AI principles and/or codes of practice. For example, Google makes recommendations on responsible practices for AI, including the principles of fairness, interpretability, privacy, and security. Also, designers of AI systems should adopt human-centered approaches.[70] Microsoft[71] has introduced a set of six responsible AI principles, focusing on fairness, reliability and safety, privacy and security, inclusiveness, transparency, and accountability.

Overall, organizations should perform their CSR when adopting AI, machine learning, and other new digital technologies to address socio-economic issues effectively.

Digital nudging and CSR

Marchiori et al.[72] define nudges as purposeful interventions that aim to change people's mindset and behavior by designing or modifying "the cues in the physical and/or social context in which they act".[72] Nudges are initiatives that can shift people's behavior toward a desired direction or state not because of financial incentives.[73–74]

In the digital economy, digital nudging is defined as the adoption of "user-interface design elements to guide people's behavior in digital choice environments".[75] Dhar et al.[76] explain that common digital technologies, such as emails, text messages, mobile applications, etc., can be used to create digital nudges that can promote employees' desired activities and performance.

Examples of digital nudges include emails sent by organizations to remind employees to use e-forms, or emails or SMS sent by banks to remind customers to opt for e-statements. These nudges can help organizations go paperless. Virgin Atlantic has also nudged its pilots to help the company save tonnes of fuel.[77]

Given the cost-effectiveness and simplicity of digital nudges, organizations can employ them to implement interventions that can be quickly implemented across the organizations to manage changes. Other benefits of digital nudges include (i) producing data that organizations can use to evaluate their intervention efforts, identify problems, and improve the process, (ii) adapting to changes in the external and internal environment, and new technologies, and (iii) creating competitive advantages via employee engagement and empowerment.[76]

Conclusion

This study has examined various concepts and models of CSR and CSR-related activities. Traditionally, CSR embraces economic, legal, ethical, and philanthropic responsibilities. Yet, these responsibilities have to be implemented in different forms in the online environment. Thus, Wade[13] discusses the four types of corporate digital responsibility, namely social, economic, technological, and environmental responsibilities although she asserted that these responsibilities should be integrated by organizations to achieve the best outcomes. It should be noted that different CSR initiatives may impact organizations differently. However, examining various impacts of CSR and CDR is not in the scope of this chapter. Therefore, future research should focus on the types and impacts of various CDR.

Given the insufficient research on CSR in the digital age, this chapter provides insights into how organizations need to address the challenges associated with CSR practices in the context of a digital economy.

References

1. Pfajfar, G., Shoham, A., Małecka, A., *et al.* (2022). Value of corporate social responsibility for multiple stakeholders and social impact — Relationship marketing perspective. *Journal of Business Research*, *143*, 46–61. Available from https://doi.org/10.1016/j.jbusres.2022.01.051.

2. Han, J. J., Kim, H. J., & Yu, J. (2016). Empirical study on relationship between corporate social responsibility and financial performance in Korea. *Asian Journal of Sustainability and Social Responsibility*, *1*, 61–76. Available from https://doi.org/10.1186/s41180-016-0002-3.

3. Sameer, I. (2021). Impact of corporate social responsibility on organization's financial performance: Evidence from Maldives public limited companies. *Future Business Journal*, *7*(1), 29. Available from https://doi.org/10.1186/s43093-021-00075-8.

4. Rexhepi, G., Kurtishi, S., & Bexheti, G. (2013). Corporate social responsibility (CSR) and innovation the drivers of business growth. *Procedia-Social and Behavioral Sciences*, *75*(3), 532–541. Available from https://doi.org/10.1016/j.sbspro.2013.04.058.

5. Friedman, M. (Sep 13, 1970). A Friedman doctrine — The social responsibility of business is to increase its profits. *The New York Times*. Available from https://www.nytimes.com/1970/09/13/archives/a-friedman-doctrine-the-social-responsibility-of-business-is-to.html.

6. Aupperle, K. E., Carroll, A. B., & Hatfield, J. D. (1985). An empirical investigation of the relationship between corporate social responsibility and profitability. *Academy of Management Journal*, *28*(2), 446–463.

7. Preston, L. E., & O'Bannon, D. P. (1997). The corporate social-financial performance relationship: A typology and analysis. *Business and Society*, *36*(4), 419–429.

8. Vance, S. C. (1975). Are Socially Responsible Corporations Good Investment Risks? *Management Review*, *64*(8), 19–24.

9. Carroll, A. B. (1991). The pyramid of corporate social responsibility: Toward the moral management of organizational stakeholders. *Business Horizon*, *34*(4), 39–48.

10. Carroll, A. B. (2016). Carroll's pyramid of CSR: Taking another look. *International Journal of Corporate Social Responsibility*, *1*(1), 1–8. Available from http://doi.org/10.1186/s40991-016-0004-6.

11. Grigore, G., Molesworth, M., & Watkins, R. (2016). New corporate responsibilities in the digital economy. In A. Theofilou, G. Grigore, A. Stancu (eds.) *Corporate Social Responsibility in the Post-financial Crisis Era*. Palgrave Macmillan, London, pp. 41–62. Available from https://doi.org/10.1007/978-3-319-40096-9.

12. Grigore, G., Stancu, A., & McQueen, D. (eds.). (2018). *Corporate Responsibility and Digital Communities: An International Perspective towards Sustainability*. Palgrave Macmillan, London, UK.

13. Wade, M. (Apr 28, 2020). Corporate responsibility in the digital era. *MIT Sloan Management Review*. Available from https://sloanreview.mit.edu/article/corporate-responsibility-in-the-digital-era/.

14. Lee, M. P. (2008). A review of the theories of corporate social responsibility: Its evolutionary path and the road ahead. *International Journal of Management Reviews*, *10*(1), 53–73. Available from https://doi.org/10.1111/j.1468-2370.2007.00226.x.
15. Carroll, A. B. (1999). Corporate social responsibility — Evolution of a definitional construction. *Business and Society*, *38*(3), 268–295.
16. Camilleri, M. A. (2017). Corporate sustainability and responsibility: Creating value for business, society, and the environment. *Asian Journal of Sustainability and Social Responsibility*, *2*(1), 59–74. Available from https://doi.org/10.1186/s41180-017-0016-5.
17. Dahlsrud, A. (2008). How corporate social responsibility is defined: An analysis of 37 definitions. *Corporate Social Responsibility and Environmental Management*, *15*(1), 1–13. Available from https://doi.org/10.1002/csr.132.
18. Sheehy, B. (2015). Defining CSR: Problems and solutions. *Journal of Business Ethics*, *131*, 625–648. Available from https://doi.org/10.1007/s10551-014-2281-x.
19. Baden, D. (2016). A reconstruction of Carroll's pyramid of corporate social responsibility for the 21st century. *International Journal of Corporate Social Responsibility*, *1*(1), 1–15. Available from https://doi.org/10.1186/s40991-016-0008-2.
20. Buchner, S. (2011). The concept of CSR — An empirical study of practitioners' CSR conceptions. Master's thesis, Linnaeus University. Available from http://lnu.diva-portal.org/smash/get/diva2:424997/FULLTEXT01.pdf.
21. O'Dwyer, B. (2003). Conceptions of corporate social responsibility: The nature of managerial capture. *Accounting, Auditing & Accountability Journal*, *16*(4), 523–557. Available from https://doi.org/10.1108/095135 70310492290.
22. Okoye, A. (2009). Theorising corporate social responsibility as an essentially contested concept: Is a definition necessary? *Journal of Business Ethics*, *89*(4), 613–627. Available from https://doi.org/10.1007/s10551-008-0021-9.
23. Votaw, D. (1973). Genius becomes rare. In D. Votaw, & S. P. Sethi (eds.) *The Corporate Dilemma: Traditional Values Versus Contemporary Problems*. Prentice Hall, New Jersey, pp. 11–45.
24. United Nations Industrial Development Organization. (2002). Corporate social responsibility: Implications for small and medium enterprises in developing countries. Available from https://www.unido.org/sites/default/files/2008-07/CSR_-_Implications_for_SMEs_in_Developing_Countries_0.pdf.
25. European Commission. (2011). Communication from the Commission to the European Parliament, the Council, the European Economic and Social Committee and the Committee of the Regions. A renewed EU Strategy

2011–14 for Corporate Social Responsibility. Available from https://eur-lex. europa.eu/LexUriServ/LexUriServ.do?uri=COM:2011:0681:FIN:EN:PDF#: ~:text=The%20European%20Commission%20has%20 previously,stakeholders%20on%20a%20voluntary%20basis%E2%80%9D.

26. Rangan, K., Chas, L. A., & Karim, S. (2012). Why every company needs a CSR strategy and how to build it. *Harvard Business School Working Paper No. 12-088*. Available from https://www.hbs.edu/ris/Publication%20Files/ 12-088.pdf.

27. Heyward, C. (Nov 18, 2020). The growing importance of social responsibility in business. *Forbes*. Available from https://www.forbes.com/sites/ forbesbusinesscouncil/2020/11/18/the-growing-importance-of-social-responsibility-in-business/?sh=7e7e1ec92283.

28. Rangan, K., Chase, L. A., & Karim, S. (2015). The truth about CSR. *Harvard Business Review*, *93*(1/2), 40–49.

29. Öberseder, M., Schlegelmilch, B. B., Murphy, P. E., *et al.* (2014). Consumers' perceptions of corporate social responsibility: Scale development and validation. *Journal of Business Ethics*, *124*(1), 101–115. Available from https://doi. org/10.1007/s10551-013-1787-y.

30. Stobierski, T. (2021). Types of corporate social responsibility to be aware of. *Harvard Business School Online's Business Insights*. Available from https:// online.hbs.edu/blog/post/types-of-corporate-social-responsibility.

31. MacGregor, S. P., Espinach, X., Fontrodona, J. (Aug 28–31, 2007). Social innovation: Using design to generate business value through corporate social responsibility. *International Conference on Engineering Design (ICED'07)*, Paris, France. Available from https://www.designsociety.org/publica-tion/25458/Social+Innovation%3A+Using+Design+to+Generate+Business +Value+through+Corporate+Social+Responsibilitytypes-of-corporate-social-responsibility.

32. Ruiz, B., & García, J. A. (2021). Analyzing the relationship between CSR and reputation in the banking sector. *Journal of Retailing and Consumer Services*, *61*, 1–10. Available from https://doi.org/10.1016/j.jretconser.2021. 102552.

33. Carroll, A. B., Brown, J., & Buchholtz, A. K. (2017). *Business and Society: Ethics, Sustainability & Stakeholder Management*, 10th edn. Cengage Learning, Boston, MA.

34. Double the Donation. Corporate social responsibility: The definitive guide. Available from https://doublethedonation.com/corporate-social-responsibility/.

35. Hutto, C. (2021). The value of corporate social responsibility in the work-place. *Inhersight*. Available from https://www.inhersight.com/blog/diversity/ corporate-social-responsibility.

36. Jackson, R. (2021). Corporate social responsibility: A simple guide. *The Giving Machine.* Available from https://www.thegivingmachine.co.uk/blog/posts/corporate-social-responsibility-a-simple-guide/.
37. Nartya, D. (2022). Business value of corporate social responsibility. *PRNews. io.* Available from https://prnews.io/blog/business-value-of-corporate-social-responsibility.html.
38. San Diago Foundation. (2020). What is corporate social responsibility? Available from https://www.sdfoundation.org/news-events/sdf-news/what-is-corporate-social-responsibility/.
39. Ahn, J., Shamin, A., & Park, J. (2021). Impacts of cruise industry corporate social responsibility reputation on customers' loyalty: Mediating role of trust and identification. *International Journal of Hospitality Management, 92,* 102706. Available from https://doi.org/10.1016/j.ijhm.2020.102706.
40. Bizri, R. (2021). The impact of CSR best practices on job performance: The mediating roles of affective commitment and work engagement. *Journal of Organizational Effectiveness: People and Performance, 8*(1), 129–148. Available from https://doi.org/10.1108/JOEPP-01-2020-0015.
41. Duc Tai, T. (2022). Impact of corporate social responsibility on social and economic sustainability. Economic Research-Ekonomska Istraživanja. Available from https://doi.org/10.1080/1331677X.2022.2046480.
42. Glavas, A. (2016). Corporate social responsibility and employee engagement: Enabling employees to employ more of their whole selves at work. *Frontier in Psychology, 7,* 796. Available from https://doi.org/10.3389/fpsyg.2016.00796.
43. Lee, J.-E., & Yang, Y. S. (2022). The impact of corporate social responsibility performance feedback on corporate social responsibility performance. *Frontiers in Psychology, 13,* 893193. Available from https://doi.org/10.3389/fpsyg.2022.893193.
44. Feng, Y., Akram, R., Hieu, V. M., *et al.* (2021). The impact of corporate social responsibility on the sustainable financial performance of Italian organisations: Mediating role of organisation reputation. *Economic Research-Ekonomska Istraživanja.* Available from https://doi.org/10.1080/13316 77X.2021.2017318.
45. Mahmood, A., & Bashir, J. (2020). How does corporate social responsibility transform brand reputation into brand equity? Economic and noneconomic perspectives of CSR. *International Journal of Engineering Business Management, 12,* 1–13. Available from https://doi.org/10.1177/18479790 20927547.
46. Swaen, V., Demoulin, N., & Pauwels-Delassus, V. (2021). Impact of customers' perceptions regarding corporate social responsibility and irresponsibility in the grocery retailing industry: The role of corporate reputation. *Journal of Business Research,* 131, 709–721. Available from https://doi.org/10.1016/j.jbusres.2020.12.016.

47. Wilkie, D. (2013). Virtual whistle-blowing: Employees bypass internal channels to expose wrongdoing. *SHRM*. Available from https://www.shrm.org/resourcesandtools/hr-topics/employee-relations/pages/virtual-whistle-blowing-bypass-internal-channels-expose-wrongdoing.aspx.

48. Bown, J. (Jul 9, 2019). How social media could ruin your business. *BBC*. Available from https://www.bbc.com/news/business-48871456.

49. Dwivedi, Y. K., Ismagilova, E., Hughes, D. L., *et al.* (2021). Setting the future of digital and social media marketing research: Perspectives and research propositions. *International Journal of Information Management, 59*, 102168. Available from https://doi.org/10.1016/j.ijinfomgt.2020.102168.

50. Mehdi, T., Clare, D., & Polonsky, M. (2015). A stakeholder approach to corporate social responsibility, reputation and business performance. *Social Responsibility Journal, 11*(2), 340–363.

51. Scherer, A. G., & Palazzo, G. (2011). The new political role of business in a globalized world: A review of a new perspective on CSR and its implications for the organisation, governance, and democracy. *Journal of Management Studies, 48*(4), 899–931.

52. Chew, H. Y., Soon, C., & Tan, D. (2021). State of digital inclusion in Singapore: A landscape review. *NUS Centre for Trusted Internet and Community and Institute of Policy Studies.*

53. Government Digital Service. (Dec 4, 2014). Government digital inclusion strategy. *Gov.uk*. Available from https://www.gov.uk/government/publications/government-digital-inclusion-strategy/government-digital-inclusion-strategy#:~:text=To%20help%20people%20go%20online,organisations%20that%20make%20a%20difference.

54. IDA Singapore. Factsheet: Overview of Digital Inclusion. *IMDA*. Available from https://www.imda.gov.sg/-/media/imda/files/inner/about-us/newsroom/media-releases/2016/0329_seniors-and-students-foster-new-bonds-through-it-bootcamp/3--overview-of-di-factsheet-mar-2016.pdf?la=en.

55. Goh, G. (Feb 9, 2021). Singapore ranks 1st in digital inclusiveness, but South-east Asia lags: report. *The Business Times*. Available from https://www.businesstimes.com.sg/asean-business/singapore-ranks-1st-in-digital-inclusiveness-but-south-east-asia-lags-report.

56. Martin, K., Shilton, K., & Smith, J. (2019). Business and the ethical implications of technology: Introduction to the symposium. *Journal of Business Ethics, 160*(2), 307–317. Available from https://doi.org/10.1007/s10551-019-04213-9.

57. Lobschat, L., Mueller, B., Eggers, F., *et al.* (2021). Corporate digital responsibility. *Journal of Business Research, 122*, 875–888. Available from https://doi.org/10.1016/j.jbusres.2019.10.006.

58. Infocomm Media Development Authority of Singapore (IMDA) and Personal Data Protection Commission (PDPC). (2019). Trusted Data Sharing

Framework. Infocomm Media Development Authority of Singapore (IMDA) and Personal Data Protection Commission (PDPC). Available from https://www.imda.gov.sg/-/media/Imda/Files/Programme/AI-Data-Innovation/Trusted-Data-Sharing-Framework.pdf.

59. Infocomm Media Development Authority (IMDA) and Personal Data Protection Commission (PDPC). (2020). *Model Artificial Intelligence Governance Framework*, 2nd edn. Info-communications Media Development Authority (IMDA) and Personal Data Protection Commission (PDPC), p. 15. Available from https://www.pdpc.gov.sg/-/media/files/pdpc/pdf-files/resource-for-organisation/ai/sgmodelaigovframework2.pdf.

60. Tan, C. (Jun 4, 2021). New e-waste recycling bins in some supermarkets and Harvey Norman outlets. *The Straits Times*. Available from https://www.straitstimes.com/singapore/new-e-waste-recycling-bins-now-available-outside-some-supermarkets-and-harvey-norman.

61. Lim, V. (Jun 30, 2021). Singapore's e-waste collection and disposal scheme: What you need to know. *CNA*. Available from https://www.channelnewsasia.com/singapore/e-waste-recycling-collection-disposal-scheme-faq-1930806.

62. Newman, D. (Nov 21, 2017). How digital transformation aligns with corporate social responsibility. *Forbes*. Available from https://www.forbes.com/sites/danielnewman/2017/11/21/how-digital-transformation-aligns-with-corporate-social-responsibility/?sh=4489298c58bf.

63. Montiel, I., Delgado-Ceballos, J., Ortiz-de-Mandojana, N., *et al.* (2020). New ways of teaching: Using technology and mobile apps to educate on societal grand challenges. *Journal of Business Ethics*, *161*(2), 243–251.

64. Elliott, K., Price, R., Shaw, P., *et al.* (2021). Towards an equitable digital society: Artificial intelligence (AI) and corporate digital responsibility (CDR). *Society*, *58*(3), 179–188. Available from https://doi.org/10.1007/s12115-021-00594-8.

65. Pasquale, F. (2020). *New Laws of Robotics: Defending Human Expertise in the Age of AI*. Harvard University Press, Boston, MA.

66. OECD. OECD AI principles overview. Available from https://oecd.ai/en/ai-principles.

67. United Nations. Do you know all 17 SDGs? United Nations. Available from https://sdgs.un.org/goals.

68. de Laat, P. (2021). Companies committed to responsible AI: From principles towards implementation and regulation? *Philosophy and Technology*, *34*(4), 1135–1193. Available from https://doi.org/10.1007/s13347-021-00474-3.

69. Partnership on AI. (2021). Creating Impact Through Community: Annual Report 2021. Available from https://partnershiponai.org//wp-content/uploads/2022/02/PAI-annual-report-2021.pdf.

70. Google AI. Responsible AI practices. Available from https://ai.google/responsibilities/responsible-ai-practices/.

71. Microsoft. Microsoft responsible AI principles. Available from https://www. microsoft.com/en-us/ai/our-approach?activetab=pivot1:primaryr5.

72. Marchiori, D. R., Adriaanse, M. A., & De Ridder, D. T. (2017). Unresolved questions in nudging research: Putting the psychology back in nudging. *Social and Personality Psychology Compass*, *11*(1), e12297.

73. Tams, C. (Feb 22, 2018). Small is beautiful: Using gentle nudges to change organisations. *Forbes*. Available from https://www.forbes.com/sites/ carstentams/2018/02/22/small-is-beautiful-using-gentle-nudges-to-change-organizations/?sh=632a22f45a8d.

74. Congiu, & L., Moscati, I. (2022). A review of nudges: Definitions, justifications, effectiveness. *Journal of Economic Survey*, *36*(1), 188–213.

75. Weinmann, M., Schneider, C., & Brocke, J. V. (2016). Digital nudging. *Business & Information Systems Engineering*, *58*(6), 433–436. Available from https://doi.org/10.1007/s12599-016-0453-1.

76. Dhar, J., Bailey, A., Mingardon, S., *et al.* (2017). The persuasive power of the digital nudge. *Boston Consulting Group*. Available from https://www. bcg.com/publications/2017/people-organization-operations-persuasive-power-digital-nudge.

77. Mooney, C. (Jun 22, 2016). Virgin Atlantic just used behavioral science to 'nudge' its pilots into using less fuel. It worked. *The Washington Post*. Available from https://www.washingtonpost.com/news/energy-environment/ wp/2016/06/22/virgin-atlantic-just-used-behavioral-science-to-nudge-its-pilots-into-saving-lots-of-fuel/.

Chapter 9

Doing Good and Doing Well: Past, Present, and Future

Mun Wei Chan

Introduction

Awareness of sustainability has been growing in recent years. Strategic communications consultancy SEC Newgate published their inaugural ESG Monitor research report[1] in October 2021, in which more than 10,000 respondents across 10 countries — including Singapore — provided their views on environmental, social, and governance (ESG) issues, commonly known as the three established pillars of sustainability.

The results showed that approximately 72 percent of the participants from Singapore were familiar with the term ESG, which is significantly higher than the global average of 51 percent. About 53 percent of the local respondents said that "ESG issues are very important when deciding whether to purchase products or services". Climate change was deemed as the most important ESG issue with 25 percent of the vote, followed by waste management (11 percent), and environmental issues in general (8 percent). Regression modeling indicated that the biggest driver behind ESG ratings of companies was "responsible and sustainable use of natural resources", followed by "action on climate change". The top three areas where most respondents agreed that companies should take responsibility were in supply chain management, looking after employees, and having processes to identify and stop unethical behaviors.

The survey results reflect the major global challenges facing countries, companies, and communities. This includes urgent climate action lest global warming renders our Earth inhospitable in the coming decades, the growing income and opportunity divide between affluent and less-affluent countries, and intra-national differences between those who make it in life and those who are left behind. COVID-19 is another global issue that has had a long whiplash since the early months of 2020, with many less-developed countries still suffering from economic disruptions, loss of lives, and limited access to vaccines and healthcare.

According to the World Bank,[2] the private sector provides up to 90 percent of jobs in developing countries. The private sector also accounts for more than 60 percent of Gross Domestic Product (GDP) in most countries. The private sector's global prominence means that companies are not only affected by sustainability-related events and shocks, they in turn can influence the trajectories and outcomes of environmental and social issues. Economic development, environmental protection, job creation, quality of life, and poverty reduction are intertwined. Bearing in mind that companies exist within a social context, this chapter will examine the following issues.

First, since the advent of companies as separate commercial entities, how has the notion of social responsibility evolved? What drives companies to give back to the communities where their operations and customers are based?

Second, what is the relationship between doing well (such as generating surpluses and returns for shareholders) and doing good (such as giving to charities and causes that do not generate any direct financial returns)? Is there a natural synergy between companies' financial performance and contributions to social good? Are there inherent trade-offs? If so, is doing good a market gap that requires regulatory intervention such as mandatory corporate disclosures and performance requirements?

Third, what does the future hold for corporate social responsibility? Does the pervasiveness of technology offer the opportunity to transform the relationship between doing well and doing good?

In the following sections, the evolution of corporate social responsibility, its relationship with sustainability, perspectives about doing good and doing well, as well as suggestions for the road ahead, with a focus on disruptive technology, are presented.

Evolution of Corporate Social Responsibility

The concept of corporations as separate entities from the owners and founders was started during the Roman Empire. The word "corporation" traces its roots to the Latin word "corpora", which means "to combine into one body".[3] There were different types of corpora during the Roman period, such as professional and religious guilds known as colleges, as well as entities called publicani that were formed to fulfill public contracts like building aqueducts, operating mines, and collecting taxes. Patterson[3] argued that corpora were formed because of natural associative tendencies toward clan, trade, and blood relations, and that in the case of the publicans, the corpora structure allowed the pooling of resources to meet contractual requirements.

As forefathers of the modern business structure, the publicani were profit-driven and influential but, unfortunately, not free from ethically questionable practices and scandals. During the Second Punic War fought between Rome and Carthage, the publicani supported the war effort by supplying ship-borne cargoes on credit, with the condition that the Roman Republic would insure these shipments and compensate the publicani for shipments that were lost at sea. Subsequently, it was discovered that some of the shipments were old ships loaded with worthless goods and scuttled at sea deliberately to claim the insurance payments. Clearly, the risk that commercial entities could behave irresponsibly is not a recent phenomenon.

The modern concept that businesses have a responsibility toward society beyond their commercial mandate is linked to the start of the Industrial Revolution in the United Kingdom in the 18th century when machinery and mass production techniques progressively replaced menial labor and hand tools. As discussed by Rafferty,[4] the Industrial Revolution brought about the best and worst of times for workers and the wider community. On the one hand, increased production led to plentiful and affordable goods for consumers, communications and transport improved significantly, medical care evolved rapidly to save lives, and there were more employment opportunities than before.

On the other hand, the growth of industrial towns and urban migration led to overcrowding, poor living conditions, and disease outbreaks. While factory workers made more money than their agricultural peers, they labored backbreaking 14–16 hours every day, six days a week, with no paid leave. Machines at the factories were often poorly maintained, dirty

206 » M. W. Chan

and hazardous, which resulted in frequent workplace injuries and even fatalities. Coal was burnt to power the machinery, and the smoke pollution was hazardous for workers and the community's health, while persistent factory emissions over many decades added to the stock of greenhouse gases in the atmosphere that contributed to our existent challenge of global warming.

The adverse working conditions during the Industrial Revolution led to three major developments. First, workers came together to join or create unions to fight for safer working conditions and higher wages. Numerous industrial actions were organized, such as the Great Railroad Strike of 1877 in West Virginia, United States, in which thousands of railway workers disrupted train movements and burnt down facilities to protest against wage cuts. The National Guard and federal troops had to step in to quell the violence, which resulted in an estimated 100 fatalities.

The second development was the government passing legislation to protect workers. According to the United Kingdom's National Archives,[5] one of the most contentious practices during the Industrial Revolution was the use of child labor. Because there were no laws prohibiting child workers, factory owners were keen to hire them as they could be paid less than adult workers, were generally more compliant, and their smaller stature was physically suitable for working in tight spaces. The United Kingdom Parliament passed the Factory Act in 1833.[6] Under the new Act, "no children were to work in factories under the age of nine. A maximum working week of 48 hours was set for those aged 9–13, limited to eight hours a day; and for children between 13 and 18 it was limited to 12 hours daily. The Act also required children under 13 to receive elementary schooling for two hours each day." Just as importantly, the Act instituted a regulatory enforcement system whereby a four-man inspectorate of factories was instituted to inspect factories and impose penalties for any practices that were illegal under the Act.

The third development was that in response to the labor unrest and the government's increased scrutiny, companies started to take a deep interest in their workers' health, safety, and well-being. It was a mindset shift from clinically looking at labor as a factor of production to the notion that happy and motivated workers would lead to higher output, better quality of work, and fewer business disruptions. Milton Hershey, the American chocolatier, businessman, and philanthropist, epitomized this progressive thinking when he started his chocolate factory in 1894 in Pennsylvania, United States.[7] He provided cheap credit for the workers to purchase their own homes and even built a leisure park — now known as Hersheypark — for the workers and their families. The milk chocolate bars from the Hershey plant were well received by American consumers and the business grew rapidly. Beyond taking care of his workers, Milton Hershey took an interest in the wider community's well-being. He and his wife Catherine did not have children of their own. They founded the Milton Hershey School in 1909 to provide a safe environment for orphaned boys and to teach them trades to make a livelihood. This was the start of Hershey's philanthropic contributions. Subsequently in 1935, the couple established the M.S. Hershey Foundation to support educational and cultural opportunities across the United States.

Corporate social responsibility took to the battlefield during the Second World War when many factories were converted to manufacturing weapons and other military equipment. As highlighted by Vergun,[8] three million civilian cars were manufactured in the United States in 1941, right before the country formally declared war on Japan. During the war, only 139 additional cars were made as the assembly lines were retooled to build guns, tanks, and other equipment for the war effort. While patriotism was a key driver for American companies to contribute to the fight against the Axis powers, Mason[9] argued that there were ideological and commercial interests in ensuring that while the government would carry out the central planning, actual production remained in the hands of private enterprises and not nationalized industries.

The concept of corporate entities adopting and practicing social responsibility, or what is now called corporate social responsibility, was first expounded after the Second World War in 1953 by American economist Howard Bowen in his book *Social Responsibilities of the Businessman*. Bowen[10] defined social responsibilities as "the obligations of businessmen to pursue those policies, to make those decisions, or to follow those lines of action which are desirable in terms of the objectives and values of our society". While businessmen are free to critique and change existent societal values, they can neither ignore nor deemphasize what are socially acceptable norms and practices. Bowen[10] further provided an institutional perspective in terms of what companies, as corporate entities, ought to do, where he articulated 11 goals to define the social responsibilities of business, as follows:

- High standard of living in terms of abundant consumption of goods and services as well as access to leisure.

- Economic progress through improvements in technology, education, skills, and prudent use of resources.
- Economic stability by moderating fluctuations in economic activity.
- Personal security offered to individual workers.
- Order in terms of a regular flow of goods and services and harmonious economic relationships.
- Justice pertaining to equitable distribution of income and wide access to opportunities for personal and economic advancement.
- Freedom of enterprise and freedom of consumer choice.
- Development of individuals through the physical environment, tasks assigned, relationships, and opportunities at the workplace.
- Community improvement that encompasses a healthy physical environment and a satisfying social environment.
- National security in having a strong economy whereby productive resources can be diverted to military production if the need arises.
- Personal integrity in how businesses have to maintain high standards of truthfulness and adherence to rules in all economic activities and transactions.

One could argue that Bowen's thinking was ahead of his time because his 11 goals can be mapped to the current environmental, social, and governance (ESG) objectives. The social and governance aspects were more prominent in Bowen's conceptualization, which is reasonable given that the current focus on climate change and other environmental issues came into the foreground only after the 1970s. The goals are also in line with the United Nations' Sustainable Development Goals (SDGs)[11] — notably No Poverty, Good Health and Well-Being, Quality Education, Decent Work and Economic Growth, Reduced Inequalities, Responsible Consumption and Production, as well as Peace, Justice, and Strong Institution. The SDGs were adopted by United Nations Member States in 2015 as a common blueprint to deliver peace and prosperity for all countries.

Corporate Social Responsibility and Sustainability

As can be seen from the foregoing discussion, corporate social responsibility, or CSR in short, has been around since businesses took on a legal status of their own during the Roman era. The form that CSR has taken is shaped by the social context and the shared and compelling concerns during that time. If the situation is to fast forward to the present day, the question would then be what salient external issues are required for businesses to act responsibly? A concomitant question is what is the relationship between CSR and the ubiquitous ESG pillars of sustainability? Are they the same thing? Has CSR evolved into sustainability?

To answer these questions, there is a need to examine how the modern concept of sustainability came about. The first development was the United Nations' World Commission on Environment and Development,[12] which was initiated in 1983 to study and propose solutions to minimizing ecological degradation from economic development. The Commission published the *Our Common Future* report in 1987, which defined sustainable development as "development that meets the needs of the present without compromising the ability of future generations to meet their own needs".[12] There are three characteristics in this macro definition of sustainability — safeguarding the long-term well-being of communities, balancing the needs of current and future generations, and using resources prudently.

The second development came almost two decades later in 2006 when the United Nations launched the Principles for Responsible Investment (PRI) report[13] in which environmental, social, and governance (ESG) issues were mooted as criteria to be integrated with the financial assessment of companies to promote sustainable investing. As of 2021, more than 3,800 asset owners, asset managers, and service providers with assets under management of more than US$120 trillion had committed to the Principles for Responsible Investment.

Over the last two decades, the two developments have merged insofar as investors and other stakeholders expect companies to manage their ESG issues well, not only as a means to manage risks and safeguard organizational resilience over time, but also to contribute to sustainable development at the societal level. In some ways, this parallels the earlier discussion on societal expectations of what commercial entities should and should not be doing.

A literature review reveals subtle differences between CSR and sustainability. Bansal and DesJardine[14] cited the United Nations' *Our Common Future* report and advocated that business sustainability is about time, in particular the need to balance access to and use of resources across generations. They cited the example of how the Norwegian sovereign wealth fund sets aside royalties from the use of natural resources for future generations. Conversely, CSR is more near-term focused on the need to balance different stakeholders' interests, such as how a socially responsible oil company would invest and build local facilities to compensate communities that have been impacted by resource extraction and environmental degradation. However, the company may or may not take a long-term view, such as the need to put in place a viable funding model for schools and hospitals that the company has sponsored to build.

Sheehy and Farneti[15] noted that while CSR and corporate sustainability have different conceptual starting points, methods, and focus areas, there has been convergence over time. However, they identified one important distinction. CSR has evolved into a form of international business regulation focused on the environmental and social impacts of business while corporate sustainability entails both strong public-oriented and weak private-oriented forms. In other words, while CSR and corporate sustainability are anchored in doing the right things for society, CSR is arguably more self-initiated by companies while corporate sustainability is more responsive in terms of external needs, expectations, and mandates. The authors went on to argue that both CSR and corporate sustainability have been drawn into the broader concept of sustainability, which they define as "a term that defines a broader public global policy agenda, forming a foundation for sustainable development".[15]

All in all, CSR and corporate sustainability are like overlapping circles in a Venn diagram with more convergence than differences. They are similar in that since pre-industrial times, companies have functioned within societies where there are contextual norms, expectations, and requirements for companies to contribute to societal needs beyond pursuing commercial interests. The insight that CSR is more self-directed is supported by how companies in Singapore still use the term to refer to ad hoc or regular acts of doing good, such as an annual golf tournament to raise money for a pre-selected charity or an employee-driven visit to an elder care center to bring cheer to the beneficiaries. Corporate sustainability, conversely, can be more purposeful, such as conducting a thorough assessment of the community's needs before developing a plan on how the company could address such needs through appropriate and sustained investments, activities, and measurements.

Doing Good and Doing Well

From what has been discussed thus far, it is fair to say that commercial entities have served the social good for a long time, be it by choice or compulsion. A question to ask is to what extent does doing good sit with doing well? Are they complementary or conflicting objectives from a company's perspective? Do socially responsible companies perform better? These questions are contemplated in the following sections.

Several studies have explored the empirical relationship between companies' financial performance and their CSR expenditure or ratings. Awaysheh *et al.*[16] examined this relationship through a statistical analysis of American companies against their industry peers using CSR ratings and financial performance ratios. They found that best-in-class CSR companies have higher levels of operating performance and higher relative valuations compared to their worst-in-class and mid-80 percent counterparts. However, whether greater social responsibility leads to better financial performance is not conclusive as the researchers noted that companies earning higher operating profits generally have more cash flows at their disposal to invest in CSR, which in turn could lead to higher relative valuations. In other words, although there is some correlation between doing good and doing well, it is plausible that companies that do well financially will naturally have the resources to do good and give back to society.

In addition, Kanter[17] argued that there is no clear dichotomy between doing good and doing well, rather, they underpin the decision-making criteria for most companies. The author suggested that companies should look for synergies between doing good and doing well. In doing so, new capabilities can be built to solve societal issues while enlarging the company's market. Incorporating social good into strategy can strengthen corporate performance over the long term in a few ways. First, it builds a positive brand in the eyes of the customers, employees, and the general public. Second, a focused and constant social purpose can be a powerful unifying force in creating a strong and cohesive corporate culture. Third, tackling societal issues can engender innovative ideas and perspectives. One relevant example can be seen in the Proctor & Gamble Company (P&G) which grew its business in Brazil by sending its employees to live in disadvantaged communities, so as to create new products and further modifications to improve residents' lives. Thinking about and solving society's daily pain points should be part and parcel of developing and implementing a firm's corporate strategy, as this would ultimately benefit both the company and the community at large.

While Kanter[17] articulated how companies ought to be socially responsible as part of running their business, there could be hurdles in the way of doing good and doing well. On this note, Mehrpouya[18] identified four factors that may weaken the relationship between responsible corporate behavior and financial performance. First, many companies are inherently short-term in their outlook, due to intense pressure from shareholders for positive financial results in quarterly reporting. As social responsibility initiatives and the resultant benefits can take time to gestate before producing tangible and intangible benefits for the company, it may be challenging to justify long-term social investments particularly if there are short-term financial performance volatilities. Mehrpouya[18] pointed to recent research which showed that about 75 percent of corporate social responsibility proposals receive less than 20 percent of favorable votes at shareholder meetings.

Second, the complexity and disaggregation of global supply chains have increased the distance between consumers and producers. As a result, some multinational corporations may not be inclined toward building solidarity "with people on the other side of the world". Such companies would focus on building a transactional and profitable relationship with their consumers, rather than take a genuine interest in global welfare and well-being issues. This perspective is at odds with Kanter's example of P&G understanding and meeting the needs of Brazilian communities. One takeaway from both perspectives is that the global marketplace can be a risk as well as an opportunity in terms of doing good across borders.

Third, Mehrpouya[18] argued that business-to-business (B2B) companies do not need to face customers directly and may be less inclined toward social responsibility and building a positive brand as compared to business-to-consumer (B2C) companies. The long-term trend toward vertical disintegration and global outsourcing could propel the shrinking of the global market share of customer-facing companies, and this could lead to a reduced need for responsible corporate behavior over time.

Fourth, the pervasive growth of monopolies and oligopolies in some industries could mean that from an economic perspective, a company has less motivation to be responsible if it has too much market concentration and power. An example is the pharmaceutical industry, which is dominated by a few multinational corporations that spend in excess of hundreds of millions of dollars to develop, patent, and sell an approved drug. As Emanuel[19] argued in *The Atlantic* magazine, one reason for excessive drug prices is that "through patent protection and FDA [US Food and Drug Administration] marketing exclusivity, the US government grants a monopoly on brand-name drugs." Thus, pharmaceutical companies are in a strong market position to set high prices and maximize financial returns even when this is socially undesirable in reducing universal access to affordable healthcare.

Mehrpouya[18] articulated the extrinsic market dynamics that make it difficult for companies to do good and do well at the same time. Another challenge is that when companies' actions are aggregated together, it could lead to unintended social harm. A manifestation of this is known as the tragedy of the commons.[20] This term, coined by University of California professor Garrett Hardin in 1968, refers to how farmers share a common piece of grazing ground for their cattle. Each farmer would send their cattle to graze the best grass as often as possible. As the farmers become more successful, they increase their livestock and the grass is eaten faster than can be replenished by nature. Eventually, the grazing ground becomes bare and can no longer feed all the farmers' cattle. Everyone suffers in the end. The tragedy of the commons is an intriguing concept as the farmers are not doing anything wrong. They are all trying to maximize their individual economic benefit by tapping on a shared natural resource, which depletes at an alarming rate in the long term. The way to address such a resource issue would be for the farmers to work out conservation and rationing practices among themselves or rely on an impartial entity, such as an industry association or the government, to set out the rules and enforcement procedures.

From a company's perspective, there could be real dilemmas in striving toward both financial performance and social good. Edwards[21] identified three conflicts between these corporate objectives. First, there is the issue of prioritization and trade-offs. An example is the sharing economy concept that reduces the use of resources and creates a more equitable society. However, this would go against the grain of a market economy that promotes unbridled competition and consumption. The second conflict is that financial performance usually takes precedence over social good. Edwards[21] cited the example of so-called impact investors that invest in businesses with a social focus, such as serving the bottom-of-the-pyramid consumers in less-developed countries. However, impact investors still need to make a financial return, which in turn limits what they can support, especially business ideas that are strong in generating community benefits but weak in monetization. Edwards[21] pointed out an interesting asymmetry between doing good and doing well, which is that there may not be a need to sacrifice financial returns to achieve a positive social impact, yet there is a need to sacrifice social returns for profit maximization. An example to illustrate this insight could be a bakery that employs persons with disabilities (PWDs). In good times, the bakery would be willing to invest in training and coaching to bring the PWD workers up to speed so that they are as productive as the other workers. However, in uncertain times, the bakery may be disinclined to recruit and retain PWD workers to reduce operating costs, which would hurt the employability of PWDs.

The third conflict is that doing good and doing well may not be interchangeable mechanisms. Edwards[21] mentioned that humanistic endeavors such as health, education, politics, civil society, and the arts should be driven primarily by shared values and not by either market economics or self-interest. There is also the issue of expertise. Most companies' core competencies are in developing and selling products and services. This may not translate directly into the ability to do good unless the social efforts are in a related area, such as an IT training company that sets aside some of its trainers' teaching hours to conduct pro bono classes for the underprivileged.

The Relationship between Doing Good and Doing Well

This section expounds on what has been discussed about the relationship between doing good and doing well. Empirically, there is a correlation between CSR and financial performance. Although it cannot be concluded that investments in CSR will result in better corporate performance, there are sound functional reasons to look for synergies between doing good and doing well.[17] Socially responsible companies are more likely to build a well-accepted brand, a cohesive ethos, and a culture of innovation, which are qualities that can help a company stand out from its competition. However, there can be external and internal dilemmas and trade-offs between doing good and doing well. Given that companies are commercially driven entities first and foremost, they would prioritize economic surpluses over social good, and they may not necessarily be the best agents to effect social improvements. Furthermore, as the tragedy of the commons has illustrated, companies' narrow and short-term self-interest may lead to overuse of common and public resources, which eventually would hurt the collective good.

Table 1 summarizes and reframes the discussion into a company-centric matrix that would be of interest to business leaders, researchers,

Table 1:   Company-centric matrix between doing good and doing well.

	Doing Social Good	Not Doing Social Good
Business doing well	This is the sweet spot from the company's and society's perspectives. The company should try to sustain and improve upon the current situation.	The company has the financial resources to do good, and may not be doing so because of a lack of knowledge or interest in social responsibility. This is where internal and external nudges, such as a CSR champion from within the ranks or government regulations, can lead to positive change.
Business not doing well	This is a common situation among social enterprises, which are businesses that aim to balance profit and social objectives. While the social enterprise can be doing good, the business model may not be robust. In this case, the social enterprise should review its mission or look for government or philanthropic grants to support its socially focused activities.	This is the least tenable situation for any company. If it is neither financially viable nor serving a social purpose, it is questionable whether the enterprise can operate as a going concern. There would be an urgent need to reboot the business model.

teachers, and students. The relationship between doing good and doing well is multi-faceted. Each box in the matrix can refer to the whole business or a specific initiative at a certain point in time. What is important from a company's perspective is to be aware of the context, explore the options for improvements, and make a decision based on desired outcomes.

The Road Ahead

While a business's raison d'être is to provide products and services to the market and aim to make a financial surplus, there are certain social expectations, norms, and rules governing what commercial entities can do, cannot do, should do, and should not do. This is a truism since the early days when companies started to have their own legal status. Going forward, one can expect greater scrutiny of the role of companies in society because of three trends — an age of extremes; science, technology, engineering, and mathematics (STEM) as drivers of large-scale environmental solutions; and information technology (IT) as a means for companies to manage their environmental and social responsibilities better.

The world is living in an age of extremes. Due to cumulative greenhouse gas emissions generated by industries, particularly in the Western nations, the average global temperature on Earth has risen by at least 1.1 °C since 1880. One degree might not seem much to the layman, but it is certainly enough to unleash extreme weather effects everywhere. As argued by Huq and Adow,[22] it is the poorer communities in the Global South, i.e., less economically developed countries located south of the Equator, that are bearing the brunt of the climate crisis. The heat wave in India and Pakistan in May 2022 destroyed wheat harvests, threatened the safety of laborers working outdoor, and subjected millions to heat-related stress and even death. Most developing countries lack infrastructure, resources, and disaster recovery systems to help their people cope as the world continues to warm.

The environmental extremes are mirrored in the social extremes of inequality. Oxfam International,[23] a United Kingdom charitable organization, reported that the top 1 percent have captured nearly 20 times more of global wealth than the bottom 50 percent of humanity since 1995. The increasing wealth of the uber-rich has been enabled by globalization and the dominance of multinational corporations in global markets, deregulation, and privatization, as well as ramping up of financial markets and asset prices. Emissions are related to social equality in that high-income countries tend to produce and consume more, which result in concomitant higher resource utilization and emission footprint compared to low-income countries. In an earlier 'Confronting Carbon Inequality' statement published in 2020,[24] Oxfam International found that between 1990 and 2015, the richest 10 percent accounted for over half (52 percent) of the emissions added to the atmosphere, which is two times more than that added by the poorest half of humanity (7 percent).

Thomas Malthus (1766–1834), an English scholar, predicted that the geometrical growth of population over time would outstrip the arithmetic growth in food production because of limited land, which could lead to mass hunger and eventually limit population growth to subsistence levels. This Malthusian theory was proven wrong in the years after the Second World War when new agricultural technologies such as new breeds of hardy and high-yield crops, pesticides, and fertilizers were invented and deployed globally. This was when the Green Revolution started in the 1960s,[25] which led to a quantum leap in food production — such as a tripling in the harvesting of cereal crops with only a 30 percent increase in the amount of land used, which in turn supported growth of the global population from 3 billion in 1960 to 5 billion in 1987.

The Green Revolution is cited as a seminal example of how STEM has played a major role in addressing mankind's big challenges. Climate change is arguably the most pressing existential challenge in the 21st century, and people would need everything that STEM has to offer. The Intergovernmental Panel on Climate Change (IPCC), a body of the United Nations that provides regular scientific assessments on climate change, published a report[26] in April 2022 on the mitigation of climate change. The report identified options that would have the highest contribution to net emission reduction. This included wind energy, solar energy, carbon absorption and storage in soil organic matter, protection of forests and other ecosystems, new buildings with high energy efficiency, and switching from fossil fuels to bio-fuels and other less emission-intensive fuels. The IPCC report made it clear that the technologies for effective climate action are already available. What is needed is for governments to play an active regulator and promoter role, such as setting a carbon price and providing efficiency incentives to nudge companies to decarbonize; companies to move toward a carbon-free future not only as a means to do well, but also to build organizational resilience for the long haul; and increased public and private investment into research, development, and deployment of carbon reduction technologies and solutions.

The third trend is how IT can enable companies to do better in doing good, particularly in managing their carbon emissions.[27] One challenge faced by many companies is the difficulty in monitoring their carbon emissions over time. The most commonly used approach is to track activity data such as mileage clocked by the company vehicles, electricity consumed at the offices and factories, and air mileage traveled by company executives. Using publicly available emission factors published by governments and other authoritative bodies, companies can convert their activity data into estimated emissions. For instance, the Energy Market Authority of Singapore publishes and updates the Grid Emission Factor (GEF) annually,[28] which measures the average CO_2 emissions emitted per MWh of electricity generated by the local power stations. The GEF for 2020 is 0.4080 kg CO_2/kWh. If a small business consumes 60,000 kWh of electricity annually, that is equivalent to 24,480 kg of CO_2 emitted at the power stations that generate and supply the electricity. Taking into account the assumption that a mature tree absorbs 22 kg of CO_2 annually, 1,100 trees would be required to sequester the company's emissions. This is where technologies such as Internet of Things (IOT) and Artificial Intelligence (AI) — whereby devices and equipment have sensors and processing software that can communicate real-time data, trends, and even anticipate failures — so that companies are well-informed to improve efficiency as well as lower costs and emissions. For instance, temperature and infrared occupancy sensors can be used to optimize thermal comfort and energy usage in buildings. The availability of data can also facilitate the setting and tracking of energy targets.

Big data, which involve "techniques to capture, process, analyze, and visualize large datasets in a rapid timeframe",[29] has enabled scientists, policymakers, and corporate executives to understand how changes in environmental variables — such as temperature fluctuations, rainfall, and humidity — can have micro and macro consequences. Governments and NGOs can use sensors and satellite imaging to track the health of forest ecosystems and their susceptibility to changing weather patterns over time. Multinational corporations committed to sustainability in their supply chains are using geospatial and real-time transport data to track where their raw materials come from and whether post-use products are adequately recycled or disposed of. Companies are also making use of meteorological data and trends to assess the physical risks posed by extreme weather to their brick-and-mortar operations around the world. Such risk assessments would allow companies to make appropriate mitigation plans, such as spreading out their manufacturing across a few locations rather than concentrating everything on a single physical plant.

Even the United Nations (UN)[30] is looking at the use of big data to help achieve the Sustainable Development Goals (SDGs) — such as tracking of online food prices to monitor real-time food security and progress toward SDG 2 of Zero Hunger, and water pump sensors to track access to clean water as part of SDG 6 on Clean Water and Sanitation. The UN aims to lead data usage for sustainable development in three ways — promoting innovation to fill data gaps, reducing the inequalities between data-poor and data-rich countries, and playing a coordination role across different stakeholders. The UN acknowledges that big data often sit with the private sector and is working toward "data philanthropy" whereby companies' data can be shared pro bono for philanthropic and humanitarian purposes. This includes a partnership with the social media giant Twitter as the millions of tweets circulating the world daily are a rich depository of people's experiences and concerns on social and environmental issues such as food costs, healthcare access, and natural disasters.

However, while big data and IT can certainly help companies become more efficient, there is growing concern about the environmental footprint of global computing. Freitag *et al.*[31] highlighted that previous estimates of IT's share of global emissions at 1.8–2.8 percent do not account for the full life-cycle and supply chain impacts of IT products and infrastructure. The researchers argued that a more accurate estimate for the sector would be 2.1–3.9 percent of global emissions. The growth in demand for computation-intensive products and services such as cryptocurrencies, blockchain, and cyber gaming has outstripped equipment efficiency such that overall emissions have increased. The researchers suggested that there needs to be greater transparency in terms of the technology giants' emission disclosures and target setting. Furthermore, industry self-regulation may be insufficient to put the sector on a realistic pathway to net-zero emissions by 2050. Beyond generating emissions, the IT sector is also a major contributor to global waste. According to a United Nations' press release in 2019,[32] the world produces approximately 50 million tonnes of electronic and electrical waste (e-waste) a year, which weighs more than all of the commercial airliners ever made. Yet, only 20 percent is formally recycled.

Conclusion

From the Roman times to the modern day, doing good and doing well have been common mantras for companies because of the indispensable role of commercial entities in producing goods and services in all societies and the expectations that companies have certain social responsibilities. Doing well is an essential goal for all businesses, otherwise they will not survive for long. However, while doing good at the same time is something desirable, it is neither easy nor a given. There can be trade-offs when companies have to deliberate between financial performance and sacrificing some of the dollars and cents for what is socially sensible. Furthermore, the summation of companies' market activities could have negative unintended consequences, such as depletion of natural resources and pollution, which could be externalities that companies are not aware of or that are not directly priced into the market transactions.

The prevailing social context has a material bearing on companies' social responsibilities. The terrible working conditions during the Industrial Revolution galvanized workers to speak up and rally together, governments to regulate, and eventually companies to respond in cleaning up their act and improving what was produced in the factory floors. Climate change and social inequality are arguably the most salient global issues of the current day. A case can be made that major companies have contributed negatively to these challenges. In 2019, the Climate Accountability Institute — an American non-profit research and educational institute — published data[33] showing that the top 20 fossil fuel companies had contributed 480 billion tonnes of carbon dioxide and methane collectively, mainly from the combustion of their products, which is equivalent to 35 percent of all fossil fuel and cement emissions worldwide since 1965. A separate study of the top 300 companies in the United States published by the Institute for Policy Studies[34] found that the average ratio between CEO and median worker pay increased from 604-to-1 in 2020 to 670-to-1 in 2021. Furthermore, the median worker's pay did not keep up with inflation in more than a third of the surveyed companies. Going forward, as the impacts of climate change and global inequality become more adverse and pressing, companies in many jurisdictions can expect greater regulatory oversight, reporting and compliance, as well as pressures from customers, investors, and the public to invest more in environmental protection and social amelioration.

Importantly, STEM and IT hold many promises for companies and governments to deal with climate change, pollution, biodiversity loss, and other environmental problems. However, as researchers from Lancaster University pointed out in 2020,[35] the idea that technological solutions — such as carbon capture and storage for pollutive industries and sustainable aviation fuel for the aviation sector — are a silver bullet to heal all of our ecological woes could have downsides in terms of downplaying any sense of urgency, delaying deadlines for climate action, and undermining company commitments to reduce emissions. Despite the Paris Climate Agreement and numerous corporate pledges to reduce emissions to net zero, the world is still in the danger zone. This is evident by the International Energy Agency (IEA)'s March 2022 announcement[36] that global emissions rebounded after the COVID-19 pandemic to their highest level ever in 2021. Furthermore, the American National Oceanic and Atmospheric Administration (NOAA)'s measurements[37] showed carbon dioxide levels continuing to rise and that current levels of above 400 parts per million (ppm) are comparable to what was last observed between

4.1 and 4.5 million years ago when sea levels were between 5 and 25 meters higher than today. At the company level, advancements in technology can help companies monitor and improve their operational efficiency, use of resources, and reporting. However, the flip side of disruptive technology and the increasing popularity of cloud-based IT services is that emissions and physical waste footprint are growing, which need to be urgently looked into by the IT sector, corporate customers, and regulators.

In conclusion, the relationship between doing good and doing well is multi-faceted from the internal company-centric and external stakeholders-centric perspectives. Notwithstanding the challenges, organizations should continue to explore, advocate, and grow the area of convergence between corporate financial performance and social responsibility as that would be a transformational step toward environmental and social sustainability as well as organizational resilience. More research into this subject, particularly in the Singaporean and Asian context, would be timely in helping companies and policymakers make informed, contextual, and sensible decisions for the corporate and greater good.

References

1. SEC Newgate. (2021). ESG Monitor 2021 — Singapore Report. Cited 22 Aug 2022. Available from https://www.secnewgateesgmonitor.com/wp-content/uploads/2021/10/SEC-Newgate-ESG-Monitor-2021-Singapore-Report.pdf.
2. World Bank Group. (2013). IFC Jobs Study: Assessing Private Sector Contributions to Job Creation and Poverty Reduction. Cited 22 Aug 2022. Available from https://openknowledge.worldbank.org/handle/10986/16979.
3. Paterson, J. L. (2013). The development of the concept of corporation from earliest Roman times to A.D. 476. *The Accounting Historians Journal*, Spring, *10*(1), 87–98.
4. Rafferty, J. P. The Rise of the Machines: Pros and Cons of the Industrial Revolution. *Encyclopedia Britannica*. Cited 22 Aug 2022. Available from https://www.britannica.com/story/the-rise-of-the-machines-pros-and-cons-of-the-industrial-revolution.
5. The National Archives, United Kingdom. 1833 Factory Act. Cited 22 Aug 2022. Available from https://www.nationalarchives.gov.uk/education/resources/1833-factory-act/.
6. UK Parliament. The 1833 Factory Act. Cited 22 Aug 2022. Available from https://www.parliament.uk/about/living-heritage/transformingsociety/livinglearning/19thcentury/overview/factoryact/.

7. Ledecky, M. Corporate social responsibility: Past, present, and future. Cited 22 Aug 2022. Available from https://everfi.com/blog/community-engagement/csr-history.
8. Vergun, D. (2020). During WWII, Industries Transitioned From Peacetime to Wartime Production. U.S. Department of Defense. Cited 22 Aug 2022. Available from https://www.defense.gov/News/Feature-Stories/story/Article/2128446/during-wwii-industries-transitioned-from-peacetime-to-wartime-production/.
9. Mason, J. W. (2017). The economy during wartime. *Dissent Magazine*. Cited 22 Aug 2022. Available from https://www.dissentmagazine.org/article/second-world-war-economy-mark-wilson-destructive-creation-review.
10. Bowen, H. R. (2013). *Social Responsibilities of the Businessman*. University of Iowa Press, Iowa City, Iowa, pp. 6–12. Available from https://books.google.com.sg/books?id=ALIPAwAAQBAJ&lpg=PT5&ots=da4fNerqsp&dq=social+responsibilities+of+the+businessman&lr=&pg=PP1&redir_esc=y#v=onepage&q&f=false.
11. United Nations. Do you know all 17 SDGs? Cited 22 Aug 2022. Available from https://sdgs.un.org/goals.
12. United Nations. (1987). Our Common Future, Report of the World Commission on Environment and Development. Cited 22 Aug 2022. Available from https://www.are.admin.ch/dam/are/en/dokumente/nachhaltige_entwicklung/dokumente/bericht/our_common_futurebrundtlandreport1987.pdf.download.pdf/our_common_futurebrundtlandreport1987.pdf.
13. United Nations. (2006). Secretary-General Launches 'Principles for Responsible Investment' Backed by World's Largest Investors. Cited 22 Aug 2022. Available from https://press.un.org/en/2006/sg2111.doc.htm.
14. Bansal, T., & DesJardine, M. (Jan/Feb, 2015). Don't Confuse Sustainability With CSR. *Ivey Business Journal*. Available from https://iveybusinessjournal.com/dont-confuse-sustainability-with-csr/.
15. Sheehy, B., & Farneti, F. (2021). Corporate social responsibility, sustainability, sustainable development and corporate sustainability: What is the difference, and does it matter? *Sustainability*. Available from https://www.mdpi.com/2071-1050/13/11/5965.
16. Awaysheh, A., Heron, R. A., Perry, T., & Wilson, J. I. (2020). On the relation between CSR and financial performance. *Strategic Management Journal*, *41*(6), 965–987.
17. Kanter, R. M. (2010). How to do well and do good. *MIT Sloan Management Review* (Fall).
18. Mehrpouya, A. (2022). Why "doing well by doing good" is not as simple as they say. *Knowledge@HEC*. Available from https://www.hec.edu/en/knowledge/articles/why-doing-well-doing-good-not-simple-they-say.

19. Emanuel, E. J. (2019). Big Pharma's Go-To Defense of Soaring Drug Prices Doesn't Add Up. Cited 22 Aug 2022. Available from https://www.the atlantic.com/health/archive/2019/03/drug-prices-high-cost-research-and-development/585253/.
20. Hardin, G. (1968). The tragedy of the commons. *Science, 162*, 1243–1248.
21. Edwards, M. (2015). Why it's time to say goodbye to 'doing good and doing well'. *openDemocracy*. Cited 22 Aug 2022. Available from https://www.opendemocracy.net/en/transformation/why-it-s-time-to-say-goodbye-to-doing-good-and-doing-well/.
22. Huq, S., & Adow, M. (2022). Climate change is devastating the Global South. *Al Jazeera*. Cited 22 Aug 2022. Available from https://www.aljazeera.com/opinions/2022/5/11/climate-change-is-devastating-the-global-south.
23. Oxfam International. (2022). Inequality Kills Report. Cited 22 Aug 2022. Available from https://oxfamilibrary.openrepository.com/bitstream/handle/10546/621341/bp-inequality-kills-170122-en.pdf.
24. Oxfam International. (2020). Confronting Carbon Inequality. Cited 22 Aug 2022. Available from https://oxfamilibrary.openrepository.com/bitstream/handle/10546/621052/mb-confronting-carbon-inequality-210920-en.pdf.
25. John, D. A., & Babu, G. R. (Feb 22, 2021). Lessons from the aftermaths of green revolution on food system and health. *Frontiers in Sustainable Food Systems*. Available from https://www.frontiersin.org/articles/10.3389/fsufs.2021.644559/full.
26. Intergovernmental Panel on Climate Change. (2022). Climate Change 2022: Mitigation of Climate Change. Cited 22 Aug 2022. Available from https://www.ipcc.ch/report/ar6/wg3/.
27. Avelar, L. (2021). How can technology help combat climate change. *World Economic Forum*. Cited 22 Aug 2022. Available from https://www.weforum.org/agenda/2021/07/fight-climate-change-with-technology/.
28. Energy Market Authority. Singapore Energy Statistics. Cited 22 Aug 2022. Available from https://www.ema.gov.sg/singapore-energy-statistics/Ch02/index2.
29. Runting, R. K., Phinn, S., Xie, Z. *et al.* (2020). Opportunities for big data in conservation and sustainability. *Nature Communications*, 11, 2003. Available from https://www.nature.com/articles/s41467-020-15870-0.
30. United Nations. Big Data for Sustainable Development. Cited 22 Aug 2022. Available from https://www.un.org/en/global-issues/big-data-for-sustainable-development.
31. Freitag, C. *et al.* (Sep 10, 2021). The real climate and transformative impact of ICT: A critique of estimates, trends, and regulations. *Patterns*, 2(9). Available from https://www.sciencedirect.com/science/article/pii/S2666389921001884.

32. United Nations. (2019). UN report: Time to seize opportunity, tackle challenge of e-waste. Cited 22 Aug 2022. Available from https://www.unep.org/news-and-stories/press-release/un-report-time-seize-opportunity-tackle-challenge-e-waste.

33. Climate Accountability Institute. (2019). Carbon Majors: Update of Top Twenty companies 1965-2017. Cited 22 Aug 2022. Available from https://climateaccountability.org/pdf/CAI%20PressRelease%20Top20%20Oct19.pdf.

34. Institute for Policy Studies. Executive Excess 2022. Cited 22 Aug 2022. Available from https://ips-dc.org/wp-content/uploads/2022/06/report-executive-excess-2022.pdf.

35. Lancaster University. (Apr 20, 2020). Why relying on new technology won't save the planet. *Science Daily*. Cited 22 Aug 2022. Available from https://www.sciencedaily.com/releases/2020/04/200420125510.htm.

36. International Energy Agency. (2022). Global CO_2 emissions rebounded to their highest level in history in 2021. Cited 22 Aug 2022. Available from https://www.iea.org/news/global-co2-emissions-rebounded-to-their-highest-level-in-history-in-2021.

37. National Oceanic and Atmospheric Administration. (2022). Carbon dioxide now more than 50% higher than pre-industrial levels. Cited 22 Aug 2022. Available from https://www.noaa.gov/news-release/carbon-dioxide-now-more-than-50-higher-than-pre-industrial-levels.

Chapter 10

Circular Business Models for Sustainable Growth

⌇

Seyed Mehdi Zahraei

The Linear Economy

Traditional industrial processes adopt a linear economy following a "take, make, use, dispose" process. In such an economy, raw materials and resources are extracted or mined and turned into products by applying energy and labor to be sold to consumers, who discard them after being used or consumed, as illustrated in Figure 1. In such an economy, value is created by producing and selling as many products as possible.

When products are discarded, the resources such as energy, labor, and knowledge invested in producing them will be wasted. Weetman[1] argues that the linear economy emerged as resources were deemed abundant and cheap and it relies on organizations striving to sell more by cutting costs, producing short life-cycle products, and encouraging consumers to buy the latest version of products. Furthermore, according to Mont *et al.*[2] consumers use many products inefficiently, which leads to products being discarded with underutilized functional potential. The authors believe it is because of the businesses' historical orientation on increasing manufacturing productivity and decreasing production costs rather than improving consumption efficiency and resource recovery from post-consumer waste.

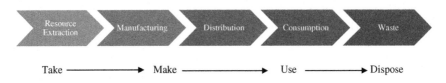

Figure 1:   Linear economy.

The Linear Economy Challenges

Although the linear economy has generated substantial growth, it has led to constraints on the availability of natural resources, the generation of waste, and environmental degradation. Brears[3] identified a comprehensive list of challenges from the linear economy. Table 1 summarizes some of these challenges.

From Linear to Circular

The linear economy model relies on unrestrained quantities of easily accessible energy and resources, making it more and more untenable as energy and resources are finite.[10] New ideas and alternative ways to evolve such production and consumption systems are needed. One such alternative is the circular economy, in which products do not simply become waste but are transformed into valuable resources that create sustainable business opportunities. In such an economy, growth is decoupled from resource consumption and materials are kept within productive use for as long as possible and are effectively looped back into the system once they reach the end of use.[10]

The Ellen MacArthur Foundation[10] characterized the circular economy as an economy that is restorative and regenerative by design and aims to keep products, components, and materials at their highest utility and value at all times. The Foundation considered three principles for a circular economy. First, *designing out waste and pollution*. That is, rather than focusing on recovering waste and exploring what to do with it; the mindset should be shifted to avoid generating waste in the first place. Second, *keeping products and materials in use* by designing for durability, reuse, sharing, remanufacturing, and recycling. Third, *regenerate the natural ecosystem* by avoiding using non-renewable resources and returning valuable nutrients to the biosphere.

Table 1:   Linear economy challenges.

Challenges	Description
Economic Growth	It is projected that the world economy will grow by 3 percent per annum over 2014–2050, doubling in size by 2037 and almost tripling by 2050.[4] If the global economy continues its linear resource consumption, by 2050, the world will need the equivalent of two planets for sustenance.[5]
Changing Consumption Patterns	A rise in income level will change individuals spending patterns. For instance, it is estimated that the share of emerging markets in total global clothing demand will rise from 35 percent in 2012 to 57 percent in 2050. Similarly, demand for housing, furniture, smartphones, tablets, and smart TVs will increase with rising income levels.
Raw Material Scarcity and Price Volatility	Due to economic growth and rising income levels worldwide, higher natural resource extraction is needed to cope with the rising demand for products. Around 90 billion tons of natural resources are extracted yearly, and the number is estimated to double by 2050. Shortages of resources coupled with their volatile prices will result in economic and social challenges that may undermine peace and security.[6]
Population Growth and Rapid Urbanization	The world's population is projected to reach 9.8 billion in 2050 out of which around 68 percent will live in urban areas, as opposed to today's rate of 54 percent. Rapid urbanization combined with population increase will result in depletion of land used for vegetation, alteration of surface water flows, increased energy consumption, and an increase in waste.
Water Degradation	By 2050, global water demand will outstrip supply by 55 percent, mainly due to a significant increase in demand from manufacturing processes, electricity,[7] and domestic water use. Around 80 percent of the world's wastewater is released into the environment without treatment, resulting in a polluted marine environment.
Waste	The world generates 2.01 billion tonnes of municipal solid waste annually. The figure is projected to grow to 3.40 billion tonnes by 2050 due to the economic and population growth discussed above.[8]
Air Pollution	The World Health Organization estimates that 99 percent of the global population breathes contaminated air that exceeds safe limits, accounting for about 6.5 million deaths yearly.[9] The extensive economic activity in growing urban areas results in higher pollution levels and greater exposure.
Climate Change	Climate change could significantly harm the economy in various forms, including climate disasters like hurricanes, changes in crop yields, and loss of land and natural resources from rising sea levels, to name a few. It is estimated that by 2060, the combined negative effect on global annual GDP could be between 1 and 3 percent under a business-as-usual emissions scenario.

Source: Adapted from Brears.[3]

The circular economy concept can be represented by the *Circular Economy Systems Diagram*, developed by the Ellen MacArthur Foundation,[11] which illustrates the continuous flow of biological and technical materials through the system to minimize systematic leakage and negative externalities. In such a system, resources are recovered and restored in the technical cycles, or regenerated in the bio-cycles, as shown in Figure 2.

In a circular economy, technical materials (such as fossil fuels, minerals, metals, and plastics) circulate within technical cycles that recover and restore products using various technologies and business models. The technical material loops, from the most to least preferred in terms of process value and energy consumption, include the following:

- **Maintenance,** the smallest loop of the technical cycle, aims to maintain and repair during use to expand the products' lifespan for as long as possible. One example would be the *iFixit* website, which teaches users how to fix electronic devices, encouraging repair instead of discarding faulty products.[12]

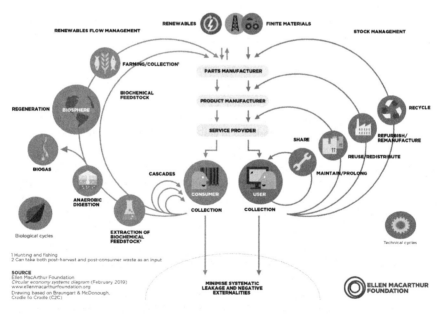

Figure 2:   The circular economy systems diagram.

Source: Copyright © Ellen MacArthur Foundation, (,) (Circular economy system diagram, 2019[11]).

- **Reuse/Redistribute** loop encourages direct reuse by remarketing a product via sharing, renting, or reselling them as many times as possible to prevent the need to create new products. For instance, *Khilonewala* is an online toy library in India with over 3,000 products providing rental services for toys, books, and games.[13] Another example is the *Singapore Freecycle Network,* which facilitates the re-use of items (i.e., computers, furniture, clothing, etc.) via donation to keep them out of the landfill and reduce waste.[14]
- **Refurbish/remanufacture** loop focuses on restoring value in a product that is not yet ready to be reused. Note that refurbishing deals more with making the aesthetics of the product look like-new again, while remanufacturing entails a more thorough process of repairing and assembling the parts so that the product functions like new. For instance, *Caterpillar* remanufactures its industrial equipment at the end of their serviceable life to same-as-new condition with a like-new machine warranty sold at a fraction of the cost.[15]
- **Recycle** loop is the least preferred option as it has a lower value process and consumes more energy. Recycling often entails spending resources and energy to deconstruct the product into small parts or its basic material level, and then again to spend resources and energy generating a new product. For instance, *Green Toys* sells children's toys made from recycled plastic milk jugs and other recycled plastic forms.[16]

Biological materials (such as water, food, wood, corn starch, etc.) are to circulate within biological cycles aiming to regenerate renewable resources and avoid negative externalities through the following ways:

- *Cascades*: In the biological cycle, reuse occurs in cascades where products are used for another application with lower quality (e.g., from solid wood to chipboard for furniture). Energy recovery should be the last option after higher-value products have been used up.
- *Extraction of biochemical feedstock* means producing biofuels (i.e., biodiesel, ethanol, green diesel, and biogas) and high value biochemicals in biorefineries using both post-harvest and post-consumer biological materials.
- *Aerobic composting* decomposes biological materials using microorganisms (such as fungi) into moist humus that returns nutrients to the soil, in the presence of oxygen. In contrast, *anaerobic digestion* is a process in an oxygen-free environment where microorganisms

decompose biodegradable material into biogas anaerobically. For instance, *The Magic Factory*, a biogas plant in Norway, uses food waste and livestock manure as resources to produce biogas.[17]

- **Return to the biosphere**: Biodegradable products are designed to decompose in the biosphere (air, water, or soil) without a negative impact. An example is *Freitag*, a Swiss company that produces biodegradable jeans.[18]
- **Farming and collection**: apart from generating biofuels and compost, farming and agricultural waste can be upcycled to create yeasts and other valuable nutrients to re-enter the production system. For instance, *Comet Bio* is a company that converts farm waste into a variety of bio-materials, including sweeteners and nutritional supplements.[19]

Benefits and Barriers of Adopting a Circular Economy

A transition toward the circular economy results in a more resilient, innovative, and productive economy.[20] Decoupling economic growth from resource consumption is the major economic benefit of adopting a circular economy. It has the potential to reduce the usage of raw materials and resources, optimize agricultural productivity while regenerating ecosystems, and decrease and, in some cases, eliminate the negative externalities and challenges arising from the linear economy model discussed in Table 1. Many social aspects would also be improved, including the development of resilient cities which provide healthier spaces for citizens to live in.[19]

The Ellen MacArthur Foundation[21] summarized the main advantages of adopting a circular economy as follows: increased economic development; extensive net material savings; reduced exposure to price volatility; increased innovation and job creation; and increased resilience in living systems and the economy.

Despite all these benefits and advantages, there are still various barriers in adopting a circular economy. Badhotiya *et al.*[22] conducted a detailed analysis of the barriers to adopting a circular economy, including social and policy, economic, and environmental barriers, as summarized in Table 2. The main social and policy barriers pertain to changing the habits and mindsets of consumers and the heterogeneous waste management regulations and policies. The high upfront investment for new

Table 2:   Barriers in adopting a circular economy.

Category	Barriers
Social and policy barriers	• Low demand and acceptance of remanufactured or recycled products • Lack of government support and legislation • Lack of top management commitment • Lack of a standard system for measuring performance • Heterogeneous waste management regulations and environmental policies • Lack of knowledge and qualified personnel • Lack of design tools for circular business models and products • Associated risk in transitioning from the linear to the circular economy • Difficulties in sorting products for reuse or recycling • Lack of thinking systematically about the impacts of individuals
Economic barriers	• High upfront investment costs and long-term economic return • Lack of appropriate partners and complexity in supply chains • High cost of establishing eco-industrial chains • Informal sector recycling processes • Need for advanced technologies and facilities • Low virgin material prices • High cost of eco-friendly material
Environmental barriers	• Lack of environmental laws and regulations • Lack of incentives to promote greener activities • Lack of availability of land for waste recovery and recycling • Low-tech waste resource management systems • Lack of adequate technologies used in landfilling and disposal methods • Safety and hygiene issues

Source: Adapted from Badhotiya *et al.*[22]

technologies and business models coupled with the uncertain return of investment are the main economic barriers. For a successful transition into a circular economy, it is essential to acknowledge, reflect upon, and overcome these barriers. In addition, it is important to note that these barriers are also an opportunity for improvement and change.

Business Models for a Circular Economy

A business model, in general, describes how an organization creates, captures, and delivers value. In other words, it is concerned with an organization's competitive strategy. Circular business models help transform linear approaches of production and consumption into circular ones to minimize or eliminate waste, externalities, and inefficiencies.[23] Five circular business models, namely *Circular Supplies*, *Product Use Extension*, *Resource Recovery*, *Product as a Service*, and *Sharing Platforms*, are discussed in what follows:

Circular Supplies

Circular Supplies, also known as "Circular Inputs", is one of the most adopted circular business models by organizations. It involves the replacement of traditional production inputs with circular alternatives such as bio-based, renewable, or recovered materials enabling partial or total elimination of waste and pollution. For instance, about 35 percent of the energy used by *Arla*, a Danish-Swedish dairy company, comes from renewable sources.[24] *Arla* also re-uses water by cleaning in its own water treatment plants. Note that implementing this business model influences the conceptualization of the product design and the manufacturing process, and affects product branding and distribution channels.[25]

Product Use Extension

This type of business models extend the life of products using design considerations, repairs, component reconditioning, upgrades, and resale, to name a few.[25] This is desirable from a circular economy point of view as products and their materials remain in the economy for longer, leading to a reduction in the extraction of new resources. OECD[25] classified product life extension models into four sub-types: classic long life, direct reuse, maintenance and repair, and refurbishment and remanufacturing, as shown in Table 3.

Lacy *et al.*[23] argue that one advantage of the Product Life Extension model is that it does not require extensive changes to an organization's existing business model but rather an extension of business capabilities or market channels where new revenue streams can be generated through resale. Examples include the resale of used items by *H&M*, *IKEA*, and *Patagonia*.

Table 3: Product life extension models.

Models	Characteristics
Classic long life	Extending product life-cycle through changes in product design.
Direct reuse	Redistributing and reusing products to ensure they attain their intended service life.
Maintenance and repair	To allow degraded products to reach their full expected life by fixing or replacing defective components.
Refurbishment and remanufacturing	To give products a new life by restoring them to their original working condition.

Source: Adapted from OECD.[25]

Product as a Service

In the Product as a Service business model, the provider typically retains ownership of the product throughout the entire lifecycle, and the products can be used by one or more customers through various arrangements[19]:

- **Pay per Period of Time:** Customers pay to access the product for a certain period of time (e.g., renting clothes from RentTheRunway[26]).
- **Leasing:** Similar to renting, however, leasing is usually a long-term commitment while renting is more of a shorter-term commitment.
- **Pay per Usage:** The customer pays for the usage of the service rather than for the period of time (e.g., light-as-a-service by Philips[27]).
- **Product Pooling:** When the product is being simultaneously used by several customers paying for the service. (e.g., carpooling service by BlaBlaCar[28]).

Lacy *et al.*[23] discussed that the Product as a Service model turns the incentive for product durability and upgrading upside-down, shifting organizations' focus from volume (i.e., selling "widgets") to performance (i.e., selling the function of that widget). In addition, organizations can generate additional value by developing long-term relationships with customers, and selling other services, to name a few.

Resource Recovery

This business model focuses on recovering materials from waste streams. Three main activities in Resource Recovery models are *collection* of the waste material, *sorting* (which involves separation of a particular waste stream into its constituent materials), and *secondary production* (by transforming sorted waste material into raw materials). The Resource Recovery business model has several variants[25]:

- **Downcycling:** Transforming waste into secondary raw materials of an inferior quality to be used as an input in a limited subset of applications. For instance, converting crushed concrete from a demolished building into road filler.
- **Upcycling:** Transforming waste into secondary raw materials to be used in relatively high-value applications. For instance, *Yuma Labs*, a Belgian start-up, upcycles plastic waste, like single-use plastic bottles and cups, into high-quality sunglasses.[29]
- **Industrial symbiosis:** Using the production by-products from one firm as production inputs by others. For example, the use of food waste from a catering firm to feed farm animals.

Sharing Platforms

This business model involves using under-utilized assets more intensively, through pooling or lending, enabled by digital technologies and the development of referral and reputational systems — which have reduced the risks associated with sharing assets and their transaction costs.[25] Housing, vehicles, and tools are among the products that often sit unused for much of their effective lives.

Note that the concept is similar to the Product as a Service business model. The difference is that the typical period of usage for sharing platforms is much shorter, and the number of users of assets in a sharing platform is much greater.[30]

According to Lacy *et al.*[23] large organizations are often slower to embrace the Sharing Platforms model as it requires a significant change to their existing business models. In contrast, start-ups are radically disrupting their respective industries (e.g., Grab, Airbnb, Uber).

Technologies Enabling the Circular Economy

Technological advances within the "4th Industrial Revolution" are the leading enablers of circular economy strategies and business models.

These innovative technologies are becoming increasingly affordable and more readily available, opening opportunities to explore solutions that weren't previously viable. Tracking mechanisms, communications systems, and operating models allow for greater product monitoring and increased ability to extend the product lifecycle. For instance, sensors can monitor individual parts of a product to anticipate failure and allow for parts to be replaced at the right time to avoid product downtime or premature disposal.[31]

Lacy et al.[23] have identified 27 key technologies that have a significant role in the transition into a circular economy. They have categorized these technologies into broad areas such as *Digital*, *Physical*, and *Biological*, as shown in Table 4. The authors highlighted that even though all of these technologies have been adopted in the industry, digital technologies have been implemented at a larger scale than physical or biological technologies.

Table 4: Technologies enabling the circular economy.

Category	Definition	Technologies
Digital	Technologies based on computers, electronics, and communication sciences that make use of the increasing volume of information and connectedness of physical resources.	Artificial Intelligence; Machine Learning; Internet of Things; Cloud/Edge; Machine-to-Machine Communication; Machine Vision; Big Data Analytics; Mobile Devices; Blockchain; Digital Anchors; Digital Twin.
Physical	Technologies based on the basic property of materials, energy, forces of nature and their interactions.	3D Printing; Robotics; Energy Storage and Utilization; Energy Harvesting; Nanotechnology; Spectroscopy; Physical Markers; Virtual Reality/Augmented Reality; Carbon Capture, Utilization, and Storage; Materials Science.
Biological	Technologies based on biological aspects such as living organisms and biological systems to create products and produces for specific use.	Bio-energy; Bio-based Material; DNA Marking; Genetic Engineering; Hydroponics and Aeroponics; Cellular and Tissue Engineering.

Source: Adapted from Lacy et al.[23]

In the rest of this chapter, several case studies are provided to highlight the role of some of these innovative technologies in enabling circular business models.

Artificial Intelligence (AI) and Machine Learning (ML)

AI augments human expertise through systems helping to generate insights from big data. Its performance, costs, and accessibility have improved as a result of significant advances in algorithmic development, big data, connectivity, cloud computing, and processing power.[32] ML is an application of AI that enables algorithms and systems to automatically learn and improve to perform new functions. The goal is to learn from data on a certain task to maximize performance. It mainly relies on neural networks and can significantly improve decision-making processes. Some applications of AI and ML within the concept of a circular economy include designing circular products or components, improving resource use, and minimizing waste.

Case 1: AI and ML at Teleplan[33]

Teleplan is an industry leader in lifecycle care solutions for consumer electronics. It plays a key role in mitigating the social and environmental externalities of the global consumer electronics industry. Their expertise is in extending the lifecycle of electronic devices using various innovative services such as returns management, testing and grading, repair and refurbishment, asset recovery, and trade-in and buyback. Sorting and grading used devices is essential for any reuse strategy. Using AI and ML, Teleplan assesses the cosmetic condition of electronic devices, differentiating between a cosmetic feature versus an anomaly such as a scratch or dent to classify used devices more accurately. By doing so, wholesalers would have higher confidence in used devices, leading to support for reuse models. Teleplan also aims to develop a product passport, capturing data points from each product serviced by them. This will be essential in handling returns efficiently and minimizing leakage (as shown in Figure 2). Where reuse or repair is not viable, Teleplan works with accredited recycling partners to maximize the materials re-entering the market as a technical nutrient (via technical loops shown in Figure 2). In 2019, Teleplan processed and made available for reuse a total volume of 23.7 million electronic devices across multiple technologies.

Internet of Things (IoT)

IoT technologies consist of interrelated wireless devices (wearables, machines, etc.) with embedded sensors which can transfer data over a network without needing human interaction. IoT can potentially extend the lifetime of assets and products, reduce their in-use consumption, and help with their effective recovery at end-of-use.[1]

Case 2: IoT at Bundles[34]

Bundles adopted the Product as a Service business model to rent washing machines and charge the users on a pay-per-wash basis, allowing consumers to pay for the performance, not the product. In such a model, Bundles not only takes responsibility for maintenance to increase the lifetime of the appliances but also handles upcycling and repairs of broken appliances to capture the value of the materials used. The performance can be improved using IoT technology to optimize machine load, temperature, cycle duration, and detergent use. The company also has another subscription model called *CoffeeBundles*, which provides "Coffee as a service". Customers subscribe to the use of a high-quality coffee machine including the delivery of coffee beans based on the amount of coffee usage and personal preferences.

Case 3: Rolls Royce's Engine-as-a-Service Model[35]

The Rolls-Royce TotalCare service removes the burden of aircraft engine maintenance from the airlines and cargo carriers and keeps the ownership throughout its life cycle with Rolls-Royce. Rolls-Royce has implemented IoT technologies using thousands of sensors in every single engine. This has enabled Rolls-Royce to execute preventive and predictive maintenance to extend the useful life of engines and optimize resource efficiency by keeping engines flying for longer. This has led to a decrease in demand for new parts and components that require complex materials and are expensive and resource-intensive to manufacture. The large amount of data gathered via IoT technologies can also be used to improve the design of engines for optimal performance and maintenance. Lastly, under the TotalCare service, Rolls-Royce will have access to products and components when they reach the end of their serviceable life. Up to 95 percent of a used aero engine can be recovered and recycled. Around half of the materials recovered are of such high quality they can be safely remanufactured for use as new aerospace components, reducing the need to procure raw materials.

Digital Twin

Digital Twin technologies are virtual representations of actual or potential physical processes or objects enabling organizations to design, visualize, monitor, manage, and maintain their assets more effectively. For instance, *Aden*, an integrated facility management service provider, created a digital twin for one of its commercial centers in Chengdu, China.[36] The virtual twin monitors and analyzes data to plan and execute maintenance and repair activities. The technology would result in about a 20 percent reduction in annual energy consumption.

Case 4: Sanofi's Manufacturing Plant Enabled by Digital Twin Technology[37]

Sanofi's Framingham production facility is a digitally enabled, continuous manufacturing facility where manufacturing processes are controlled through state-of-the-art analytical techniques that forecast and control variations to improve performance and ensure quality. The digitized manufacturing process is about 80 times more productive than a traditional factory and makes medicines in less time for twice the number of patients. This has helped Sanofi to achieve an 80 percent reduction in CO_2 emissions and energy consumption per year, a 94 percent reduction in the use of chemicals, a 91 percent reduction in water footprint, and 321 tons of waste reduction per year.

3D Printing

This technology creates three-dimensional objects from digital models by printing successive layers of material. One of the main potentials of this technology is the 3D printed spare parts that can be used to extend the life of other products. For instance, *Aectual*, a Netherland-based start-up, creates circular and customizable interior furniture & architectural finishes made from bio-based and recycled materials using 3D printing technology.[38]

Energy Storage and Utilization

This technology prolongs the life span of batteries, replaces existing chemical-based raw materials with organic substances, or increases their storage capacity.[23]

Case 5: Renault's Circular Economy Car Factory[39]

In late 2020, Group Renault established *Re-factory*, the first dedicated circular economy factory in Europe for vehicles and mobility devices, in collaboration with an extensive network of partners to support innovation across the entire life-cycle of vehicles and create sustainable, accessible, carbon-free mobility solutions. The goal is to achieve a negative CO_2 balance by 2030. The Re-factory ecosystem is organized around four interconnected and complementary activity centers:

- Re-trofit: Extending the life of vehicles by reconditioning them, converting combustion motor vehicles to less carbon-intensive energy versions, and using 3D printing to manufacture rare parts facilitating the reconditioning process.
- Re-energy: Production, storage, and management of green energies by optimizing the first life of batteries, giving used batteries a second life, and managing end-of-life batteries and the exploration of new energy sources such as hydrogen.
- Re-cycle: Optimizing resource management via dismantling end-of-life vehicles, remanufacturing parts, and reusing and recycling materials.
- Re-start: Enhancing and developing skills and accelerating innovation in the circular economy by hosting an incubator for start-ups and partners and a university and training center.

Carbon Capture, Utilization, and Storage (CCUS)

CCUS captures carbon dioxide (CO_2) from industrial processes (e.g., fossil-fuel power plants) or fuel combustion and transports it via pipeline, ship, rail, or truck to a storage site. The captured CO_2 can be used to create new services or products or be stored deep underground.

Case 6: Boundary Dam Coal CCUS Project[40]

The Boundary Dam CCUS Project, located in Saskatchewan, Canada, is the world's first commercial-scale, post-combustion CCUS project on a coal-fired power plant aiming to make a viable, technical, environmental, and economic case for the continued use of coal. This project transformed an aging coal-fired power unit into a reliable, long-term electricity producer capable of capturing 90 percent of emissions, reducing greenhouse gas emissions by one million tonnes yearly. The CO_2 captured from the coal unit will be injected

(Continued)

Case 6: (*Continued*)

into an oil field nearby to extract more oil from the oil field. Any leftover CO_2 is stored in a saline aquifer (an underground, deep salt-water reservoir). Similar CCUS technology can be scaled and applied to most of the world's coal plants to reduce greenhouse gas emissions from large power sources worldwide.

Bio-based Material

This technology utilizes substances derived from living (or once-living) organisms to create new materials. These substances could include biopolymers and other natural fibers created partially or wholly using plant feedstock.[23]

Case 7: Bamboo Veneer Lumber by Widuz[41]

Widuz, founded in 2019 in Singapore, is developing a new class of renewable and sustainable construction materials called BVL™ (Bamboo Veneer Lumber), a patented high-performance structural composite made from bamboo fibers. BVL™ is up to three times stronger than timber, and unlike timber, BVL™ is not susceptible to decay or degradation and is much more dimensionally stable. Due to its exceptional strength-to-weight ratio and durability, BVL™ is suitable for use as structural elements (e.g., beams, columns, trusses) in the construction of buildings in place of other non-renewable construction materials such as concrete, timber, and steel. BVL™ will help address the supply constraints of construction materials to meet the future global demand for housing and contribute to the transition toward a circular economy using only biobased materials and nature-based solutions. Note that bamboo grows extremely fast and is in abundance in many parts of the world. Besides, bamboo releases 35 percent more oxygen than the equivalent number of trees and can sequester up to 12 tons of carbon dioxide from the air per hectare per year. As a result, through bamboo plantations' development in the long-term and when the harvested bamboos are further turned into BVL™ products, Widuz will be able to contribute more to the mitigation of global greenhouse gas emissions, especially within the construction sector.

Case 8: Unibio[42]

Unibio is a pioneering venture operating in the biotechnology sector with core competencies in fermentation technologies. Its bio-industrial innovations not only enable saving water and energy in a highly sustainable manner but also allow protein production to be decoupled from the volatile agricultural sector and fishing industries. The U-Loop® fermenter is a proprietary continuous-flow microbial fermentation technology converting natural gases, including biogas, into a highly concentrated protein product, Uniprotein®, that can be used as a direct supplement in animal feeds. It can substitute fishmeal, a traditional feed component and an increasingly scarce resource. Uniprotein® makes it possible to reduce deforestation and over-fishing of the oceans, helping to decarbonize the planet.

Case 9: Piñatex [43]

Ananas Anam, the maker of Piñatex, has developed an innovative natural textile made from waste pineapple leaf fiber. These leaves are a by-product of the pineapple harvest, therefore the raw material requires no additional resources to produce, and their use creates an additional income stream for the farming communities. After the pineapple harvest, suitable plant leaves which are left behind are collected in bundles and the long fibers are extracted, washed, and dried. The dried fibers go through a purification process to create fluff-like pineapple leaf fiber to be mixed with a corn-based polylactic acid to create Piñafelt, a non-woven mesh which forms the base of all the Piñatex collections. The rolls of Piñafelt are then shipped by boat from the Philippines to Spain or Italy for specialized finishing. Piñatex is suitable for use across fashion, accessories, and upholstery, and has been used by over 1,000 brands worldwide including Hugo Boss, H&M, and the Hilton Hotel Bankside.

Materials Science

An interdisciplinary field that combines chemistry, engineering, and physics for material innovation. This technology utilizes substances derived from living (or once-living) organisms to create new materials.[23]

Case 10: SEPPURE [44]

SEPPURE, founded in Singapore in 2018, is a clean technology company that has developed innovative chemical-resistant nanofiltration membranes for more sustainable industrial chemical separation processes. Chemical separation processes account for 15 percent of the world's energy consumption and around 10 percent of the world's greenhouse gas emissions. By replacing the industrial-scale thermal distillation with a pressure-driven membrane process, SEPPURE can reduce CO_2 emissions and energy consumption by up to 90 percent. This would result in about a 50 percent deduction in associated operating costs. The company's unique and patented technology results in robust membranes that show exceptional performance such as high selectivity, high solvent permeability, excellent chemical and temperature tolerance, as well as outstanding durability for different applications. SEPPURE's chemical-resistant membrane technology is enabling a circular economy through resource recovery and more energy-efficient industrial separation processes.

Case 11: Close the Loop Group [45]

Close the Loop Group, an Australian-based company, focuses on end-to-end solutions across the creation, collection, recovery, and re-use of materials deemed challenging to recycle and often end up in landfills. In 2018, they managed to recover 39 million pounds of material from landfill; these include soft plastic/flexible packaging, print consumables, cosmetics, eyewear, and phone cases, to name a few. Close the Loop mixes these materials with asphalt and recycled glass to make a road surface that could last up to 65 percent longer than traditional asphalt. The mix uses the equivalent of 168,000 glass bottles, 530,000 plastic bags, and the waste toner from 12,500 printer cartridges in every kilometer of road laid.

Case 12: Dyeing Technology at DyeCoo [46]

DyeCoo, a Netherland-based company, is the global first supplier of chemical and water-free dyeing technology that has proven to be sustainable, clean, efficient, zero-waste, and profitable. It has developed CO_2-based dyeing technology, which uses supercritical CO_2, which has a very high solvent power, to dye the fabrics instead of water or other chemicals in a closed loop system where 95 percent of the CO_2 is re-used through recycling. The technology roughly reduces the usage of 50 million liters of water and 250 kgs of chemicals per 1000 tons of production.

Summary

The linear economy has led to waste generation, environmental degradation, and constraints on the availability of natural resources. Circular business models and strategies can help transform linear approaches of production and consumption into circular ones to minimize or eliminate waste, externalities, and inefficiencies. Technological advances from the 4th Industrial Revolution are the leading enablers of circular economy strategies and business models. Several case studies are provided to emphasize the role of these innovative technologies, such as AI, ML, IoT, digital twin, energy storage and utilization, 3D printings, CCUS, and bio-based materials, in facilitating such a transition into a circular economy. As illustrated in the case studies, these technologies could help in the design of circular products, enhancing manufacturing processes, increasing efficiency, improving data transparency and asset tracking, reducing reliance on resource-intensive materials, and eventually keeping products and materials at their highest utility and value at all times.

References

1. Weetman, C. (2021). A circular economy handbook: How to Build a More Resilient, Competitive and Sustainable Business. KoganPage, London, UK.
2. Mont, O., Plepys, A., Whalen, K., & Nußholz, J. L. K. (2017). Business model innovation for a circular economy: Drivers and barriers for the Swedish industry — The voice of REES companies. *Mistra REES*.
3. Brears, R. C. (2018). *Natural Resources Management and Circular Economy*. Palgrave Macmillan, London, UK.
4. PWC. (2015). The World in 2050: Will the shift in global economic power continue? Available from https://www.pwc.com/gx/en/issues/the-economy/assets/world-in-2050-february-2015.pdf.
5. European Commission. (2011). Roadmap to a resource efficient Europe. Available from http://eur-lex.europa.eu/legal-content/EN/TXT/PDF/?uri= CELEX:52011DC0571&from=EN.
6. Environmental Scarcity and the Outbreak of Conflict. *PRB*. Available from https://www.prb.org/resources/environmental-scarcity-and-the-outbreak-of-conflict/.
7. Understanding the relationship between energy and water. ExxonMobil. Available from https://www.exxonmobil.co.uk/Energy-and-environment/Environmental-protection/Sustainable-water-solutions/Understanding-the-relationship-between-energy-and-water#Wateruseacrossindustries.

8. Trends in Solid Waste Management. The World Bank. Available from https://datatopics.worldbank.org/what-a-waste/trends_in_solid_waste_management.html.

9. Air pollution. World Health Organisation. Available from https://www.who.int/health-topics/air-pollution#tab=tab_1.

10. Ellen MacArthur Foundation. (2013). Towards the Circular Economy. Available from https://www.ellenmacarthurfoundation.org/assets/downloads/publications/Ellen-MacArthur-Foundation-Towards-the-Circular-Economy-vol.1.pdf.

11. Ellen MacArthur Foundation. (2019). The butterfly diagram: Visualising the circular economy. Available from https://ellenmacarthurfoundation.org/circular-economy-diagram.

12. ifixit. Available from www.ifixit.com.

13. Khilonewala. Available from http://khilonewala.in/.

14. Singapore Freecycle Network. Available from https://www.freecycle.org/town/Singapore.

15. Circular Economy. Caterpillar. Available from https://www.caterpillar.com/en/company/sustainability/remanufacturing.html.

16. Green Toys. Available from https://www.greentoys.com/.

17. Fagerström, A., Al Seadi, T., Rasi, S., & Briseid, T. (2018). *The Role of Anaerobic Digestion and Biogas in the Circular Economy*. J. D. Murphy (ed.) IEA Bioenergy Task 37, 2018: 8. Available from https://www.ieabioenergy.com/wp-content/uploads/2018/08/anaerobic-digestion_web_END.pdf.

18. Freitag. Available from https://www.freitag.ch/en.

19. Circular Economy Institute. Circular Economy Specialist Certificate. September 2021.

20. An economic opportunity worth billions — Charting the new territory. The World Bank. Available from https://reports.weforum.org/toward-the-circular-economy-accelerating-the-scale-up-across-global-supply-chains/an-economic-opportunity-worth-billions-charting-the-new-territory/.

21. Ellen MacArthur Foundation. (2016). Intelligent Assets: Unlocking the circular economy potential. Available from https://emf.thirdlight.com/link/1tb7yclizlea-116tst/@/preview/1?o.

22. Badhotiya, G. K., Avikal, S., & Soni, G. (Feb 15, 2022). Analysing barriers for the adoption of circular economy in the manufacturing sector. *International Journal of Productivity and Performance Management, 71*(3), 912–931.

23. Lacy, P., Long, J., & Spindler, W. (2020). *The Circular Economy Handbook, Realizing the Circular Advantages*. Palgrave Macmillan, London, UK.

24. Stronger Planet: Sustainable operations. *Arla Foods*. Available from https://www.arla.com/sustainability/sustainable-operations/.

25. OECD. (2019). *Business Models for the Circular Economy: Opportunities and Challenges for Policy*. OECD Publishing, Paris, Fr.
26. Rent a runway. Available from https://www.renttherunway.com/.
27. Philips' light-as-a-service offering. (Nov 22, 2016). *Smart Cities World News*. Available from https://www.smartcitiesworld.net/news/news/philips-light-as-a-service-offering-1137.
28. BlaBlaCar. Available from https://www.blablacar.co.uk/.
29. Yuma Labs. Available from https://www.yuma-labs.com/about-us.
30. Modak, P. (2021). *Practicing Circular Economy*. CRC Press, Boca Raton, FL.
31. PWC. (2017). Spinning around taking control in a circular economy. Available from https://www.pwc.com/gx/en/sustainability/assets/taking-control-in-a-circular-economy.pdf.
32. DHL. (2019). Logistics trend radar: Delivering insight today, creating value tomorrow. Available from https://www.dhl.com/discover/en-global/business/market-intelligence/logistics-trend-radar.
33. Teleplan. (2019). Enabling the Circular Economy. Sustainability Report. Available from https://www.reconext.com/wp-content/uploads/2020_CSR-Report.pdf.
34. A model offering multiple benefits for multiple electronic products: Bundles. *Ellen MacArthur Foundation*. Available from https://ellenmacarthur foundation.org/circular-examples/a-model-offering-multiple-benefits-for-multiple-electronic-products.
35. Power by the hour. *Rolls-Royce*. Available from https://www.rolls-royce.com/media/our-stories/discover/2017/totalcare.aspx.
36. Accelerating sustainability with virtual twins. (Jan 26, 2021). *Accenture*. Available from https://www.accenture.com/us-en/blogs/industry-digitization/accelerating-sustainability-with-virtual-twins.
37. Factory of the Future. (2020). *Sanofi*. Available from https://www.sanofi.com/en/about-us/our-stories/sanofi-takes-a-step-into-thefuture-of-making-medicine.
38. Aectual. Available from https://www.aectual.com/.
39. Refactory: The Flins Site Enters the Circle of the Circular Economy. (Nov 25, 2020). Renault Group. Available from https://www.renaultgroup.com/en/news-on-air/news/re-factory-the-flins-site-enters-the-circle-of-the-circular-economy/.
40. Boundary Dam Carbon Capture and Storage Project — Canada. United Nations Climate Change. Available from https://unfccc.int/climate-action/momentum-for-change/activity-database/boundary-dam-carbon-capture-and-storage-project.
41. Widuz. Available from https://www.widuz.com/.

42. Unibio. Available from https://www.unibio.dk/.
43. Ananas Anam. Available from https://www.ananas-anam.com/.
44. SEPPURE. Available from https://seppure.com/.
45. Close the Loop. Available from https://www.closetheloop.com.au/about-us/.
46. Dyecoo. Available from https://dyecoo.com/co2-dyeing/.

PART V

LEADING IN THE DIGITAL ERA

Chapter 11

Leading the Company of the Future

⚬⚬

Karin Sixl-Daniell

You manage things; you lead people.

— Grace Hopper, Computer Pioneer and Rear Admiral

Management and leadership are not identical: A manager does not necessarily have to be a good leader, vice versa, a good leader does not necessarily have to be a good manager. The distinction between pure management and leadership can be defined in such a way that management is primarily about execution, while a leader is also concerned with how this is done. Leaders who, in contrast to pure management functions, act as role models or provide inspiration and do not merely perform routine functions, are also seen as such leaders. They should also be able to lead the organization in such a way that it adapts to the respective environment in the best possible way.

The years since early 2020 have brought tremendous change and need for adaptations to the whole world. COVID-19 and its consequences have led to unprecedented disruptions affecting organizations and individuals alike, be it in Asia or around the globe. Millions of deaths were brought upon mankind and lockdowns, circuit breakers, shutdowns, and the like took a toll on business life. This was the case both from the company as well as the employees' perspectives, with companies having to at least temporarily shut down across the globe and employees having to make amends with no or a reduced salary.

Supply chains were (and are still) interrupted. Further disruptions due to war and further diseases are likely to extend this phase so that the Leader of the Company of the Future needs to be equipped appropriately to be able to respond to those new requirements for leadership in times of uncertainty, fear, and anxiety. This chapter outlines the concept of leadership and what it means to lead the company of the future. It further presents the shift in leadership needs as well as the importance of organizational culture for leading the company of the future.

What is Leadership?

The concept of leadership is understood in very different ways. Over the last 60 years, at least 65 different classifications have developed that address the dimensions of leadership.[1] One group of definitions sees leadership as a focus of group processes. The leader is at the center of the group, its changes and activities, and embodies the will of the group. Another group of definitions conceptualizes leadership from a personality perspective, where leadership is a combination of specific qualities and characteristics that individuals possess. These characteristics enable the leader to motivate other individuals to achieve goals. Others define leadership as an activity that a leader performs to initiate change in the group. Another dimension focuses on the power relationship that exists between the leader and the follower. From this perspective, leaders can exercise power to bring about change in others. Leadership can also be seen as a transformative process that leads the follower to achieve more than what is actually expected of them. There are also scholars who look at leadership from the perspective of skills, specifically at certain skills and abilities that an effective leader should possess.

Despite the different definitions, certain elements can be found in most definitions. Leadership is a process that cannot be limited to a particular quality or trait of a person. Leadership as a process also implies that the leader influences the follower. However, this also applies vice versa. Leadership is therefore not a linear process or a one-way street, but an interactive process. When leadership is defined in this way, it is not limited solely to the formal leader, but can be exercised by all group members. In addition, leadership involves influence — this is about how the leader affects those who follow and is a necessary condition for leadership. In summary, leadership is a process whereby an individual influences a group of individuals to achieve common goals — an important notion for Leading the Company of the Future.

A leader can be designated, such as by holding a formal position in the organization. Other persons may act as leaders because other group members perceive this person as the most significant in their group. This type of leadership is therefore not related to position, but is formed through communication. These are people who are verbally involved, informing, inquiring about others' opinions, initiating new ideas and being firm but not intransigent. The notion of power is related to leadership as power is a component in the process of influence. Many people see the exercise of power, such as influencing the attitudes or thoughts of others, as part of leadership. However, research with a focus on power in leadership is limited. Exercising power through coercion is a special case of the power available to leaders — coercion often involves the use of threats and punishment, which is the reason why leadership by coercion must be considered separately. Coercion serves the pursuit of one's own interests and is not leadership. Instead, it is merely exercising the aspect of *power* but not leading as it lacks respect for others and the human(e) aspect and may involve elements of toxic leadership.

Leadership and management resemble each other in various ways: Both involve exerting influence, working with other people, and achieving goals. Nevertheless, there are differences: the theories of leadership can be traced back to Aristotle, whereas management has its beginnings in the Industrial Revolution. The primary function of management is planning, organizing, hiring, and controlling and Kotter[2] described the central function of management as ensuring order and stability. Although traditionally, leadership was equaled to management, differences crystallized themselves, and therefore, a move from a purely mechanistic and transactional nature of management (pay for work) to a different stage in leadership developed.

While rigid authoritarian approaches may have worked in the past, studies have shown that there is a shift to quality of life being in the focus as well as a rise in individualism around the globe. There is a universal trend of the workforce showing a tendency to an increased emphasis on work–life balance (or "life–work balance"); lower birth rates in many countries reveal a problem with aging societies while, simultaneously, there are fewer people active in the workforce. Furthermore, a trend dubbed "The Great Resignation" or "The Great Attrition" can be observed. In the years since the emergence of the COVID-19 pandemic, millions of employees worldwide have left their jobs and moved to different sectors. Examples include, but are not limited to, shifts from hospitality to construction, from banking to lifestyle brands, from the medical sector to yoga. Many a times, employees leave employment without a new job offer in hand.

According to a McKinsey study, only two-thirds of people who left their jobs did so with a new job offer in hand, while only one-third left employment without a new job offer. The same study also showed that an average of 40 percent of surveyed employees from Singapore, the United Kingdom, Australia, the United States, and Canada stated that they are at least somewhat likely to switch employment within the next three to six months. This is the case across all sectors, with the educational sectors showcasing the lowest percentage (32 percent) and the hospitality industry standing at 47 percent. Employers are well aware of this trend as two-thirds of employers surveyed stated that they expect elevated and/or increased voluntary turnover. Of the employees who said they are at least somewhat likely to quit their current job, a third said they would do this only with a new job offer in hand, while two-thirds stated they would do so without new employment lined up. This results in a lack of talent, a phenomenon that can again be observed all over the globe which, together with the emphasis on more work–life balance and individualism, leads to new and bigger challenges in and for leadership of the Company of the Future. Importantly, leadership has to focus on the human aspect in order to be successful for all stakeholders in an organization.

Making High-Quality Decisions in the Company of the Future

We constantly make decisions. Every day, each person makes numerous decisions, consciously or unconsciously, in business or in personal matters. Even more so, this is the case in leadership. Often, however, these decisions are made under the influence of heuristics and/or biases of which individuals usually are not aware. Heuristics are shortcuts which the human mind uses in order to arrive at decisions. When misapplied, these heuristics can prove costly when the shortcuts turn out to be harmful for both organizational outcomes as well as personal matters. Hence, these heuristics must be known to a leader in order for the leader to be able to recognize them and avoid them. Some of these heuristics are:

Framing: Every situation can be framed in a positive or negative manner, similar to a glass half-full or glass half-empty approach. Depending on the situation and the framing of that situation, a decision can turn out to be the exact opposite than if it were framed the other way round.

Availability Bias: Often, individuals assess the frequency, likelihood, or probable causes of an event on the basis of which occurrences of that occasion stand out most clearly in the individual's memory. The availability heuristic proposes that events that are vivid and induce emotions will be more easily recalled than occasions that are bland or vague. However, there are factors that can incorrectly increase the event's importance and vividness, causing an overestimation of the occasion's likelihood of recurring. Examples would be people overestimating the likelihood of shark attacks because such attacks are prominently featured in the news, or the likelihood of plane crashes occurring when in fact planes are the safest mode of transport.

Representativeness Bias: Individuals assess the frequency, likelihood, or probable causes of an event on the basis of the similarity of that occasion to their stereotypes of similar events. The representativeness heuristic, if misapplied, can lead to discrimination (e.g., gender, ethnicity, religion, etc.) as the entire group may be judged by one or two persons that are erroneously believed to be representative of the group in question. An example for representativeness bias would be a stereotype held against Person A by Person B based on their perception of a particular group of which Person A is a member.

Overconfidence: Individuals often have unjustified levels of confidence in their own skills, judgment, and knowledge. Furthermore, many people tend to overestimate the likelihood of positive events while at the same time underestimating the probability of negative occurrences.

Confirmation Bias: This heuristic can be explained as "You only hear what you want to hear" — only information supporting existing views is taken into account, while information contradicting held beliefs is dismissed. This can be seen in political discussions as much as in the way statistics are interpreted and used for an individual's or group's goals.

Self-Serving Bias: Most individuals have come across this tendency to avoid accountability for failures while at the same time claiming unwarranted levels of responsibility in the case of success. For example, it can be observed in instances where students blame teachers for bad exam grades when, in fact, they have not studied enough. If, however, the exam went well, the same person will not attribute their success to the teacher, but rather to their intelligence, hard work, etc. It can also be seen in companies when a project does not go as planned and only very few people wish to be associated with that project. If, however, the same project goes very well, the number of people who want to be associated with the project immediately goes up.

Anchoring: Anchoring occurs when individuals jump to conclusions by using irrelevant — but known — data to make a decision. This happens when decisions are influenced by often irrelevant information. An example for this would be having people think about their (US) social security number and then asking them an entirely unrelated question such as how much they are willing to pay for a particular good. Research has shown that if the last two digits of the social security number are higher than 50, people are willing to pay significantly more for the same product than people whose social security number ends in a number lower than 50.[4]

Another example would be sales prices where the original price serves as an anchor for making a buying decision, even if the "original prices" had been artificially increased before the sale or were entirely made up.

All these heuristics may distort an individual's decision-making ability. A leader needs to be aware of them and how they influence their decision-making abilities to be able to act against them. It becomes evident that the quality of decisions can be distinctly negatively influenced if awareness of these heuristics is lacking and a leader "falls" for them. A Leader of the Company of the Future needs to be well-versed in them to ensure high-quality decisions. Ensuring high quality decisions goes hand in hand with ethical decision-making. This is an area that is often overlooked but is of significant importance for leading the Company of the Future. There are decision-making aids for ethical reasoning, one of which is shown here.[5] These decision-making aids center around the following questions:

1. Have you defined the problem accurately?
2. How would you define the problem if you stood on the other side of the fence?
3. How did this situation occur in the first place?
4. To whom and to what do you give your loyalty as a person and as a member of the organization?
5. What is your intention in making this decision?
6. How does this intention compare with the probable results?
7. Whom could your decision or action injure?
8. Could you discuss the problem with the affected parties before you make your decision?
9. Are you confident that your position will be as valid over a long period of time as it seems now?
10. Could you disclose, without qualms, your decision or action to your boss, your CEO, the board of directors, your family, society as a whole?
11. What is the symbolic potential of your action if understood? If misunderstood?
12. Under what conditions would you allow exceptions to your stand?

Asking these questions, reflecting on them, and answering them is a thoroughly helpful approach when Leading the Company of the Future in order to ensure ethical decision-making with the human factor in mind.

Developments in Leadership Important for Leading the Company of the Future

Unsurprisingly, ethics have found their way into the discussion of Leadership. While a mechanistic and autocratic approach like in *Taylor's* or *Fayol's* approaches in the early 20th century was the norm, various approaches to leadership were developed over the years. These ranged from a discussion of leadership styles such as e.g., autocratic, democratic, and laissez faire (*Lewin*), to *Weber's* addition of a bureaucratic style. This was expanded on by Tannenbaum and Schmidt's *Leadership Continuum*[6] that discussed further variances between leadership styles. The authors described a leadership continuum that distinguishes between the poles of authoritarian and democratic, and other styles such as patriarchal, informative, consultative, cooperative, and delegative. On one side of the continuum is the authoritarian leadership style, in which the superior alone decides and orders. This is followed by the patriarchal leadership style, in which the superior decides but also tries to convince the employees of this decision before giving orders. The third area on the continuum can be seen as informing (the supervisor decides but allows questions about this decision to gain acceptance), followed by the consultative style (the supervisor informs employees about upcoming decisions, allowing employees to express their opinion before the final decision is made). On the continuum toward more decision-making freedom for employees, the cooperative style is heavily present (i.e., development of proposals by/ with employees, with the supervisor then deciding which proposal should be implemented). This is followed by the delegative leadership (i.e., group or employees decide after the supervisor has identified the problem and defined a scope for decisions) and the democratic leadership (i.e., group/ employee decision, with the supervisor acting as coordinator).

Blake and Mouton[7] developed the *Managerial Grid*, which focuses on leadership approaches, along two axes labeled people-centered and task-centered. The combination of the positions based on the two axes would showcase an approach to leadership which could range from "impoverished" (for those not focusing on tasks nor people) to "country club" (for those focusing on people but not tasks) or "team management" for those focusing on both tasks and people. Such leadership obviously requires an involved leader who focuses on more than one dimension in their work. Moreover, Hersey and Blanchard[8] established a model they categorized *Situational Leadership,* which involves leaders adjusting their leadership behavior based on the respective follower's readiness and abilities. In this model, a differentiation between Telling, Selling, Participating, and Delegating is necessary, based on the individuals involved. These four aspects of leading can be explained as follows:

Telling: Communication is one-directional, from the supervisor to the employee; the focus is on a low relationship orientation combined with a low task orientation. This approach is used when the employee is neither able nor motivated.

Selling: High task orientation. This approach is used when the employee is not capable but motivated and the employee is presented with arguments as to why it makes rational sense to accept the task and perform.

Participating: Joint decision-making process between employees and superiors, where the superior leads but solutions are worked out together in a collaborative manner.

Delegating: The supervisor defines the goals while the employee carries out tasks independently; this approach is used if the employee is both capable and motivated.

In order to be effective, the leader needs to observe closely whether the chosen leadership style is successful for the respective task given. If the chosen style does not lead to the desired success or generates inadequate results, the degree of participation should be reduced, and closer monitoring should take over with instructions given. As such, flexibility and adaptability are key to successful leadership. These approaches highlight the move from the above-mentioned transactional nature of work toward an approach that looks beyond the basic and obvious (pay for work) taking place.

A Shift in Leadership Needs

In the Company of the Future, leading in traditional and autocratic ways will not prove positive and emerging keywords such as Agile Leadership, Authentic Leadership, Empathetic Leadership, Ethical Leadership, Servant Leadership, and Transformational Leadership — to name only a few — have been added to the mix. These concepts are detailed in the following:

Agile Leadership is based on agile methods in software development (self-organizing teams) and focuses on an agile mindset. Static and rigid mindsets will not work when Leading the Company of the Future due to unpredictable events requiring flexibility, agility, nimbleness, autonomy, and adaptability. Disruption, as a result, will be the norm, not an exception. With an agile mindset, organizations are not seen as static and organized in rigid structures. Rather, self-organized teams are in focus as organizations are viewed as open systems with such systems seen as both dynamic as well as stable, thus flourishing even in rapidly changing environments. The necessity and success of an agile mindset could be seen throughout the COVID-19 pandemic, when agile leaders acted swiftly to adapt business models to a new (and often changing) environment. Such adaptations opened up newer and more innovative options for organizations, leading to better organizational performance. This kind of agility and nimbleness will also be required in the Company of the Future. Organizations across the globe have learned to embrace agile approaches and created new ecosystems and platforms, with Alibaba, Amazon, or ING being prime examples for this approach; those not embracing agile approaches will no doubt have competitive disadvantages.

Authentic Leadership is needed in the Company of the Future: Leaders who walk the talk, are self-aware as well as self-reflecting, and who take in feedback while remaining original. The importance of authenticity could be seen clearly in recent times, including the lack of, in statements and at occasions by business and political leaders alike.

Empathetic Leadership focuses on the importance of actually showing as well as living empathy. During the pandemic, this has gained even more importance as hundreds of millions of people were affected by changes in their employment and/or paycheck status all over the globe. The necessity for empathy in the workplace has risen to new heights. Understanding the needs and feelings of employees has received higher significance and is necessary in order to ensure employees remain part of an organization. This empathy translates into increased organizational performance as employees feel valued and understood, while simultaneously, feeling a certain bond to an organization that was understanding in time of need and did not simply opt to lay off people in order to save costs. Empathetic leadership increases employee loyalty. Once these businesses restarted after various circuit breakers, lockdowns, and the like due to the COVID-19 pandemic, such organizations had (and still have) a distinct competitive advantage as they have the necessary workforce ready, as opposed to those organizations that let employees go and now still face issues in rehiring, leading to losses.

Ethical Leadership is another concept important for Leading the Company of the Future. Along with digital disruption, coupled with the rise of artificial intelligence (AI), it becomes even more important for leaders to emphasize that respect for ethical values and dignity are at its core. By acting ethically, such leaders can be role models and have a multiplying effect on ethical behavior in their organization, effectively nudging others to emulate their behavior.

Servant Leadership is about the sharing of influence by putting individuals and their needs first and therefore leading as a "servant" to ideas in order to reach organizational goals while not adhering to old, transaction-based, concepts. Greenleaf,[9] who coined the term in 1970, wrote

The servant-leader is servant first... It begins with the natural feeling that one wants to serve, to serve first. Then conscious choice brings one to aspire to lead. That person is sharply different from one who is leader first, perhaps because of the need to assuage an unusual power drive or to acquire material possessions... The leader-first and the servant-first are two extreme types. Between them there are shadings and blends that are part of the infinite variety of human nature. The difference manifests itself in the care taken by the servant-first to make sure that other people's highest priority needs are being served. The best test, and difficult to administer, is: Do those served grow as persons? Do they, while being served, become healthier, wiser, freer, more autonomous, more likely themselves to become servants? And, what is the effect on the least privileged in society? Will they benefit or at least not be further deprived?

(Greenleaf, 1970, p. 6)

Servant leaders inspire others to go beyond the obvious, beyond what is expected — because of their concern for others, contributing to overall success and goal achievement.

Transformational Leadership[10] focuses on four Is — Inspirational Motivation, Idealized Influence, Individualized Consideration, and Intellectual Stimulation — in order to transform followers' approaches to tasks. These four Is ensure that followers are motivated to perform at superior levels, leading to equally superior organizational performance.

Inspirational Motivation requires creating and communicating a vision as well as adequately setting goals that act as an inspiration. While dedication and effort are required to achieve such goals (often stretch goals), these goals are achievable and serve as a doable challenge.

Idealized Influence refers to a leader acting as a role model with followers trying to copy them and their behavior. The leader is admired and charismatic, and hence exercises influence. This aspect of transformational leadership focuses on leaders "walking the talk" and showcasing traits followers see as inspirational and ideal. While generally seen as positive, this aspect may be problematic when applied in political settings (e.g., dictators) or cults.

Individualized Consideration focuses on the importance of adequate genuine attention and consideration given to followers to ensure their development. Mentoring is as much part of individualized Consideration as are carefully selected tasks to be delegated to followers to aid them in their personal and career growth.

Intellectual Stimulation is another focal point in Transformational Leadership. Followers are encouraged to be creative, to use intellectual stimuli in order to advance their thinking and to not remain in static mind-sets. Instead, challenging the status quo, thinking out of the box, and innovativeness are encouraged. This automatically necessitates an adequate error culture where errors can be made and learned from for organizational success.

All these aspects enhance employee well-being, motivation, employee happiness, positive work behaviors, and lead to better overall organizational performance. Transformational Leadership is not viewed as the opposite of transactional leadership as there are aspects of transactional leadership also found in transformational leadership (after all, employees do get paid in return for their work), but rather as an approach going far beyond a mere transactional nature of interactions.

Some authoritarian aspects in leading in crises led to further discussions in areas such as *Paradoxical Leadership:* A leader should be able to handle seemingly paradox or conflicting needs such as followers' individual needs (e.g., empowerment) in parallel with organizational needs (e.g., to exert authority and power over employees) and to reconcile and integrate these opposing aspects to ensure effective guidance and leadership. The tension between such contradicting elements needs to be observed closely in order for leaders to succeed in the complex and dynamic environments they face across the globe.

This has become more evident in recent years, with a lack of adequate leadership skills seen as a contributor to the aforementioned "Great Attrition" or "Great Resignation" wave that has been witnessed all over the globe. There have been plenty of reasons for employees to voluntarily leave employment, often without even having a new offer in hand (or to consider leaving without a new offer in hand) and the McKinsey study mentioned earlier showcased this. Aspects such as living in a desirable location, starting a business, access to technology were not seen as important for both employees as well as employers. Instead, work–life balance came out on top. Furthermore, leaders do not seem to grasp what is important for employees and hence cannot steer the boat accordingly. Employers mentioned poor health (physical as well as emotional) and compensation as main reasons for employees leaving when in fact these aspects were not the most important ones for employees. For employees, the most important aspects were a lack of being valued by and in the organization and/or their managers as well as a lack of sense of belonging. More than half of the respondents stated these three reasons as the main points why they chose to voluntarily leave employment. This was followed by factors classified as "somewhat important" by employees: having caring and trusting teammates, potential for advancement, and a flexible work schedule. Employers and employees equally think that work–life balance is "most important"; the aspects of caring for family, the manageability of the workload, as well as feeling engaged by work are seen as "somewhat important" by both employers as well as employees.

Another aspect which has been discussed in literature is leader warmth[11] as an important factor in leadership. Leader warmth refers to a person's concern for others, "employees' well-being, expression of support, and display of trustworthiness and friendliness)".[12] Consideration for others forms an integral part of leadership. Leaders of the Company of the Future will hence need to be close to their teams in order to understand them best and to motivate them best. Inflexible authoritarian approaches cannot and will not work. Instead, a combination of aspects from leadership approaches mentioned above will likely work best.

Organizational Culture and the Company of the Future

The previous discussions already hint at the fact that leadership and organizational culture are intertwined. Organizational culture needs to be actively shaped and managed accordingly to enable the Company of the Future to prosper. On this note, Edgar Schein,[13] MIT professor and one of the most prominent scholars on Organizational Culture, commented that

> *The culture of a group can now be defined as: A pattern of shared basic assumptions that the group learned as it solved its problems of external adaptation and internal integration, that has worked well enough to be considered valid and therefore, to be taught to new members as the correct way to perceive, think, and feel in relation to those problems.*

Culture can be described as accumulated learning. Not all aspects of organizational culture are visible; some are clearly visible such as artifacts (i.e., architecture, corporate design, colors, layouts, uniforms), while others are not visible such as espoused values or hidden assumptions (e.g., basic beliefs, habits). Symbols, routines, rituals, stories and myths, organizational structures as well as power structures are all part of organizational culture. Managing all these parts and leading accordingly are important, yet sometimes daunting, tasks for a leader. It is important to note that every organization *has* a culture, whether it is a culture that is conductive to innovation, one that embraces organizational learning, or a negative example of organizational culture where employees do not share knowledge, where there is a lack of trust, or an error culture that is not conducive to innovation, to name only a few.

It is also vital to appreciate that there is a link between organizational culture and organizational performance. As mentioned, managing all the aspects of organizational culture can be daunting, yet good leadership is essential in creating and maintaining organizational culture that has shown successes. Still, all too often, organizational culture and its role in organizational performance and economic success are underestimated, despite studies having found Organizational Culture to be the value driver in firms in the United States, ahead of Finance or Production. Hence, it becomes clear why managing organizational culture is fundamental for a leader, as it is linked to the organization's performance (i.e., financial performance), which in turn is something against which leaders get measured. When contemplating how to actively design and manage organizational culture, a leader of the Company of the Future needs to consider a number of aspects. These include, inter alia:

How is leadership done?
Which behaviors are shown/lived?
How is the working day organized for the employees?
What kind of appreciation is shown in the organization?
Which values are lived and shown?
Are there role models? Who? Why? Who are not? Why?

It is important to note that both the formal as well as the informal organization are important aspects of organizational design and organizational culture. The formal organization consists of structures that have been formalized. This includes organizational structures, charts, and processes. The informal organization, on the other hand, does not necessarily go hand in hand with the formal structures, relationships, and processes in an organization. The informal organization is dynamic rather than static, often (not always) easier to change than the formal organization and does not adhere to organizational charts. Although both aspects occur in every organization, the latter is not sufficiently paid attention to in many organizations. Often, leaders only focus on the formal organization and might not realize the full force and impact of the informal organization when making decisions or putting together project teams. Not paying attention to the informal organization can prove to be a very costly mistake as people — as the informal organization — can make or break many an effort in an organization. A good Leader of the Company of the Future needs to pay attention to both the formal as well as the informal organization. As organizational culture influences employees' and leaders' actions, which affects how employees behave and which norms they adhere to, actively designing and managing organizational culture can create a competitive advantage, including being able to attract and retain talent, further strengthening organizational equity, performance, and success.

Conclusion

Leading the Company of the Future means leaders need to show concern for their followers. As seen in the previous years of the pandemic lockdowns and circuit breakers, another important aspect to pay attention to is employee mental health. Empathetic leaders are essential to aid employees in navigating the rough seas induced by COVID-19 to ensure smooth sailing for all stakeholders.

As the COVID-19 pandemic continues to spread, mental health has seemingly become a focus of deliberations. Lack of face-to-face interactions, outdoor activities, and similar issues brought on by isolation have led to an increase in mental health issues as employees were confined to their homes during extended periods of working from home. Some might have an extra strain to bear by e.g., looking after home-schooled children or elderly parents. Numerous unplanned changes in the external environment and internal organizational conditions impacted existing work requirements, which proved to be very taxing for many and took a toll on many people's mental health.

Good leaders will need to keep in mind that stress can be a driver for improving or deteriorating the mental health of employees, as it can have both positive (driving performance) as well as negative aspects (limiting performance). Managing stress in the workforce, in combination with a greater focus on work–life balance, will be a distinctive success factor when Leading the Company of the Future. Leading the Company of the Future requires the leader(s) to exhibit considerable interpersonal and managerial skills. As mentioned above, authentic, empathetic, and agile leadership is needed to ensure smooth sailing — all this while remaining sharp and on point with observations, walking the talk, and acting as a role model in order to be able to be a truly transformational Leader of the Company of the Future.

The challenge of leadership is
to be strong, but not rude;
be kind, but not weak;
be bold, but not bully;
be thoughtful, but not lazy;
be humble, but not timid;
be proud, but not arrogant;
have humor, but without folly.

— Jim Rohn

References

1. Northouse, P. (2016). *Leadership*. SAGE, Thousand Oaks, CA.
2. Kotter, J. P. (1990). *A Force for Change: How Leadership Differs from Management*. Free Press, New York.
3. De Smet, A., Dowling, B., Mugayar-Baldocchi, M., & Schaninger, B. (2021). The 'great attrition' or 'great attraction'? The choice is yours. *McKinsey Quarterly*, September 2021.
4. Ariely, D., Loewenstein, G., & Prelec, D. (2003). "Coherent arbitrariness": Stable demand curves without stable preferences. *Quarterly Journal of Economics, 118*, 73–105.
5. Nash, L. (1981). Ethics without the sermon. *Harvard Business Review*.
6. Tannenbaum, R., & Schmidt, W. (1973). How to choose a leadership pattern. *Harvard Business Review*.
7. Blake, R. R., & Mouton, J. S. (1964). *The Managerial Grid*. Gulf Publishing, Houston, TX.

8. Hersey, P., & Blanchard, K. H. (1977). *Management of Organizational Behavior — Utilizing Human Resources*, 3rd edn. Prentice Hall, New Jersey.
9. Greenleaf, R. K. (1970). *The Servant as Leader*. Robert K. Greenleaf Publishing Center.
10. Bass, B. M., & Riggio, R. E. (2005). *Transformational Leadership*, 2nd edn. Psychology Press, London.
11. Cuddy, A. J. C., Glick, P., & Beninger, A. (2011). The dynamics of warmth and competence judgments, and their outcomes in organizations. *Research in Organizational Behavior*, *31*(2011), 73–98.
12. Kong, D., Park, S., & Peng, J. (2021). Appraising and reacting to perceived pay-for-performance: Leader competence and warmth as critical contingencies. *Academy of Management Journal*. AMJ, 0, https://doi.org/10.5465/amj.2021.0209.
13. Schein, E. (1993). *Organisational Culture and Leadership*. Wiley, New Jersey.

Chapter 12

Rethinking Strategy for the Digital Age

Eng Joo Tan

The Nature of Technology

Technology has radically altered the way businesses operate today. Among other things, it has increased a firm's speed of execution and ability to scale, while simultaneously lowering market frictions and experimentation costs. Furthermore, technology has the potential to enable businesses to create much value and, in some cases, entirely new markets. Many businesses have harnessed the power of technology to great success, including notable examples like Adobe, Microsoft, Tencent, and Amazon.

At the same time, the democratizing nature of technology, which allows for highly inclusive access, suggests that new competitors today may have profiles that incumbents in an industry would not traditionally view as competitors. For instance, Sea Limited has been awarded a digital full bank license yet it looks nothing like, and operates very differently from, a local bank in Singapore. The greater reach facilitated by technology also means that competition can, quite literally, come from anywhere. Paradoxically, technology is double-edged in that the very technology that a business can leverage for economic benefit can also be leveraged by copycat competitors in quick order. Consequently, competitive dynamics have become much more fluid, and the competitive landscape has never been more fraught with uncertainty.

Why Strategy Needs Rethinking for the Digital Age

A lot of what we know about strategy today is based on coming up with a plan to position a firm advantageously relative to competitors. However, many classical strategic management concepts have been turned on their heads in the digital age and applying conventional strategy frameworks without critical analysis can be dangerous and run contrary to competitive advantage.

Consider environmental scanning using the Five Forces analysis, often used to gain insight into the profitability of an industry.[1] Central to the framework is the concept of an industry but, with industry lines blurring, it is increasingly unclear how granularly an industry should be defined for such an exercise to be meaningful. More importantly, an analysis of the Five Forces appears to provide at least an incomplete, if not flawed, understanding of the competitive dynamics of digital businesses. For example, a buyer of a product in an e-commerce marketplace like Alibaba's Taobao is not actually a buyer of Taobao's services (although a seller of a product may be if the seller uses the platform's advertising services), and such buyers cannot be neatly classified as one of the five competitive forces, yet these participants clearly affect the profitability of e-commerce marketplaces in a meaningful way.

Now, consider the growth-share matrix, originally conceived as a corporate-level strategy framework to provide guidance on how to allocate capital among a firm's portfolio of business units.[2]

By classifying each business unit along two dimensions — its industry's growth and the firm's market share (as shown in Figure 1) — a company can direct the cash generated from low-growth businesses with dominant positions toward select high-growth businesses with less dominant positions to increase their market shares. However, this strategy is predicated on two assumptions — that cash is needed to fuel growth and, hence, is required by high-growth businesses and that a higher market share leads to greater cash-generative ability. Neither of these assumptions necessarily holds true today.[4] Many digital businesses are asset-light, often requiring little to no cost to serve the additional user, creating a disconnect between capital intensity and scalability. Further, a dominant market share need not translate to high profits, much less strong cash flows. For example, even though Uber has a dominant position in many

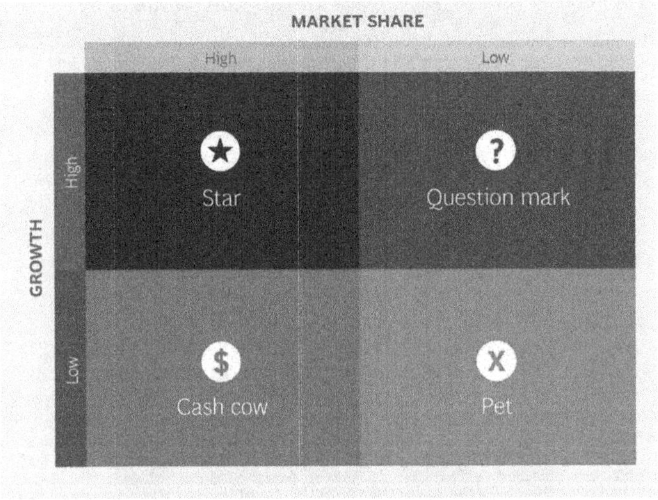

Figure 1:   Growth–Share matrix.[3]

markets that it still competes in (it has exited a few), it has never turned an annual operating profit since its founding in 2009.

The growth–share matrix could be refined by assigning businesses along the additional dimensions of their cash-generative ability and capital intensity, but this comes with greater complexity and ambiguity. Under the original framework, "cash cows" (low growth, high market share firms) are the primary providers of funding but, under this refined framework, funding can come from "stars" (high growth, high market share firms) that also have low capital intensity. There is also greater ambiguity in applying such a refined framework: Is a "star" that has low cash-generative ability really a star?

Data are also changing the way corporate-level strategies are executed. For instance, Chinese tech giant Tencent has invested in many of the companies that develop the mini-programs within its WeChat super-app, as shown in Figure 2.[5]

Tencent's access to app analytics data allows it to assess which of the mini-programs are gaining traction among its base of over a billion users and to reallocate its capital investments from the losers to the winners. As Tencent has complete control over its social communications platform, it can also direct traffic to mini-programs of companies that it has invested in to improve the odds of their success or to realize synergies within its portfolio of businesses.

Figure 2:   Screenshot of the mini programs in WeChat.

Alternative Approaches to Strategy

At a minimum, some of the conventional strategy frameworks appear to be in dire need of a refresh. To be sure, not every firm should be throwing out the conventional strategy playbook, as classical strategies continue to be relevant for some segments of today's economies.

This begs the question of when strategy-as-usual is appropriate and when (and how) classical strategies need an update. A key determining factor is the predictability of a firm's business climate.[6] For firms operating in business environments that can be predicted with relative certainty (e.g., beverages), many of the standard strategic planning tools and frameworks continue to be highly relevant. However, as many digital businesses are operating in highly uncertain environments, two alternative approaches to strategy have come to the fore: adaptation and shaping through the use of ecosystems.

Adaptation in the Face of Hypercompetition

If a firm has little ability to influence its business environment, then it is imperative to employ strategies that help the firm adapt to its fast-changing environment. Strategic planning cycles should become shorter as learning from experimentation and iteration is not only less costly with the help of technology, long-drawn strategic planning exercises are not well-suited to a volatile business environment. In a technology-fueled hypercompetitive environment, one in which competition is more intense, the ability to achieve a sustainable competitive advantage has been called into question.[7] Instead, what may be more realistic is the ability to maintain a successive string of temporary competitive advantages, pivoting from one to the next as competitors start to chip away at a pre-existing competitive advantage.[8] Adaptive strategies require that firms be able to transition seamlessly between exploring, exploiting, and exiting business opportunities. That is, a firm should develop the prescience to anticipate where they will soon be in the lifecycle of a competitive advantage, so that it can continue taking advantage of existing business moats that will hold up well, plan a measured exit from businesses in which its competitive advantages are eroding, and explore new opportunities where it may have a competitive edge. A successful transition requires both an innovative and risk-taking culture, as well as an ambidextrous organization — one that is structured to concurrently run a legacy business that is under attack alongside an up-and-coming business that has yet to experience the ravages of competition.

Disruptive Innovation

Competitive edge in a volatile business environment also stems from the firm's ability to monitor the environment for disruptive innovations.[9] The term "disruptive innovation" is often used by industry practitioners to refer to any commercializable invention that radically alters the positioning of competitors in an industry. Such usage is too broad to convey the important process through which a technological innovation seeks to disrupt.[10] Disruptive innovation is dangerous precisely because it occurs insidiously: A new entrant to the market gains a toehold in a segment (usually low-margin) of a product market that is largely ignored by incumbents, who find it much more profitable to serve the mainstream and higher-margin segments of the market. The new entrant's offerings are usually novel but inferior to existing offerings, so industry leaders continue to make investments that sustain their technological edge instead. The nature of technology, however, is such that significant performance enhancements can be had for a fraction of the original cost with the passage of time. Soon enough, the new entrant's offering provides value that is sufficiently acceptable that it gains mass-market adoption, while the incumbents are forced upmarket as their offerings are now much too premium for the average consumer. By the time the incumbents realize this, the new entrant has already become a formidable competitor.

A classic example is how Netflix successfully disrupted the video rental industry, in which incumbent Blockbuster once held a dominant position. In the beginning, the de facto way to watch movies at home was through the rental of video cassette tapes by visiting physical stores owned by Blockbuster, which was founded in 1985. In 1998, then-startup Netflix launched its online DVD rental subscription service, which delivered and collected the DVDs via mail. What made this possible was technology that enabled a compact form factor for the DVD. At the time, DVD player ownership was not widespread, and this service did not appeal to the mainstream customer but rather to a niche segment of savvy internet users, so Blockbuster did not consider it a significant threat. However, with greater adoption, prices of DVD players decreased and, together with the superior content quality of DVDs vis-à-vis video cassette tapes, online DVD subscriptions spiked as a larger proportion of the video rental market took to Netflix's service. Blockbuster was late to the party, as it launched its own online DVD rental subscription service only in 2004. Interestingly, in January 2007, Netflix disrupted the industry (and itself) yet again, by launching an online streaming service. As before, streaming was inferior to DVD rental because of low streaming speeds, high bandwidth costs, and a much smaller available selection of streamed titles compared to DVD titles. However, technological improvements would lead to higher streaming speeds at lower bandwidth costs, eventually making online streaming subscriptions the de facto way to watch movies at home today. This would also prove to be the final nail in the coffin for Blockbuster, which did too little too late and filed for bankruptcy in 2010.

A key lesson is the importance of staying vigilant in a hypercompetitive environment, to assess whether innovations by new entrants will eventually be good enough for the mainstream market and, if so, to compete with the new entrant down-market early on, by appealing to the fringe group of customers, before the new entrant gains market traction.

Cooperation in the Face of Uncertainty

Faced with an unpredictable business environment, cooperative strategies may be more important than competitive strategies. Firms can cooperate even with their competitors by thoughtfully choosing the specific dimensions on which to compete and the specific dimensions on which to collaborate. For example, competitors can form a consortium to negotiate bulk discounts from an otherwise powerful supplier. Business ecosystems have emerged as a popular cooperative structure to share risks and resources, and this structure also facilitates a scale that is otherwise unachievable by a standalone firm, thus allowing the collective entity to wield some level of influence over its business environment.

Ecosystems and Networks

Business ecosystems feature so prominently in today's competitive landscape that any contemporary strategy playbook would be remiss to ignore them. Fundamentally, a business ecosystem connects different actors for a common economic purpose, which makes otherwise independent players interdependent. The risk- and resource-sharing benefits of such networks come at the expense of control, which is typically achieved through some means of coordination. A networked business structure is not novel (e.g., MasterCard payment network). However, it is widely used today not only because of greater uncertainty in the business environment, but also because technology has significantly reduced the costs of coordination by making it faster and easier to communicate, thereby facilitating the building of such ecosystems.

Types of ecosystems

Broadly, there are two distinct types of business ecosystems — a solution ecosystem and a transaction ecosystem.[11]

In a solution ecosystem, a firm coordinates the efforts of several third-party firms to add complementary products to a core product that solves a specific business problem. Such ecosystems tend to exhibit modularity in that the complementary products are designed independently, yet they add to the overall solution in a coherent manner. The ecosystem contributors often have to make ecosystem-specific investments and the customer often gets to decide on the combination of complementary products to use with the core offering. An example of a solution ecosystem is Xiaomi's ecosystem that delivers a smart home solution by coordinating the efforts of manufacturers of different smart consumer products around its core mobile phone offering.

A transaction ecosystem, on the other hand, serves as a marketplace to matchmake participants for the purpose of buying and selling products and services, or of exchanging information. Technology facilitates the building of such an ecosystem because it reduces both the search and transaction costs. These ecosystems tend to benefit from network effects, which can be direct or indirect. With a direct network effect, the ecosystem offering becomes more valuable as the number of participants on the same side of the market increases whereas, with an indirect network effect, the ecosystem offering becomes more valuable as the number of participants on another side of the market increases. An example of a transaction ecosystem that benefits from both direct and indirect network effects is the professional networking platform LinkedIn — the value of the platform increases with each additional professional that uses it; also, an increase in the number of professional users makes the platform more valuable to corporate employers and vice versa.

Arguably, many powerful business ecosystems today are hybrids — Apple's operating system and its network of third-party developers who create optimized apps constitute a solution ecosystem, while its App Store, which allows users to buy said apps from the developers, constitute a transaction ecosystem.

Ecosystem design

Given that many of the most valuable firms today are organized as business ecosystems, an important question is how ecosystems should be designed to maximize the chances of success.[12]

A necessary, but hardly sufficient, condition for ecosystem success is to create enough value with the ecosystem. In other words, it should address some pre-existing pain point or meet some previously unidentified need to such an extent that some party would be willing to pay for the value proposition. Whether the value created is enough depends on whether it could be distributed among all the key actors necessary in the ecosystem in such a manner that is deemed fair by these actors to incentivize their continued participation. If the problem addressed by the ecosystem is not important enough to solve, then the key actors will not want to participate in such an ecosystem, which will lead to its failure.

Identifying the parameters of a minimum viable ecosystem is a crucial first step.[13] For solution ecosystems, this entails identifying the key types of complementors that are needed to deliver a core value proposition, before adding modules to increase the appeal of that value proposition over time. For transaction ecosystems, this entails building a localized marketplace that is self-sustaining, before extending the marketplace boundaries. A self-sustaining marketplace is one in which the volume of transactions is large enough to prevent net marketplace participant churn — just as network effects are virtuous in a growing ecosystem, they can be deleterious to growth when the ecosystem shrinks. After all, if a marketplace becomes more valuable to participants as the number of participants increases, it follows that the marketplace's value diminishes as the number of participants decreases, further fueling an exodus from the marketplace.

Determinants of network quality

The value of a network depends on factors that determine network quality; namely, the quality of nodes and the strength of the connections.

First, the quality of a network node can be thought of in terms of the number of existing connections to the node (e.g., influencers with many followers on Instagram). It can also be thought of as the number of connections the node can potentially establish. For example, content produced by creative users on short-form video hosting service Tiktok is more likely to be shared and propagated throughout the network, with some of it getting built upon by other content creators. The number of potential connections is a function not only of the motivation of the node to connect with others but also the motivation of others to connect with it. For instance, entry-level professionals are highly motivated to connect with C-suite executives on LinkedIn but not the other way around. Thus, the nodes that provide the largest number of potential connections are middle management, who are motivated to climb the corporate ladder and who can benefit from stronger relationships with junior managers.

All else equal, the greater the number of nodes in a network, the stronger the network effects. If we hold the size of the network constant, a greater number of quality nodes implies greater network density, which means a larger proportion of possible connections are actual connections, which in turn implies stronger network effects as well.

Second, the strength of the connection can be thought of in terms of the strength of the relationship that the connection represents or the engagement level as the nodes interact. For example, Facebook launched by connecting students at Harvard and connecting two parties only upon mutual agreement. The strong connection, facilitated by the close relationships, increases the value that is derived from the subsequent interactions.

Engagement levels depend on the frequency of the interaction, as well as its directionality. Unsurprisingly, the more frequent the interactions, the more value the connection provides to the users. A team composed of members working on a project that requires close collaboration is likely to find Slack, a popular workplace communication tool, more valuable than one in which its members can function relatively independently of one other. Also, watching a pre-recorded video on YouTube is less engaging than, say, participating in a Twitch live stream because communication for the former is largely one-way whereas that for the latter is two-way, which may explain YouTube's introduction of live streaming in 2008.

Of course, many of the factors affecting network quality are inherently determined by the reason for connecting people in the first place, although product and platform features can augment the core value proposition of the business ecosystem.

The chicken or the egg

Network effects are clearly important to the health of an ecosystem. However, they can pose an initial challenge for many ecosystems that are just starting out. This is especially evident for two-sided marketplaces because sellers will not want to participate in the marketplace unless there are sufficient buyers and vice versa. This has been described as a chicken-or-egg problem.[14]

To begin, it is important to identify the actors instrumental to the ecosystem's core value proposition that are the most difficult to onboard.

An actor would be instrumental if the ecosystem's core value proposition cannot be delivered without the actor on board. In general, the actors that are most difficult to onboard are those that have little to gain from being on board or those that have to make sizeable ecosystem-specific investments. For a solution ecosystem like the Sony PlayStation, Sony would have to secure buy-in from key game developers who would like assurance that there would be sufficient demand for the gaming console to warrant developing a game for it. For a transaction ecosystem like an e-commerce marketplace, the supply-side typically needs to be solved first, since sellers are usually much more vested in the marketplace than are buyers because the livelihood of the former can depend on whether they thrive in the marketplace.

Next, once this key group of actors have been identified, a variety of methods can be employed to onboard them. One method is to subsidize this group, at least during the launch phase, possibly at the expense of other groups. Uber, for example, incentivized drivers to sign up by guaranteeing them earnings upon their meeting of conditions like a minimum acceptance rate. Another method is to provide low-cost or, in many cases, no-cost services or tools that may appeal to this group. Airbnb, in a bid to help its early hosts present their homes in the best possible light, paid for on-site professional photography. A third method is to attract this group from a competing ecosystem that has already built such a group. For instance, using automated emails, Airbnb solicited hosts who listed their short-term vacation rentals on Craigslist to entice them to cross-list on the Airbnb platform.

It is worth noting that many of the onboarding efforts at launch are not sustainable at scale. Airbnb would not have been able to continue engaging professional photographers at a larger scale. OpenTable, an online service for restaurant reservations, onboarded restaurants through a brute force approach — by using a sales team to get buy-in from restaurant owners, one restaurant at a time. Since this approach is clearly labor- and cost-intensive, the quality of the node that is onboarded is crucial. In OpenTable's case, this meant restaurants that were popular so that there is likely a large pool of potential users looking to make reservations.

Scaling

Once one side of the market has been kick-started, it is time to work on the other side of the market, alternating between developing one side and the other until network effects kick in. The key here is to maintain an optimal relative size between the two sides of the market. Didi, China's largest ride-hailing service, likely had to maintain a minimum ratio of driver to riders as it set up its ecosystem. Also, at this juncture, important decisions have to be made about how inclusive the ecosystem is going to be. If rapid scaling is a priority, then the ecosystem will need to be less exclusive, but this may require giving up control and the quick growth may occur at the expense of quality. If quality is of greater initial importance, as is the case with many ecosystems, access fees can be charged, or greater due diligence can be exercised to onboard high-quality participants.

As the network expands, more potential participants start to learn about it from existing participants and have greater propensity to join the network because of the increased value they derive from being part of a larger network; their participation further increases the network's value, creating a virtuous cycle. Often, network effects are generated alongside a data flywheel, which is typically facilitated by technology. The data flywheel describes another virtuous cycle wherein the greater the number of participants, the more data can be collected about the participants and how they interact within the ecosystem and with the product, and that data can then be harnessed for actionable insights to improve the platform or product, which then attracts more participants, and so on.

Reaching this stage of critical network mass is paramount for financial viability because customer acquisition costs can be lowered; it is also at this juncture that the orchestrator of the ecosystem (i.e., the coordinator of the different ecosystem actors) can potentially scale back on subsidies. At the same time, the value created by the network can more easily be monetized, which deals with whom to charge and what to charge for. For solution ecosystems, monetization can mean charging more for the solution or complementary services, while for transaction ecosystems, it can mean charging for access or premium access, charging a transaction fee for usage, or charging for advertising. Apple, for instance, monetizes its streaming service Apple TV+, a component of its smart home solution ecosystem, by charging a monthly subscription fee. Further, it monetizes its transaction ecosystem, the App Store, by charging app developers up to 30 percent on purchases made.

The intrinsic qualities of the product served by a network will determine the extent of reach of that network. Many networks are modular in nature in the sense that they are really a network of networks. Solution ecosystems can be grown one incremental component at a time. For instance, Xiaomi can grow its ecosystem by adding complementary categories to its Internet-of-Things product portfolio over time. Similarly, many transaction ecosystems are localized in the sense that the market participants share close, usually geographic, proximity. The vast majority of users on Tinder, for example, are unlikely to want to date someone else from the other side of the world. So, while Tinder may provide its services worldwide, it is effectively a network of city networks; in fact, it was rolled out from one university to the next at the beginning. Once a localized network has been largely developed, the learnings from developing that network can then be applied to replicate the development of subsequent localized networks, before building cross-network connections.

Maturity

Network value does not grow exponentially with scale indefinitely. Just as network effects help to propel the network's growth when its size reaches a certain critical mass, beyond a certain point, large networks will face their own set of problems which, when left unchecked, can cause participant churn. An e-commerce platform with too many sellers may be overwhelming and contribute to a poorer shopping experience as buyers have more difficulty finding what they need or want. Large social media platforms have to contend with a proliferation of spammers and trolls, requiring users to sift through irrelevant and objectionable content in order to access relevant, agreeable content. Fortunately, these problems can frequently be solved with good network design through some combination of participant policing and effective algorithms.

A related problem is that the technology that enables the rapid scalability of digital businesses also potentially leads these businesses into unchartered legal waters. The ensuing disruption of incumbents and other stakeholders can lead to significant pushback, as Uber experienced with the taxi industry, and attract greater regulatory scrutiny on anticompetitive grounds. Likewise, Meta Platforms Inc. (formerly known as Facebook) faced similar pushback with its acquisitions of Instagram and WhatsApp. These problems can be avoided by growing in a measured fashion so that quality problems do not spiral out of control, taking ownership of the responsibility that comes with scale and market dominance, and anticipating regulatory and stakeholder concerns by working with the relevant parties to address such concerns.

Case study: Pinduoduo

Many of the key ideas discussed in this chapter can be exemplified through Pinduoduo, China's third largest e-commerce platform by gross merchandise value. Pinduoduo was founded in September 2015, at a time when the Chinese e-commerce market was dominated by a duopoly of Alibaba and JD.com. Given the mature e-commerce landscape in China at that time and the dominance of the incumbents, many industry experts were of the opinion that there would not be room for a third player of any significance. It is against this backdrop that Pinduoduo grew from a standing start to having 823.8 million annual active users by March 2021, accomplishing in less than 6 years what Alibaba took 22 years to do. For context, China has a population at the time of this writing of about 1.4 billion people, of which about 68 percent are between the ages of 15 and 64. This implies that Pinduoduo has captured the vast majority of the addressable e-commerce market to date.

How did Pinduoduo accomplish this growth feat?

It is worth noting that Pinduoduo initially focused on the lower-tier cities, which were relatively overlooked by the incumbents. At the beginning, Pinduoduo limited its offering to agricultural produce and targeted young mothers. This specialized offering represented an excellent product–market fit because young mothers in these cities are responsible for the purchase of fresh produce and, being price-sensitive, find the low-cost fresh produce that sellers offer in Pinduoduo's marketplace appealing. At the time, fresh produce was not deemed to be well-suited for e-commerce and thus was underrepresented as an offering category on the incumbents' platforms. Yet, the focus on this low-cost niche by Pinduoduo is reminiscent of the beginnings of disruptive innovation.

As with many two-sided marketplaces, Pinduoduo had to develop both the supply-side and demand-side to build out the ecosystem. However, unlike many two-sided marketplaces, which tend to focus solely on generating cross-side network effects, Pinduoduo's innovation was to generate strong same-side network effects for the transaction ecosystem.

On the demand side, Pinduoduo pioneered social commerce using a group-buy mechanism. With group buy, buyers can purchase items as a group from a seller at a deep discount from the list price for a purchase by a solo buyer. What made this especially compelling was that the buyers in a team were often not strangers but, rather, part of a social network. Also, as Pinduoduo started off as a mini-program on the WeChat platform, a prospective buyer could form a team with his social network using WeChat; the integration with WeChat also facilitated payment for purchases made on Pinduoduo. In addition, the platform's recommender algorithm makes it easy for buyers to share the purchases and their feedbacks with friends, which increases the friends' propensity to buy due to the greater value of social (as opposed to stranger) validation. In fact, there were "power" sharers, those nodes which have strong influence over the buying behavior of nodes connected to them. The quality of interaction among same-side nodes is high given the strength of pre-established relationships, which makes buyers more likely to share their purchases, keeps the level of engagement high, and motivates buyers to open the app frequently. The low price point of grocery offerings also increased buyer adoption as they represented low-risk transactions. Thus, the direct network effect generated by the group buy mechanism and the data flywheel promoted strong growth on the buy-side.

Interestingly, the group buy mechanism helped to develop the supply side as well. By aggregating buyer demand and allowing sellers to decide on the minimum team size to be eligible for the group buy discount, Pinduoduo enabled sellers to negotiate volume discounts with their suppliers to offer their products at a significantly lower price. Also, the data on aggregated demand afforded sellers valuable insights into optimizing their supply chains and their product lines. This consumer-to-manufacturer model thus allowed for greater scale economies, and the savings could then be passed on to the buyers. It is important to note that Pinduoduo was able to easily onboard sellers by charging them a fee of only 0.6 percent on transacted value, which is substantially lower than the commission rate of two to eight percent (depending on product category) that is charged by JD.com.[15] This, in turn, translated into lower prices for the sellers' offerings.

The value proposition of Pinduoduo is clear — offering a marketplace for low-cost products to a target demographic looking to get a good deal. While it could create value, how was Pinduoduo able to monetize enough of that value for itself to ensure its economic viability?

For starters, the group-buy mechanism allowed Pinduoduo to keep its customer acquisition costs, the bane of many digital businesses, low. Existing buyers on the platform, in their attempt to meet the minimum team size to be eligible for the group buy discount, effectively acquire new customers for Pinduoduo when they share deals and manage to persuade their friends who are not on the platform to sign up.

While a low transaction fee of 0.6 percent may not seem financially sustainable for Pinduoduo, most of its revenue is derived from fees charged to sellers who advertise on its platform. Prepayments by advertisers, as well as team purchasers, allowed Pinduoduo to maintain a sizeable float that can be invested in the money market. The company keeps its business asset-light by operating a primarily third-party model, which means it does not sell its own products and, hence, does not own inventory; this has the added benefit of reassuring sellers that Pinduoduo is not in competition with them, as is the case in a first-party model, in which the marketplace operator has a data advantage because it has greater visibility on e-commerce traffic and developing trends. Also, Pinduoduo kept its business asset-light by exploiting third-party logistics, which had excess capacity at the time, instead of acquiring or developing its own logistics infrastructure.

All these factors contributed to the stratospheric growth of Pinduoduo's transaction ecosystem in a short span of time. However, such rapid growth comes with a host of attendant problems. For instance, the growth was so rampant that Pinduoduo maxed out the excess third-party logistics capacity and had to liaise with distribution centers to support customer pickup for localized produce; fortunately, this allowed for lower delivery costs since the last mile is fulfilled by the customers themselves. Also, with a proliferation of sellers, new sellers may not have a chance to peddle their goods effectively compared to established sellers, since the products of the latter have higher volume and more reviews. Pinduoduo solved this by actively managing the ratio of sellers in a given category that a prospective buyer sees and by developing an algorithm that democratizes the likelihood of product views, making them less reliant on seller vintage. In addition, with a greater number of sellers, counterfeit products also became more commonplace, which Pinduoduo mitigates by requiring sellers to post deposits against which stiff penalties are applied in the event of such transgressions.

It may be tempting to follow Pinduoduo's playbook to grow all transaction ecosystems, but one should note that Pinduoduo operated in an environment at a time that was highly conducive to its growth strategy. The communal culture in China facilitated the formation of teams to take advantage of group buy discounts since people were accustomed to doing things together. It also helped that Tencent provided the WeChat platform for ease of sharing deals and paying for purchases in a country with the highest smartphone penetration in the world. Lastly, the excess capacity in third-party logistics at the time allowed Pinduoduo to expand quickly without significant capital expenditures.

For all its success, Pinduoduo is at a crossroads today. While it has clearly solidified its position as the third largest e-commerce player in China, displacing the top two incumbents will prove to be a much bigger challenge. Certainly, the average order value on Pinduoduo's platform will increase as buyers in lower-tier cities become increasingly affluent with the economic development of those cities. However, it is unclear whether prior innovations can allow Pinduoduo to dominate the first- and second-tier cities, which are the strongholds of Alibaba and JD.com. Further, these incumbents are unlikely to wait idly as Pinduoduo eats their lunch.

Defense

Thus far, this chapter has discussed value creation and value monetization for the orchestrator of an ecosystem. But how can the value be protected from being dissipated away by competitors and other stakeholders of the ecosystem? Put differently, why are some business ecosystems profitable yet others are not?

Technology and the integration of capital markets have lowered the barriers to entry and allowed competitors to not only imitate both product and system innovations at breakneck speeds, but also improve on them to lure an ecosystem's participants to switch or to multi-home (i.e., participate in multiple ecosystems of the same type concurrently).

One strategy would be to continuously stay ahead of competitors in creating value through network effects. This constitutes a form of switching costs in the sense that participants would have to give up the differential value should they switch to a competing network. However, the ability to succeed at staying ahead depends on how network value changes with network scale or density, which in turn depends on the nature of the product in question. For example, the marginal value that an additional driver adds to a rider begins to diminish at a much lower network density for Uber than the point at which the marginal value that an additional host adds to a guest begins to diminish for Airbnb. This is because a differentiated ride experience is much less important to a rider than a differentiated rental home experience is to a guest, and the variety of car makes and models available is much fewer than the variety of vacation homes available. Furthermore, a network of loosely integrated networks is more vulnerable to attacks, as new entrants can choose the localized network that they have the strongest chance of successfully competing against as a starting point of attack. In contrast, a single deeply integrated large network is much harder to compete against, since potential competitors would have to expend sizeable resources to build a competing network with overlap of some significance. For these reasons, Airbnb is much harder to compete against than Uber and it shows in their bottom lines.

If the point of diminishing marginal value occurs at a small scale or density, and this has occurred for multiple players with significant network overlap, then network effects are no longer an effective form of switching costs, if they even were to begin with. Even if there are network effects and there is minimal network overlap, it is challenging for the ecosystem orchestrator to capture much value for itself if participants can multi-home relatively seamlessly, as is the case for both riders and drivers with ride-hailing. Another strategy would be to design features to keep participants continually engaged with the ecosystem. Pinduoduo, at 823.8 million annual active users, has arguably reached network saturation and has significant network overlap with Alibaba, which has a user base of a similar size. Although groceries are essentials, making them high repeat purchase items, Pinduoduo users do not have to shop with Pinduoduo given that they can multi-home relatively frictionlessly. To mitigate this, Pinduoduo has gamified its platform with social games, so that users will open its app often and increase and prolong their engagement with it because of the social glue that holds its users together. Pinduoduo has also designed its platform to be browse-centric instead of search-centric, focusing on the discovery as opposed to the intentional aspects of shopping, so that users will spend more time on its platform.

Will these measures work? Perhaps only time will tell.

Concluding Remarks

The concepts shared in this chapter have only scratched the surface of how competition works in the digital age. This chapter underscored the notion that strategy in a networked world is very different from strategy in a brick-and-mortar world and provided some of the important building blocks to approach strategy in the digital era. There remains much to be learned in what will undoubtedly be a very exciting time for strategic thinkers.

References

1. Porter, M. E. (2008). The five competitive forces that shape strategy. Harvard Business Publishing, Brighton (MA) (Updated 2023 March 3; cited 2022 September 14). Available from https://hbr.org/2008/01/the-five-competitive-forces-that-shape-strategy.
2. Henderson, B. D. (1970). The product portfolio. Boston Consulting Group, Boston (MA) (Updated 2022 September 20; cited 2022 September 14). Available from https://www.bcg.com/publications/1970/strategy-the-product-portfolio.
3. Boston Consulting Group. What is the growth share matrix? Available from https://www.bcg.com/about/overview/our-history/growth-share-matrix.
4. Reeves, M., Moose, S., & Venema, T. (2014). BCG classics revisited: The growth share matrix. Boston Consulting Group, Boston (MA) (Updated 2022 September 20; cited 2022 September 14). Available from https://www.bcg.com/publications/2014/growth-share-matrix-bcg-classics-revisited.
5. Tech in Asia. (2019). (WeChat Mini Programs Home Screen). Cited 2022 September 14. Available from https://www.techinasia.com/wechat-homescreen-instant-apps.
6. The strategy palette. Boston Consulting Group, Boston (MA) (Updated 2022 May 31; cited 2022 September 14). Available from https://www.bcg.com/capabilities/corporate-finance-strategy/strategy-palette.
7. D'Aveni, R. A. (1994). *Hypercompetition* (Illustrated ed.). Free Press, New York City (NY)
8. McGrath, R. G. (2013). *The End of Competitive Advantage: How to Keep Your Strategy Moving as Fast as Your Business.* Harvard Business Review Press, Brighton (MA).
9. Bower, J. L., & Christensen, C. M. (1995). Disruptive technologies: Catching the wave. Harvard Business Publishing, Brighton (MA) (Updated 2023 January 12; cited 2022 September 14). Available from https://hbr.org/1995/01/disruptive-technologies-catching-the-wave.
10. Christensen, C. M., Raynor, M. E., & McDonald, R. (2015). What is disruptive innovation? Harvard Business Publishing, Brighton (MA) (Updated 2022 April 19; cited 2022 September 14). Available from https://hbr.org/2015/12/what-is-disruptive-innovation.
11. Pidun, U., Reeves, M., & Schüssler, M. (2019). Do you need a business ecosystem? Boston Consulting Group, Boston (MA) (Updated 2023

February 10; cited 2022 September 14). Available from https://www.bcg.com/publications/2019/do-you-need-business-ecosystem.

12. Pidun, U., Reeves, M., & Schüssler, M. (2020). How do you "design" a business ecosystem? Boston Consulting Group, Boston (MA) (Updated 2023 February 01; cited 2022 September 14). Available from https://www.bcg.com/publications/2020/how-do-you-design-a-business-ecosystem.

13. Adner, R. (2012). *The Wide Lens: A New Strategy for Innovation*. Portfolio Penguin, New York City (NY).

14. Chen, A. (2021). *The Cold Start Problem: How to Start and Scale Network Effects*. Harper Business, New York City (NY) (An Imprint of HarperCollins Publishers).

15. Dalela, S. The ultimate guide to Pinduoduo marketing. GoDigitalChina AS, Oslo (NO) (Updated 2022 October 7; cited 2022 September 14). Available from https://www.adchina.io/pinduoduo-marketing-guide/.

Index